On the Trail of a Lion
Ahmed Shab Massoud
Oil Politics and Terror

On the Trail of a Lion
Ahmed Shab Massoud
Oil Politics and Terror

A.R.Rowan

Edited by Aaron Rain

Library and Archives Canada Cataloguing in Publication

Rowan, A.R., 1952–
On the trail of a lion: Ahmed Shah Massoud, oil, politics and terror /
AR. Rowan ; edited by Aaron Rain

ISBN: 978-1-965407-58-5

1. Rowan, A.R., 1952--Travel. 2. Massoud, Ahmad Shah. 3. Afghanistan-
-History--1989-2001 4. Revolutionaries--Afghanistan--Biography. 5.
Remote Communities Development Foundation. I. Rain, Aaron II. Title

DS371.43.R68.A3 2005   958.10'46   C2005-906234-7

Publishing by Mosaic Press 2005

Independently published 2023

Copyright © A.R. Rowan, 2006

ISBN: 978-1-965407-58-5

email: ronaldpublishing@outlook.com

To those supportive people who, when I was stumbling, moved me forward – not the least of whom is Kasmira, a beacon on the path of perseverance.

ACKNOWLEDGEMENTS

This book would not have been possible without the continual dedication of my dear friend Wenda-Dawne who carried the ball on her own without support for sustained durations.

Aaron Rain was instrumental in getting my thoughts on to the page.

Sam made valid contributions when they were needed no matter when I requested them.

And my family, particularly my daughters, all of whom were essential.

A.R. Rowan,
November 2005

TABLE OF CONTENTS

Introduction

Part One: On the Trail

Part Two: The Emirate of Afghanistan

continued over

Part Three: A Murder and Its Wake

FORWARD

A generation has grown up since this book was first published. The world has seen a lot of changes since then, certainly not all of them for the better. The spectre of imperialism still haunts Afghanistan and the Middle East. In order to move forward, we need to understand these changes.

For me personally, there have been some very sad changes. Aaron Rain, whom I had known for more than half a century, has died. He was much more than an editor and a prime mover in first getting this book published.

Farzana, an organizer, fixer and faithful sister, who opened so many doors for me through connections she made, has also passed away. Bless their souls.

History is filled with the stories of those who would not listen to reason nor nature. One day they wake up thinking, "What happened?"

There are clues that we in the West turned our eyes away from what was actually happening. We enjoyed the benefits and spoils of colonialism, far too many of us echoing the words of Ebenezer Scrooge, "Are there not workhouses?" The result is hundreds of thousands of migrants marching through Africa then Europe in search of a better life, and far too many Tiny Tims washing ashore from the Mediterranean, face down in the mud.

Let us review what has happened.

A series of errors

When I wrote this book, my prediction of the return of the Taliban was controversial. Both my editor and publisher strongly disapproved of including it. But here we are.

The cruel mass murder of 9/11 highlighted some social wounds in the world. Osama bin Laden, the accused mastermind of the attack, has been gone so long that millennials would probably have to Google him to answer a question about him.

The inability to distinguish the Muslim religion of 1.5 billion from the acts of a few criminals also created a double standard at places like airport security screening for at least one very polarized decade.

Led by the United States, the Western allies decided to avenge this act of terrorism by men who were from Saudi Arabia by invading Iraq and hunting down Al Qaeda in Afghanistan.

America's longest war took the lives of at least 2,400 Americans and 150,000 Afghans, most of them civilians. Not to mention the $2.3 trillion in US dollars that was spent. The question that dominated Vietnam in the 60s and 70s, echoed in Afghanistan. "What are we doing here?"

Back in 1981, as Maggie Thatcher crossed the border from Pakistan into Afghanistan, shaking hands with Afghan border guards, her quip to President Zia Ul Haq about how "We had better leave while they're friendly", was a point the US in 2002 might have been wise to take note of.

Visionaries and nationalists like Massoud and Haji Qadir wanted unity not foreign soldiers in Afghanistan.

Actions have consequences

History may have turned out quite differently, had the US and its allies simply stuck to their proclaimed mission of hunting down the leaders of Al Qaeda and chased out the Taliban for a while.

The Iraq War dominated the military effort and stripped away focus from Afghanistan, leaving duffle bags full of cash around the countryside and the social infrastructure projects in tatters.

The rampant corruption, I witnessed firsthand, when for $20, I was allowed to skip the Security Check line-up at the Kabul Airport. The conspicuous transfer of military equipment and structural assets from Afghanistan to Iraq predicated the tragic outcome.

Obama expanded the use of drones in the tribal areas of the Pakistan/Afghanistan border area, causing indiscriminate collateral damage. This was designed to cover the West's retreat but instead it fanned a fire and handed the Taliban the best recruitment tool they could hope for.

For every civilian slaughtered, 3,000 rose up to avenge them. No one cared if the Taliban would let girls go to school. They were given bullets and/ or a suicide vest to strike back at those who had oppressed them.

In August 2021, the Taliban swept into Kabul, while people fell out of wheel wells of departing transport planes, trying to escape. In August of 2022, just outside Kabul, Zahwari as Bin Laden's second-in- command, was killed by an American drone as he hailed the morning sun.

Results are far-reaching

Prior to the invasion, Hussein's Iraq had the best infrastructure in the Middle East. Libya was a functioning country. Now Iraq, Libya and Afghanistan have been reduced to rubble. In 2004, my daughter Mae used her school P.A. system to ask why the children of Fallujah, Iraq had to suffer. If something cannot be easily explained to a 10-year-old does it actually make sense?

Afghans make up a large portion of the endless masses who leave all that they know and love to escape the destruction left in the wake of yet another failed Western experiment. As poet Warsan Shire, a refugee from Somalia has written, "no one leaves home unless / home is the mouth of a shark". Some of those who didn't leave home in Afghanistan have been reduced to selling their underage daughters or maybe a kidney to stave off starvation or survive an Afghan winter.

Disruption and pain do not stop because the privileged stop paying attention and shift their focus elsewhere. Perhaps many may have recognized that their privilege rides on the backs of such people whom the wealthy have been trying to keep out of their own countries.

And perhaps the Middle East is no longer the West's flavour of the month.

A new focus.

Though China recently brokered a peace deal between Iran and Saudi Arabia, Western eyes are mainly set on the Pacific.

China has been building ports in Pakistan, Burma and elsewhere. Inside China a vast system of high-speed train routes has been built including into neighbouring countries such as Laos.

A key component of China's Silk Road initiative throughout Asia and Eurasia is their train's gage changing wheel sets. A coincidence perhaps but their infrastructure now is buttressing Afghanistan, a country historically known as the crossroads of the world.

The spider's web criss-crosses Asia and throughout the Pacific. China has caught up in the technological arms race, including outer space.

China is a formidable contender in an imperial power struggle. The pages of history are still turning and maybe we still have time to change patterns of war fought vicariously through corruption and the blood of innocents, even in Africa. A big ask?

This book is not a point of departure nor arrival. It is a waystation, an attempt to understand what has happened, so we can try to move forward

Enjoy learning while reading. It's later than you think!

INTRODUCTION

I don't remember exactly what drew me to the East. Perhaps it was an adolescent' natural curiosity. I do know what kept me coming back. The rich cultures and religions of India and Nepal, with their various sects and vivid costumes, particularly appealed to me. On my first trip to Nepal, I watched thousands of reclusive Hindu devotees stepping out of the forests for their annual Shivarati festival, clad only in loincloths. These deeply spiritual people, known as Saddhus, lead a meager existence in rural lowlands and some of the highest mountains on earth. Unique experiences like this made me feel as though I had discovered a new world. Indeed I had. I found such unusual sights were not limited to India or Nepal. Thought-provoking cultural treasures highlighted my every journey.

My travels also took me to Pakistan, back in the early 1980s. A great many Afghan refugees lived there at the time due to the Soviet invasion of their own land. Some had settled in Iran and Tajikistan as well. While the authorities of these two countries severely restricted the movement of their Afghan refugees, the Pakistani government showed considerably more sympathy. It even allowed the Afghans to work in the transport industry. The nation's highways teemed with Afghan truck drivers.

During one of my trips to Pakistan, I found myself parked beside a dusty truck 'adda' for several days, while trying to get my mini-bus repaired. The "adda" was a large yard used mainly for parking, servicing, and scrapping industrial vehicles. Because the waiting list for repairs was long, my visit there allowed me to rub shoulders with some of the operators of the big rigs. The men in competition for the mechanics' attention were an ethnically diverse group. Many of them were Afghans. I would occasionally join a small group for a snack and some tea, or "chai." This was where I first learned about the charismatic Ahmed Shah Massoud of Afghanistan, an accomplished military commander roughly my own age.

I listened closely as these drivers spoke of political complicities, military strategies and guerrilla warfare. Commander Massoud had done the impossible they said; he had united the warring tribes of Afghanistan into an alliance that was successfully thwarting the Soviet occupiers. The drivers unraveled story after story about a legend-in-the-making and his rag-tag army which was fighting for Afghan independence. The almost mythical tales of valor engaged my imagination.

As the decade progressed, the Cold War slid up a notch on the global insanity meter; nuclear technology ruled the day. The blood-bath in Central America raged on and the conflict in Israel spilled over into Lebanon, complete with US military intervention. It riled me that billions of innocent souls around the globe were suffering just to satisfy the greed of a few.

The Soviet troops disappeared from Afghanistan by 1990-91. International media coverage of the ravaged country left with them. My interest, however, did not. A communist rogue had been left in charge and the leaders of various Afghan political parties sought to depose him. The CIA had innundated the country with weapons. They may as well have saturated the land with nitro-glycerin. My travels in Central Asia had allowed me to witness a great many changes in other countries, but none were as interesting as the developments in Afghanistan.

In 1992, Massoud's militiamen and their fellow guerillas toppled the Soviet puppet regime left behind in Kabul. Massoud took the all-important office of Defense Minister. Those of us who heard about the victory hoped this weary nation would finally find some peace. It did not. It immediately fell into the throes of a civil war. While the international press covered a similar clash in Sarajevo, innocent civilians were dying by the thousands in Kabul and few took notice.

The mayhem in the Afghan capital lasted for more than three years before a totally unexpected development unfolded. A Muslim fundamentalist movement, the Taliban, surfaced out of Kandahar region and established its hold on the country's south within a few months. Their momentum was staggering. It would take them only a year to capture the majority of the country, including Kabul.

I asked myself where did these Taliban come from. They had seemingly grown out of a vacuum and achieved military prowess.

Before long, I read an unconfirmed report that the CIA had formed a covert alliance with Saudi Arabia and Pakistan to bolster the Taliban in order to dominate Afghanistan. An American–controlled oil giant sought to build a pipeline through the nation and a pliable government was required. It made perfect sense to me. But still, most of this was more rumour than established fact.

Ahmed Shah Massoud and his men were hemmed into a shrinking territory in the northern provinces by the summer of 1997. They continued to battle the Taliban aggression, with an ever-changing coalition of military generals and their fighters. These forces, which would come to be known as the Northern Alliance, were badly outnumbered and outgunned by a dedicated foe. It was then that I first decided to travel to this remote, war-torn country – a land I would discover had been literally forgotten by time.

The Remote Communities Development Foundation (RCDF) is a charity some acquaintances and I established back in the late 1980s. It trains nurses in places that have negligible access to health care and provides some medicines, as well. As I wanted to help in Afghanistan in any way possible, I would seek out the legendary Massoud and offer to assist his people. I also was compelled to learn the real story of Afghanistan, one that I felt would be different from the Western media version.

This has taken me many years – but this book is a result of that effort.

I have divided this book into three sections. The first is an expanded version of excerpts from my 1997 travel diary. For the second, I have constructed a memoir from notes I took during my journey in 1998. The third consists of my journals of my visits to Afghanistan prior to the end of 2003 and reflections on what I have learned. Massoud's history is scattered throughout. Enjoy.

A.R.Rowan
November, 2005.

This map is not precise and used for general reference only

PART ONE

ON THE TRAIL

CHAPTER 1

UNITED ARAB EMIRATES and UZBEKISTAN:
AUGUST 9-18, 1997

Without warning, a cloudless, blue sky transforms itself into an intimidating gray. Boats in the creek race for cover. Today's heat practically sears the flesh and the breeze provides little relief. The wind picks up again, flinging dust and debris into the air — maybe a sign of the chaos that awaits me. God only knows.

This is Dubai, United Arab Emirates, not my ultimate destination. Yesterday, I phoned the Uzbekistan embassy with the hope of carrying on my journey. I was told that getting a travel visa for the country could strand me here for the better part of a week. This was unacceptable. A personal appearance at the embassy, only a couple of hours ago, fortunately cut the red tape. I leave shortly. While waiting for my cab, I catch a final glimpse of the view from the front of the hotel. It's hardly flying weather. I hope this witch's brew blows over in a hurry.

I board my plane at 2:00 p.m. The flight to the Uzbek capital, Tashkent, lasts longer than I would have thought, somewhere between three and four hours. Inside the arrivals terminal, I study the Uzbekistan customs brochure. The pamphlet features an older picture of this airport that flatters its present reality. I doubt that whenever the photo was taken, the tarmac exhibited such gaping potholes or an army truck carrying passengers to the terminal. These days it's a harsh environment, not well suited for tourists. It looks pretty bombed out.

The customs officers here poke their suspicious noses into all manner of business. They even assess the value of rings on the fingers of returning vacationers. Foreigners such as I must declare all funds and the full value of any jewelry or gadgetry we carry. Before they allow us to leave the country, they will compare the entry inventory with our current economic status. Too big a difference could result in questions. One might be suspected of illegal activity. Still, I think I might look a little too rich for their liking. I carry quite a bit of extra money for duties I must attend to in Thailand, for my charitable foundation. I therefore decide to declare a more modest total, not realizing it could hurt me down the road.

After the unnerving customs process, a friendly local approaches me. He offers to guide me through the remaining airport procedures and chaperone me to my hotel. He also converts $100 American for me at a 100 Uzbek soames to the buck, which he states is the normal rate. The man insists on receiving nothing for his help, so I leave him with only a company pen. His gesture strikes me as inordinately kind and selfless for a while.

I settle into my room before attempting to gather some information. My first stop is the tour agency right here on the same floor of the hotel. I run several questions by an ethnic Korean gentleman who works there, before interrogating him about currency exchange locations. This man claims to be from Vladivostok, a Russian city by the Korean border.

When he inquires about the rate I might expect, I say 100 to 1, the same one dispensed by my airport helper. He says his agency can manage this, so I convert another $500 American. He proves quite accommodating in other ways as well, offering useful details about Tashkent and promising to show me around town. The same afternoon, I discover that the true rate of exchange is 150 to 1, a sobering little detail.

My accommodation in Tashkent includes three varieties of bugs. One resembles a cockroach, another I believe to be a spider of some sort, and the most interesting looks like an overfed centipede. This doesn't bother me much, but the nail heads poking through the floorboards rip my socks and hurt my feet. Nonetheless, I can't upgrade my room because this is the last deluxe suite in the house.

One of my reasons for touching down in a little-traveled part of the globe like Uzbekistan is the ancient architecture. While I am here, I will try to drum up some business for the recycling company I work with back home in Canada. More importantly, I would like to distribute some medicines among displaced Afghan refugees. It would particularly please me if I could offer them a healthcare training program.

My interest in Afghanistan and its people is epitomized by the exploits of an Afghan revolutionary named Ahmed Shah Massoud. Massoud attained a legendary status in Afghanistan for heroics against the Soviet Army in the 1980s. In and around the Panjshir Valley, a mountainous region north of Kabul, thousands of needy folk still consider him a warrior who represents their passion to resist tyranny.

This is the land he calls home. The Soviet threat no longer exists, but a government called the Taliban has recently brought the bulk of the country under an oppressive new rule. Only a few northern areas, all under the protection of Massoud and his military commanders, remain free from capture. The Panshjir Valley is among them. With living conditions worsening due to the civil combat, the villagers turn to Massoud, their war hero, to find solutions. Although time often alters perceptions, he once possessed a Robin Hood mystique in a region that knew little of English folklore.

Tales of this famous Afghan first started to drift my way around the beginning of the Soviet occupation of Afghanistan in 1981, when distinctly fierce fighting saturated the Panjshir Valley. Massoud was always in the thick of it. In periods of intense attack, he would hide most of the women and children safely in mountain caves, while the combatants organized defensive strategies in trenches dug through village huts. When helicopter gun ships swooped low to terrorize and seek out resistance, his men would try to snag them with manually hurled cables. This sometimes enabled them to finish the task of bringing the choppers down with their old recoilless rifles. Such innovative techniques helped his small but effective militia acquire a significant portion of its weapons.

Massoud's success against such overwhelming odds did not go unnoticed. His name quickly circulated the globe. Within a few years, every major newsroom in the West would have a file on the "Lion of Panjshir." The British press dubbed him the "potential second Tito." The Wall Street Journal would eventually brand him "The Afghan who ended the Cold War." And I would like to know the man personally.

I realize it might be too much to expect to meet Massoud in Uzbekistan, but it's likely I'll come across some of his countrymen here. I know for certain that quite a few Afghans have recently fled into Pakistan and Iran. Refugees from the northern areas, where Massoud's forces currently fend off the ever-encroaching Taliban, probably reside somewhere up in these parts. But I find it hard to know where to start looking. Either here, Tajikistan, Turkmenistan, or some other "stan." There have been many convoluted coups and civil wars pushing Afghans out of their own country to become strangers in some of the lands surrounding them. This place seems too "under control" to be a potential gathering spot for refugees, but perhaps I can pick up a few clues. I have aspired to meet Ahmed Shah Massoud for years now. I believe I'll live to regret it if I don't give it my best shot.

Hotel employees clamor to exchange my money the next morning at the hotel. I do not expect to see this because it's illegal. A maid nonetheless knocks aggressively on my door with a bundle of soames in her hand and her floor manager presses the issue when she sees me in the hallway. These women naturally propose the standard rate for the poorly informed or impatient foreigner. I refuse to do business with them. I have managed to get myself swindled twice already, thank you. Since I really do need some more funds changed, I approach the clerk in the gift shop where I have already stocked up on fluids for the next two days. He seems to be a talkative fellow. Perhaps he can offer me some information. It turns out that he can, but the news isn't good. "Not much Afghan around here," he says with a thick accent. "Over there; Afghanistan," he exclaims, waving his arm in a direction presume to be south.

I carry on to the second floor lounge to probe the bartender. All get from him is polite smiles. I continue my inquiries for the rest of the day, but they lead nowhere.

After my second night at the hotel, I realize I haven't heard the regular call to prayer that characterizes Muslim lands. The haunting chant usually emanates from a variety of mosques and resonates through city streets at about 4:30 a.m. Reception soon tells me that the city uses only its most prominent locations for the ritual. The call will likely go unnoticed unless one is close by.

The daylight hours leave me with a few impressions. Nearly all the buses I see run with their engine flaps open, some of them bent right out of shape and hanging permanently ajar. Yet I understand that Tashkent, the largest municipality in Central Asia, showcases a comparatively up-to-date railroad/subway system. The roads certainly impress me when compared to the crater-hewn thoroughfares of India and Pakistan. The Soviets obviously invested some money in the republic.

Uzbeks with Uzbek ancestry are known as Turkic people, not to be confused with Turks. Turkic people are any who speak a language from the Turkic family of languages. This includes the Uzbek and Turkish languages, but also involves many different tongues and residents of many different countries. Some linguists place the many Turkic tongues in a broader grouping called the Altaic family of languages. The lands where Turkics live stretch from Eastern Europe, north to Siberia and east to Western China. This region very much includes Central Asia, but more Turkics live in Turkey than in any other single country. Perhaps 150 million strong, most of them practice the Sunni Muslim religion. Others however, in countries such as Iran and Azerbaijan, are Shi'a Muslims.

One of the other guests at the hotel is a Canadian from the international aid organization, "Medecins Sans Frontieres" (Doctors Without Borders). He works as part of a group investigating environmental and health concerns around the Aral Sea. This crucial body of water, shared by Uzbekistan and Kazakhstan, has shrunk in half from irrigation and overuse in general. It is no longer one sea but two, and because of the lower water levels, the higher salinity has killed most of the fish. Even the weather has changed as a result. Yet the dependency of the countries using the water, such as Turkmenistan, Uzbekistan and Kazakhstan, cripples authorities from rectifying the situation. The cotton industry, which uses plenty of water, is the biggest culprit says the doctor. It also adds tons of pesticides into the diminishing water table. This has had a disastrous effect on local environments and agricultural sustainability, very much like the developing countries that use this industry to pay off their military debts to the US. Most of Uzbekistan's cotton is marketed in Russia.

I admire the workers of "Medecins Sans Frontieres" partially because I help run a small charity with complementary aims (the RCDF). I also respect the fact that they do their work without a hidden political agenda or any religion peddling. Many other Western NGOS export workers who have little to no respect for the spiritual practices of those they try to help. They force their Western faiths on vulnerable aid recipients as though the existing religions of these people are little more than justifications for colonization.

I recently sat beside an American NGO worker on one of my flights to East Asia. This young man was exhilarated to be bringing "civilization" to an area so completely destitute, he alone held the power to determine life or death – or so he implied. Medicines, wells, seeds and plows were all part of the arsenal of bartering chips in his chauvinist agenda. He commented, "Even though the villagers don't know it, I control each and every one of their lives from right here in my laptop."

An American I once met in Laos told me he was walking door-to-door spreading "the good news." He referred to himself as a "lamplighter." He said he was waiting to hear if the Laos government had accepted his application for NGO status. I had already spent quite a bit of time in Laos, and knew for certain that they did not allow any of this type of foreign preaching. I doubt very much this fellow had written anything at all about his proselytizing on the application form. If so, he would have found himself on his way home shortly after we spoke. Most Westerners do not understand how much umbrage it causes people of developing countries when foreign aid comes wrapped in a proselytization package. The Taliban could not understand why the developing world did not applaud them when they arrested some Christian proselytizers who were surreptitiously passing religious literature to locals. The Christians were working with an aid group called "Shelter Now." From the perspective of a non-Christian in the developing world, proselytization may seem part of a war package. The mainly Buddhist country of Sri Lanka is in the process of passing a law that will hand out stiff punishments to those who proselytize.

I spoke with a Laotian refugee in Thailand who claimed he formerly worked with USAID. This is an NGO I understand provides legitimate cover to CIA operatives working on foreign soil. I lightheartedly remarked that forty percent of his duties probably entailed covert operations such as blowing up bridges at night. He at first looked shocked that I could say such a thing. However, he soon winked and said, "More like eighty percent at night." Maybe the man was just playing along with me, but I didn't think so at the time. What bothers me in every one of these instances is the dishonesty and hypocrisy involved. But regardless of my past experiences with NGO employees, I feel fortunate to meet a fellow Canadian working on the Aral Sea project, providing a genuine service for humanity.

I turn on the television on my third morning in the hotel and hear that one of my favorite musicians has died. He couldn't have been much older than me. The man was a Pakistani by the name of Nusrat Ali Khan. He sang a type of Sufi music called "Qawwali" and performed it around the world, to adoring fans everywhere. I hold artists such as this – humans whose work brings the East and West together – in the highest regard. I don't mind admitting that news of his death moves me to tears on this day.

In the afternoon, I try to get some business done. I pass along a promotional brief about my recycling company to the ethnic Korean tour rep who works at the hotel travel agency. It sparks his interest and he offers to circulate it for me. He sounds very enthusiastic about the idea of participating in a business that could result in a better environment - an avant-garde thinker. This could work, so I agree. Later on in the day, I tell the tour guide I have scheduled a meeting with a Pakistani businessman who has also expressed an interest in my company. He reacts as though this betrays our newly formed business alliance. The embarrassing situation reminds me how little I know about Central Asian etiquette.

My four days in Tashkent yield just about everything short of a refugee camp. I like the city, but staying here longer would not help me accomplish my mission.

I join a throng of travelers heading in a southwesterly direction, to a town called Samarqand. There we are greeted by the most remarkable architecture I have ever laid my eyes on. Some of the majestic structures, including a domed temple, have been coated with mosaics that glisten in the sun. The alluring patterns even cover some of the roads. This place is as dazzling as the fabled Land of Oz.

Late in the fourteenth century AD, Samarqand and a vast territory surrounding it belonged to a ruthless conqueror named Timur I Leng. The word "leng," which was eventually replaced by "Lane" in most historical accounts, means "lame" in Uzbek. This was in reference to his left foot, lame from birth. Many of the artisans responsible for the uniqueness of Samarqand, Timur Lane's headquarters, were abducted from their own lands by his army. Even though few men in history have slaughtered as many innocents as the infamous Uzbek, he is still lionized by many people in Uzbekistan. Some of them consider the county's current ruler, President Islom Karimov, a far less honorable man. Karimov, born right here in Samarqand, runs an administration with a human rights record that includes allegations of rampant torture and boiling people alive.[1] This controversial Uzbek ruler holds democracy in very low regard. He's becoming a great friend of the United States these days.

I attend an outdoor dance performance in a lavish courtyard during my second evening in Samarqand. The performers invite everyone to join in for the finale and I cautiously take them up on the offer. I cannot help but reflect on the similarity between this presentation and a dancing exhibition some years ago by the First Nations peoples in Alert Bay, BC. Not only was the audience there encouraged to participate as well, but also the facial features of the dancers here closely resemble those of the Canadian natives. Uzbeks with Mongolian facial features were not an uncommon sight in Tashkent. I see a lot more of them here in Samarqand. Because this town was a major stop along the Silk Road, developed largely by Genghis Khan and his Mongols, the facial characteristics do not surprise me. Many Hazara ethnics in Afghanistan have a similar Mongolian look about them.

Most Westerners consider the Silk Road strictly ancient history. Yet less than two hundred years ago, Napoleon Bonaparte sought to control it. Today it is coveted by the US. American strategy planners are drafting a plan for a major military buildup throughout the Silk Road Corridor, from China all the way to the Mediterranean. The interest centers on Central Asian oil and gas, possibly the most substantial sources left on the planet. The Americans say they need it to maintain their standard of living. They have already gained the upper hand in bidding and now they want to begin constructing the pipelines necessary for its transport. The White House believes in a sovereign right to protect its investment. This is where the military comes in.

Controlling the Silk Road and Central Asian fossil fuel will do more than provide lucrative investment opportunities for the American military/industrial complex. It will keep the precious resource out of the hands of rivals such as Russia and China, crippling the two main countries that stand in the way of US plans for a global empire. Furthermore, the upcoming war on terror (this would not get underway for another four and a half years) will give the US an excuse to deploy thousands of troops right on the doorstep of both nations. And In less than two years the ominously aggressive objectives to control the Silk Road and its oil will be tabled in US congress as The Silk Road Strategy Act.

I leave Samarqand on my second morning in the city. I would like to continue exploring the historic sites, but priorities other than tourism now start to bear down on me. The plan is to head further southward, this time to Termez, a smaller town right on the river that borders Afghanistan.

During last year's visit to Yemen, I discovered buses frequently left early, a lingering memory. I therefore get to the depot a half-hour ahead of the 6:30 a.m. departure time. No other passengers have arrived yet, so I take a look around. A worker transfers a number of sheep from the hold of one bus to that of another. A woman at the other end of building moves about waving a straw-like stick, soon right up under my chin. The intoxicating smoke weaves its way up to my nostrils. This is a type of incense used for good luck blessings, which she distributes for as much or as little as one might pay. I am familiar with the practice, having seen it in other Asian lands.

Twenty minutes go by and no one joins me. A cab driver then punches his horn to get my attention. He shouts out the window that the southbound bus will not turn up today. I consider this a minor annoyance rather than a major setback, since it's nothing new for me on roads less traveled.

The first of my drivers explains the trip to Termez will involve three separate cabs and drivers operating in relay fashion. The men will split the fare. The main reason for the relay system probably involves licenses required to drive through certain jurisdictions lying in between Samrqand and Termez. This would not surprise me at all in tightly controlled country like Uzbekistan. In many countries, taxis, or even private vehicles, need permits to cross provincial or district boundaries. But the relay system also assures the drivers stay within a reasonable distance of home, and it helps them conserve fuel as well. Because the government rations petrol right now, it's a wise plan.

The heat of the desert sun filters into the car as we drive. We pass a young shepherd boy preparing and selling yogurt by the side of the road. The boy, looking very alone in a vast expanse of desert, spends more time lazing under a self-made lean-to than serving customers.

In several places, men with strange conical hats linger by the side of the road. The third of my cabs employs a radar detector that proves useful, as we speed through a trap. We reach the Termez provincial boundary shortly before our destination. Here, another surprise lies in store. It's the Russian 201st Mechanized Division military checkpoint. These guys aren't here to fool around; they've got a tank on either side of them. Short and plump guards, far less intimidating, were tending the roadblocks further north. The government obviously wants to keep a firmer grip on the comings and goings down here on the Afghanistan border. The fact that it puts a Russian military outfit in charge shows who is really in control of security.

One reason for all of the security in this country is the Islamic Movement of Uzbekistan (IMU), a grass roots organization that wants to transform the land into a Muslim state. The movement began in the Ferghana Valley, on the Uzbek/Kyrgyz border. Many of the members of this group, consisting of Uzbeks and other Central Asians, have benefited from Osama bin-Laden's training centers in Afghanistan.

The movement, led by a man named Juma Namangani, is still in its fledgling stages. Soon, however, it will gain notoriety for a series of well-coordinated bombings in Tashkent. The Kyrgyz secret service will also accuse the organization of controlling heroin smuggling from Northern Afghanistan into the surrounding lands of Central Asia. President Islom Karimov of Uzbekistan has attracted many enemies, but the Muslim fundamentalists of the IMU might be the most deadly.

My cab reaches Termez less than an hour after we leave the Russian military checkpoint. I soon find out that the only person who can speak English around here is a ten-year-old boy working at the hotel. The man at reception can utter a few words, but not enough to communicate anything of value. My frustrations are mounting.

The next morning, after the sun blasts a wake-up call through the gap in my curtains, I make my way over to the local market. It seems like this would be a good place to find Afghans, if there are any to be found. Here, I spy a unique looking elderly man with tribal clothes and a fur hat. He looks like someone with more experience in desert dust bowls than urban centers – possibly an Afghan. I trail him for a while, hoping to eventually take a photo. I finally get his attention. He eyes me with suspicion at first, but soon warms up and gives me a knowing smile. I snap my shot before he returns to haggling in an animated and aggressive fashion.

I next move on to the tomb of a famous Sufi saint named Mohammed Ali Hakim. He was a medieval scholar who founded a Sufi order. A window at the rear of the tomb looks out onto a lovingly groomed garden. Not far beyond, the land gradually dips down onto the riverbank and then rises up again on the other side of the water – Afghanistan. The land on both sides of the river belonged to a larger country named Bactrium, back in the days of Alexander the Great. Several hundred years later, both Islam and Buddhism flourished here, side by side. The congregation of religious expression must have influenced modern day Sufism. Paying tribute to the memory of Bactrium, the Afghan province directly to the south still bears another of its ancient names, Balkh.

This is such a picturesque setting. An artist could sit here for hours on end, laying brush to canvass. But as I take in the sensual expanse, a feeling of bewilderment suddenly washes over me. Here I stand, practically a stone-throw from the country that has lured me here. And not a solitary Afghan has crossed my path.

CHAPTER 2

UZBEKISTAN and TAJIKISTAN:
AUGUST 18-22, 1997

For me, travel in distant lands represents emotional peaks and valleys. The natural highs that accompany new discoveries are interspersed with sporadic bouts of loneliness. Moments of uplifting conversation in turn relieve these. A unique occurrence will occasionally help me gain a moment of clarity somewhere beyond my normal range of experience. This can help balance the entire situation. But right now, my sense of purpose for coming here feels like it's slipping away.

My wife and daughters now wait for me in Bangkok, while I lag behind schedule. I can't even phone them; the telephones here are inefficient and expensive. Most of the people I have spoken to don't know a word of English. I get a fairly clear impression that even if they did, all they would tell me is how much they dislike the Afghans. Adding salt to these wounds, I have accomplished next to nothing. Except to learn that the border has been sealed for some time and that not even NGOs can cross the "Freedom Bridge" leading into Afghanistan.

My most logical destination from here appears to be Tajikistan. If the refugees who lived in Afghanistan's northern provinces did not flee for Uzbekistan, they would have settled in Tajikistan. Most Tajiks speak Dari (Persian) and so do most Afghans, although often as a second language. Massoud's father came from Tajikistan. Massoud's people in the Panjshir Valley are almost all of Tajik ethnicity. There must be Afghans inside the country.

The only realistic departure point for an entry into Tajikistan is Tashkent. According to the schedules I have studied, I cannot readily fly into the country from here, and any overland route would take too much time. The train from Termez to Dushanbe, for instance, leaves only a few times a week. Tajik officials might not let me in, either, without getting a visa from their embassy in Tashkent. I must get back to the Uzbek capital as soon as possible. From there I can hire a driver to take me to a Tajik city called Kojund. I do not want to waste another day driving back up north, so I will fly back to Tashkent tomorrow.

A tense atmosphere greets my early morning arrival at the Termez airport. Plain-clothes authorities drag a distraught fellow, bound by the wrists, onto a waiting aircraft. Another English-speaking ticket holder, seemingly well connected but overly inquisitive, latches onto me. He claims to know a lot about Afghanistan. Maybe I can use some of his information, but I don't like the fact that he buzzes around making and taking telephone calls from airport business desks. It disturbs me enough that I don't want him around me. I finally shake him off, but now it's time for the airport officials to search my carry-on bags.

I have recently been scanning a couple of paperbacks pertaining to my travels. One of them contains details on Uzbek history that the woman sifting through my bags does not appear to care for. The account presents Timur Lane, the country's national hero from centuries past, in a very unflattering light. It portrays him as more of a butcher than the glorious leader still heralded by many Uzbeks.

The Russian security officer demonstrates more than a casual interest in the book, a possibility that would never have occurred to me, not even remotely. She takes her time, really getting into it. Because slandering a head of state or legendary figure can mean trouble in many eastern countries, I start to squirm a little. Finally, however, she motions me ahead. I wonder had she not been of Russian descent, but an Uzbek official, if the encounter might have ended differently. Once again I have trouble distinguishing who is in charge of security around here.

While up in the air, my thoughts drift toward the city at which I will once again momentarily arrive. I recall the Pakistani businessman I spoke to about my recycling company. We talked about other things as well. He explained that the gas rationing in Uzbekistan stemmed from a dispute with Kazakhstan, which supplied them with fuel from its massive reserves. He then went on to say that Uzbekistan also possessed mineral wealth, having signed a $1.3 billion deal with Enron for exploitation rights less than a year ago. As of yet, the natural gas remains untapped.[3]

Kazakhstan might have as much or even more oil than Saudi Arabia. The oil and also the massive border that the nation shares with the Russian heartland make it a geo-political prize as a business and military partner. The US has already made considerable progress on both fronts, mostly at the expense of Russia.

With huge dividends at stake for a number of struggling nations, Central Asian oil deposits have become big news in business and political circles. The oil would certainly not be recent news to American intelligence agencies, but it has altered the politics of the region considerably. Later this year, Zbigniew Brzezinski, a former American National Security Adviser, would release his book called "The Grand Chessboard." In it he described how the control of present day Eurasia was the key to world supremacy. He also claimed that conquering Central Asian oil was the key to establishing this control. With the American public's disapproval of US military expansionism, he concluded that his plan unfortunately couldn't be put into play "except in the circumstance of a truly massive and widely perceived direct external threat."

After the Pakistani gentleman and me had exhausted other subjects, I made some favorable comments about Massoud. He countered that I was entitled to my opinion, adding that Afghanistan contributed nothing to its section of the globe other than guns and narcotics.

It did not take long for me to see that this man's point of view reflected a strong cultural bias. According to persistent rumours, the Taliban own tons of weapons. These arms get into Afghanistan via Pakistan and its intelligence agency, the ISI (Inter-Service Intelligence Agency). The Taliban government that he respects uses poppy production and the ensuing heroin manufacturing to support itself financially. By clearly supporting the Taliban, Pakistan – possibly inadvertently – helps to perpetuate the violence in Afghanistan. Yet the country sees itself as a stabilizing force.

Pakistan, in this very year, is identified as the world's most terrorist-friendly country. It allegedly hosts sixty-three training camps for Sikh and Kashmiri separatists alone. Others prepare hardcore dissidents for operations inside India.[4] A number of them are largely for "Arab" Afghans. It has been widely reported that notorious Afghan military commanders Gulbuddin Hekmatyar and Rasoul Sayyaf have at times supervised a number of these training facilities, located just inside Pakistan's border with Afghanistan.[5] These two Afghans have spent time as both allies and adversaries of Ahmed Shah Massoud, as well as each other.

The Pakistan government officially claims to be shutting down the training camps, but the ISI seems much more interested in nurturing them. This is partly because the CIA, with its Saudi friends, has been working hand-in-hand with the ISI for about twenty years to facilitate its political designs in Afghanistan and neighboring lands. Ultimately, the training provided by the insurgent camps comes in handy for all concerned. Some of the graduates can be manipulated to stir up trouble precisely where and when it serves the CIA's agenda. Some of the camps originally created by the ISI and CIA during the Afghan Soviet war, both in Afghanistan and Pakistan, are still in operation today. They still might even have the same landlords. These "terrorist" training centers could be compared to the School of the Americas in the USA.

Certain rebel factions in Pakistan's North West Frontier Province moved over the border into Afghanistan several years ago. Perhaps it was a matter of timing. Here Osama bin-Laden, subsequent to banishment from both his Saudi homeland and Sudan, ran some of the world's largest terrorist schools. Although his main camp, Duranta, allowed only Arabs to attend, the schools attracted fundamentalist Muslims from everywhere. They trained for duty not only in Afghanistan, but other places, such as Kashmir. Some of the graduates did not take long to demonstrate, rather dramatically, what they had learned under Osama's tutelage. It all started in Saudi Arabia. Two attacks, in 1995 and 1996, claimed the lives of twenty-four US military men. Some called the violence a blowback.

As soon as I get back to Tashkent, I reduce my travel load and obtain a visa from the Tajik embassy. At the embassy, I encounter the first people who I consider potential Afghans. But I get little opportunity to communicate with them and I feel temporarily intimidated by my inability to express myself in anything but sign language. Tomorrow I will cross the Tajikistan border and attempt to locate Afghan refugees for the final time.

I emerge in the town of Kojund around noon the next day. This requires two taxi rides, the first dropping me at the pedestrian border crossing and the other hauling me the rest of the way. The second cab drops me off at a bank. I realize now that by not declaring all of my funds when I first arrived in Central Asia, I could face a touchy situation when I leave the Tashkent airport for home.

Bank personnel help me out as much as they can under the circumstances, but it's not enough. To show their compassion, two tellers invite me to lunch. You would never see this where I live. An English professor joins us, and after eating he takes me to the local museum for a couple of hours. Here, I learn about the father of all Western medicine, Abu Sina, or "Avicenna." He invented new concepts in surgery by working on stolen cadavers, about a thousand years ago. Avicenna's discoveries advanced the Muslim world a few hundred years beyond Europe in the medical field.

I continue to ask questions about Afghan refugees and Massoud after leaving the museum – questions that once again draw blanks. I finally scratch out a letter requesting pertinent information and send it to an NGO in Dushanbe, this country's capital. I will unfortunately not receive a reply until I get home, if at all.

This nation's capital, Dushanbe, sits in the southern portion of the nation, across the Hindu Kush Mountains. If I could have spared a few extra days, maybe I would have considered flying there directly from Tashkent instead of making a quick trip here to a smaller northern location. But the bottom line is I just don't know where the refugee camps are. I didn't know then and I don't know now. The only options remaining for me are to stay here overnight or go directly back to Tashkent. I will catch a taxi back right away, even if I have to travel through the night. There seems to be enough government control in Uzbekistan that I do not need to worry about security. I would come to know much more about the nation's policing efforts.

Tajik police accost my cab just south of the border, waving us over from the side of the highway. They rummage through my belongings, asking questions in a gruff manner. They don't subject me to a body search, but it's a fairly intimidating shakedown. My driver tells me these thugs were probably less concerned that someone might be running drugs, guns or whatever, than with the possibility one might attempt such an enterprise without having first greased their palms.

I find myself grounded for one final day at the Tashkent Hotel before the next flight out. The boss of my Korean friend at the tour agency invites me to join him and his family for an afternoon at a nearby lake.

Along the way, we pass a sizeable group of people lined up outside of an ordinary house. It's a designated sugar rationing station, I am told. The government has monopolized cane sugar due to a shortage. Other agricultural concerns exist as well. Soldiers were stationed at wheat farms during harvest time, to make sure none of the crop was pilfered for black market sale.

My companions pick their boy up at a summer camp that looks not unlike the one I take my daughter to, half way around the world.

It's called "Simurgh." The simurgh is a mythical bird quite revered in their culture. It even appears on Uzbek currency.

We spend the afternoon at a cottage on an artificial body of water named the Qayroqqum Reservoir. It's situated very close to where Krygystan, Tajikistan and Uzbekistan all meet. The reservoir has been created by the drainage overflow from a part-natural dam that lies nearby. The water ultimately derives from the Syr River system. The cottage does not belong to this family but offers comfortable quarters for us all. The adults report that this is the hottest day of the year, creating a perfect opportunity to go swimming. Cooling off, I relax and take in my surroundings. An elderly neighbor beats the hard earth with a hoe, seemingly acclimatized to the blistering sun. A bird perches on the back of an either apathetic or friendly horse. The sky is free of cloud and azure like the blue mosaic found throughout Muslim lands. I am grateful for the moment.

Ultimately, my uncompromising vegetarianism strains the occasion, as it leads my hosts to believe they have poorly accommodated me. It also leaves me dining on medicinal tea to prevent intestinal cramps. Still, everyone enjoys the outing.

Darkness falls shortly after we return to town. It's time for me to start packing. I find myself worrying about the rest of the undeclared funds I still possess. My banking efforts in Kojund attained only partial success, so the balance remains lumped in one of my pockets. If the authorities at the airport decide to pat me down really well, they will wonder why I am leaving the country with more money than I claimed to have on the way in. The fact that I dare to conceal it will not amuse them either. Intensifying my paranoia is a bit of hotel gossip about a French patron who recently plotted a similar maneuver. Apparently he still resides in town, several days past his scheduled departure date. His funds have been confiscated while he awaits legal resolution. It was also mentioned that the officials who caused his troubles did not demand a bribe, which the Frenchman believed to be rather "stupide" of them.

I don't determine my strategy until morning. If I declare all of my money and try to explain the discrepancy as a misunderstanding, I will probably at least miss my flight. I decide to take the silent route. All I can do is apply maximum resourcefulness when I hide the cash.

Things work out fine. The customs people accept my claim at face value. I can now board the plane.

CHAPTER 3

MASSOUD:
1953 to 1980

Ahmed Shah Massoud was born in 1953 in Jangalak, a small village near the foot of the Panjshir Valley in Afghanistan. The third of six children, he enjoyed a fairly normal childhood with an education that included the fundamentals of the Islamic faith. His father, a Tajik native, graduated from military college and moved the family around to accommodate his career as a police commander. Later, he became a mid-level official in the Afghan military. His assignments often carried him into the borderlands of Afghanistan, always teeming with criminal activity. It was an occupation intriguing enough to have perhaps fed a young boy's imagination.

Ahmed Shah received his high school education at a French school in Kabul named Lycee Istiqlal. The French he learned here would help him later in life. At the impressionable age of nineteen, he enrolled at the Russian college, Kabul Polytechnic Institute. It was an extremely impressive facility built by the Soviets in the 1960s, with teaching materials only in Russian. Perhaps a few friends knew that his interest in the school involved more than just the curriculum and social activity that such establishments offered. Maybe no other interest existed at first. In any event, the shift to higher learning resulted in a far different experience for the young man than his family would have expected. Massoud bonded with vigilant students who paid far less attention to their studies than the politics of their country. The winds of change were blowing freely in the capital city of Afghanistan.

The president of the nation was a man named Mohammed Daoud Khan. He had been prime minister in the 1950s, before seizing leadership of the country from his cousin, King Zahir Shah, in 1973. He then quickly moved to abolish the monarchy. Daoud's reformist leanings and long-term relationship with the Soviet Union had dredged up considerable unrest, especially in Kabul. Protest mattered little to the Afghan president. He continued to hold modernization and development as a priority over Islamic creed. As tensions heightened, Daoud proceeded to ban activities of the many Islamic opposition parties. This suppression of freedom soon pushed the brittle conflict to a breaking point.

Massoud allied himself with one of the few ethnically mixed student opposition groups, the Jawanan-e-Mussulman, or "Muslim Youth." They opposed Daoud passionately. A plan for an insurrection was made under a man named Habib Rahman, but the government found out about it.[6] Authorities jailed Rahman, while Massoud fled to Pakistan with some of his cohorts.[7]

This would not only defuse the situation, but would also buy the young men some time and space to formulate a viable plan against the president. The departure from his homeland terminated Massoud's flirtation with higher education after only a year. It also altered the course of his life. Ahmed Shah Massoud was now on the path of becoming the legendary "Lion of Panjshir."

Exiled in Peshawar where nationalism festered, the young commander found himself in close quarters with others of similar mind. One of them was the esteemed leader of Jamait-i-Islami, Burhanuddin Rabbani. Rabbani had helped to found the "Muslim Youth" at Kabul University. A passionate Muslim and respected theology professor, Rabbani practiced a methodical approach to winning the loyalty of his disillusioned people. He was very much a media savvy man, likely the result of education and travel. He seemed to understand it would require time, dialogue and consistency to build the people's trust. Rabbani's platform was a voice for the sanctity of Islamic principles, the most important concern amongst the many. He stressed protection of Islamic teachings and an honest representation for all. Nevertheless, spreading the word would have to go hand-in-hand with a passionate opposition to Daoud's oppressive policies. This was risky business. Daoud punished his detractors very severely, despite initiating some humane national programs.

To what extent Pakistani intelligence assisted these young men with their mission, few can claim with certainty. It appears that the ISI trained Massoud and others to stir the pot in strategic areas of Afghanistan. Pakistan also wanted to rid itself of the Soviet influence so close by. The strategy would hopefully overwhelm regional governments and simultaneously disperse central command's forces, clearing the path for a coup d'etat in Kabul. Even if the students devised the plot entirely on their own, they would have known ahead of time that the people in the border regions of Peshawar, Pakistan, would lend a sympathetic ear. The territory was traditionally full of hot-blooded fundamentalists with an historical affiliation to Afghan politics. If the young men had come in search of weapons and manpower, it was precisely what they found.

The plan that was agreed to dispatched Massoud to the Panjshir Valley, the land of his birth. The young man's former neighbors initially met him with enthusiasm, but only until heated speeches grew into controversial actions. The valley folk then developed apprehensions about the increasing likelihood of government reprisal. Other members of the "Muslim Youth" attempted to carry out the most perilous phase of the overall strategy, the coup. They failed. A number of Ahmed Shah's colleagues were not only captured, but also executed. Whatever details of the scheme the government had not yet gathered wind of surely spilled out at this point. With support dwindling to the extent that his own people had started to raise arms against him, Massoud's only recourse was to escape into the mountains with his life. He stayed there for several months.

Ahmed Shah eventually returned to the Peshawar, while others in the fledgling political party viewed his escape with suspicion. Certain members had convinced themselves that one of the key players must have tipped Daoud off, and they had started to point fingers. A menacing degree of paranoia swirled around the Muslim Youth Party camp for a while. Some accounts even suggest that Massoud spent some time under house arrest.

One of those who started to quarrel with Massoud at this point was a fellow collaborator named Gulbuddin Hekmatyar. The two of them accused each other of not holding up their end of the coup. This would be the beginning of a lengthy adversarial relationship between the two.

Most Afghans would eventually come to view Daoud Khan, the once unpopular Afghan president, as a strong leader. One could count Ahmed Shah among them. As an older and wiser warrior, he would regret his attempt to wrestle power away from the man. Massoud eventually realized that Daoud had implemented long term programs aimed at decreasing ethnic sensitivities and boosting national pride – a much needed political strategy in a country divided by ethnic rivalries and tribal warfare. The president had also distributed funds equitably across the land. Massoud would come to acknowledge that Daoud was the only one in contemporary history who had committed himself to upgrading and improving the lives of his countrymen. Quite sadly, no such sentiment had blessed Daoud Khan's rocky tenure as Afghan president back in the 1970s. When all was said and done, it would not be Daoud's eagerness, but rather his lack of inclination to take sides in the Soviet–US political wrangling, that precipitated his demise.

Some resentment toward Massoud's role in the botched control bid festers in certain Afghan circles to this very day. But shortly after the mission failed, he resigned from a fractured and dissension-filled Muslim Youth Party. He probably concluded that such a radical road to change would simply not work in his native land. The disheartened young warrior demonstrated sharp instincts in calculating this move, for the party would now collapse, at least temporarily.

The Soviets were still very much in the picture. They had grown increasingly agitated at Daoud Khan's insistence on Afghan independence. The president welcomed aid from both the US and the USSR. A high-ranking Russian official visited him personally, in a last-ditch effort to extort cooperation. The Russian premier was now demanding Daoud's compliance to Soviet objectives in Afghanistan. A rumour would circulate that when Daoud heard the order, he responded by lighting an American cigarette. This signified a shift in allegiance. The moment of impertinence probably cost the Afghan leader his life.

President Daoud Khan and his family of seventeen were massacred in a coup by their own military in the spring of 1978. It was a bloody ordeal that took up to 2,000 lives – an event no doubt manipulated by Moscow. A local communist faction called the People's Democratic Party of Afghanistan (PDPA) assumed control, but dissension would quickly develop. The two government groups involved, the Parcham and the Khalq, both wanted the upper hand. The ensuing battle resulted in the Khalq Party ruling the country. Nur Mohammed Taraki became the president of the Revolutionary Council and chairman of the party. His close friend, Hafizullah Amin, became the first prime minister of Afghanistan. The two of them signed a friendship pact with the Russians before the year's end. To seal the agreement, the Soviets shipped him arms and advisers to help smash a raging resistance, especially within traditional tribal communities. The government was now at war with its people. Afghan prisons, already known for their horrors, became overcrowded torture facilities and death camps for rabble-rousers. The Communist Democratic Republic of Afghanistan was born.

In February of 1979, the American Ambassador to Afghanistan, Adolph Dubs, was kidnapped. He died shortly after in a failed rescue attempt. Taraki's government accused Kabul's small Maoist party, one of a large and confusing array of political factions now vying for control. The group apparently did not care for the Americans' growing interest in the nation's power struggle. Tensions were now escalating in all directions.

An anti-communist rebellion grew out of control in western Afghanistan's most populated city, Herat, only a month later. Taraki quickly moved to put out the fire, sending in troops from Kabul. But once they got there, many of these troops, now under the guidance of a local military officer named Major Ismail Khan, decided they would join the side of the masses. They started executing communists, whom they held responsible for the trouble in their country. Chaos set in. Reinforcements were summoned from the capital, including Soviet helicopters, and five thousand Afghans died in the melee. Taraki looked like a fool. Ismail Khan, on the other hand, would eventually be rewarded for his foresight. He would go on to become the highly respected leader of Herat and the governor of the surrounding provinces. But first he would fight as Mujahideen, for a sovereign Islamic Afghanistan.

Taraki died in a power struggle about six months later, at the hands of his prime minister, Hafizullah Amin. For his own sake, Amin should have rejected the leadership role. Afghans saw only another Soviet implant in power and could not have cared less what he had to say. When a few months passed and Amin showed little ability to control the rampant hostility, the Russians ran out of patience. The time had arrived to grab this fractious nation by the throat and beat it into submission. In December of 1979, about 30,000 Red Army troops rolled into Afghanistan. They executed Hafizullah Amin and installed Babrak Karmal, the man who had led the Parcham Party before the Khalqs exiled him. The next few weeks would unleash a full-scale attack on Afghanistan.

Early in 1980, a mature Ahmed Shah Massoud marched home again from Pakistan to the Panjshir Valley, followed by a gathering militia of Muslims ready to repel the Soviet invader. An imperialist superpower had suddenly entered their homeland, so Afghans would now put petty grievances aside. Everyone in the Panjshir rallied around Massoud this time. Unlike his first assignment on home ground, five years earlier, his date with destiny would not be denied.

Almost no one realized it at the time, but the Soviets had just been lured into cooperating with the US agenda. In the words of Zbigniew Brzezinski, then US National Security Adviser:"It was July 3rd 1979 that President Carter signed the first directive for secret aid to opponents of the pro-Soviet regime in Kabul. And that very day I wrote a note to the president in which I explained to him that in my opinion this aid was going to induce a Soviet military intervention...We didn't push the Russians to intervene, but we knowingly increased the probability that they would...That secret operation was an excellent idea. It had the effect of drawing the Soviets into the Afghan trap...the day that the Soviets officially crossed the border, I wrote a note to President Carter. We now have the opportunity of giving to the USSR its Vietnam".[8]

The fact that hundreds of thousands of innocent Afghans would surely die in the process was obviously beside the point.

The United Nations and the Organization of Islamic Nations did not take long to voice their disapproval of the Russian military assault in Afghanistan. Moscow insisted its army would remain only as long as it took them to repel the foreign elements trying to sabotage the friendly Kabul regime. The Kremlin told their troops that these insurgents consisted of mercenaries from Pakistan and Israel, led by the CIA.

Soviet military strategists must have thought that victory over a mere twenty five million who possessed little in the way of an army, modern technology, or even electricity, would be only a matter of time. Probably not much of that, either. As in all wars, there would be a certain amount of death and destruction. But to them, as with most invaders and occupiers, the end would justify the means. It was necessary to tear down before everyone could rebuild the country together, along Soviet lines. Perhaps the Russians believed the resistance in Afghanistan would be minimal. It seemed reasonable to assume that in regions such as the Panjshir Valley, clusters of peasants still mired in the Dark Ages surely couldn't mount much of a threat. Occupying a space even smaller than Texas, USA, the size of the country would certainly not pose a problem. And with three Soviet republics bordering its north, surely they would achieve infiltration with the ease of penetrating a next-door neighbor's backyard. But even though nothing could alter this latter advantage, the former assumption would prove to be a lethal miscalculation. Back in the nineteenth century, the British had learned this very same lesson the hard way. The war would ultimately drain the

Soviet Union's power and influence so badly, it would open the door to Eurasia for the USA's industrial/military complex.

The one technique proven to unify Afghans is to assail their country. United against invaders, they tussle with the ferocity of a pit bull protecting her litter. It was with this ingrained spirit and an array of guerrilla warfare tactics that Massoud and his men confronted the communists. Foreign weapons supplies shipped through Pakistan would assist to a small degree, but such provisions served many other areas first. The ISI, who distributed them, did not support Massoud's vision for Afghanistan. They consequently kept him well down their list of those who deserved arms the most. This forced the commander to somehow supplement his munitions aid. Stores of guns from grounded helicopters and captured soldiers helped considerably.

Massoud was not a commander who led his men from the sidelines. A chunk of shrapnel injured his leg early in the fighting, while under fire in the famed Salang Tunnel. Fortunately it did not cause enough damage to keep him out of action for long.

After the war had dragged on for a while, the Mujahideen discovered that war-weary Russian vets sometimes found the temptation of the region's heroin and hashish very difficult to resist. The drugs-for-arms deals benefited the Afghans on more levels than one a masterful barter. The trade also helped establish connections with the Russian military for the eventual smuggling of heroin through Tajikistan.

Resistance efforts of the Panjshir militia paid off by December of 1980, when the Soviets left the bulk of the valley for the first time. Their withdrawal followed a month-long skirmish fought by almost every available man and woman for miles around. But the communists made the Panjshiris pay dearly in casualties. They also delivered the severest message possible before their retreat. Buildings, homes, vehicles and anything of value were torched to a crisp. As they buried their dead, many thousands of destitute Afghans faced the scourge of a brutal mountain valley winter without shelter. Food and fuel were scarce as well. Still, the evacuation signaled regional victory for the home side, if only temporarily. Massoud took the opportunity to restructure his team. This gave birth to an inner circle named the Supervisory Council of the North, the Shura-i-Nazar.

News of the Massoud-led success quickly spread to Kabul, inspiring deeper insurrection elsewhere. It also perked the ears of journalists around the globe, such as the well-known BBC anchor, Sandy Gall. Some of them cancelled previous assignments, opting to pursue the freshly crowned "Lion of Panjshir."

CHAPTER 4

TORONTO, CANADA:
DECEMBER, 1997

Thoughts of Afghanistan have never drifted far from my mind since I flew home from Thailand, about three months ago. I have decided I will keep trying to aid Northern Afghans even if a meeting with Massoud continues to elude me. The effort will hopefully increase my chances of tracking down the elusive character.

Knowing some Persian will open doors for me once I arrive in Tajikistan. If I manage to cross the border into Afghanistan, it will help me even more. I have therefore hired an Iranian woman to teach me some of the language. Her name is Farzaneh and she has proven to be a sound investment. Right away, her curiosity about my interest in the Persian language led to a lengthy conversation. More banter after each lesson has developed into a friendship. For some time now, we have been networking to access useful information. She has turned out to be a top end diplomat, something you might expect from someone who comes from distant blood ancestry of a royal court in Persia's peacock throne.

I have also begun to acquaint myself more intimately with Afghan history and culture. Much of what I read on Afghanistan mentions the importance of the "Durand Line." The Durand Line is the name of the somewhat haphazardly marked 1500–mile border between Afghanistan and Pakistan. The British imposed this border on Afghans in 1893, after being defeated by them in two different wars. It was named after Sir Mortimer Durand, the colonial Foreign Secretary of British India at the time of "the Great Game". British India would later become the country of Pakistan. Harper's Magazine, in 1862, would say the following about the British occupation of Afghanistan: "The practical exercise of power was in the hands of servants of a soulless corporation on the opposite side of the globe, whose predominant feeling was contempt for the people over whom they were placed."[9]

The Durand line took a large strip of turf belonging to Afghanistan and gave it to British India. Over a century later, modern–day Pakistan has continued to keep the region under its jurisdiction. The land was initially transferred to separate many of Afghanistan's Pushtun tribes from one another, weakening the nation. The Afghan loya jurga, or tribal council, of 1949 decreed the Durand Line invalid, but it still stands as the official border between the two countries. Many of the ethnic Pushtuns who live in the disputed FATA territory today still identify with Afghanistan as their true ancestral home, even though they possess Pakistan citizenship. Some can enjoy a better standard of living by remaining in Pakistan, and so they stay. But they do not forget that the soil they live on belonged to the country of their origin just over one hundred years ago. They are Afghans who live in a country called Pakistan simply because a British bureaucrat drew a new line on a map and scratched out the old one.

The Durand Line is a very capricious issue for these Pushtuns. The mid-western borderlands where they live are known as North West Frontier Province. In the mosaic of provinces that form Pakistan, the NWFP is the only one whose name does not reflect the ethnicity of the people residing there. Its many Afghan Pushtuns would very much like to see the province called "Pushtunistan." The name "Frontier Province" falls well short of inspiring pride. Pakistan bureaucrats, however, feel that allowing such a name change would almost amount to granting the Pushtuns their independence from Pakistan. Much of what Pakistan gained by the imposition of the Durand Line over a hundred years ago would be lost. So, many Pushtuns of Pakistan remain locked in a long simmering debate with the Pakistan government. Afghanistan and Pakistan fought a war over "Pushtunistan" in 1962.

My research also divulges that four major ethnic groups co-exist within the country, but dozens of others are found in smaller numbers as well. These groups usually have their favorite leader who most of them rally behind. For instance, most Uzbeks support General Dostum, another Uzbek. Many Pushtuns support Gulbuddin Hekmatyar. Most Tajiks favor Massoud, while many Hazaras get behind General Dostum. Quite a few Hazaras also support a leader named Mazari. Afghans with Tajik bloodlines, like Massoud, represent about a quarter of Afghanistan's population, the most predominant ethnic minority. The Hazaras, supposedly descended from Ghengis Khan, comprise about twenty percent of the nation, with the Uzbeks and others accounting for another twelve. This leaves the Pushtuns, out of which the Taliban has not only grown, but from which it also receives the bulk of its support. They account for about thirty eight percent of the population, but this figure is deceiving.[10] The many Pushtuns who live on the other side of the Durand Line, in the Federally Administered Tribal Area (FATA) of Pakistan's North West Frontier Province, would raise this figure to fifty percent or higher if included in the tally. And they consider themselves Afghan. The fact that Pushtun students from the FATA are allowed to attend Afghan schools and universities shows the political clout that these Pushtuns still retain in the present political climate of Afghanistan.

Most Hazaras practice a division of the Islamic religion known as Shi'a (or Shi'ite). Some smaller Shi'a Muslim groups also reside in the land. However, the majority of the country practices the Sunni Muslim faith, which these Afghans consider to be a purer form of Islam. Many more Sunnis than Shi'as can be found throughout the world. The Shi'as are focused largely in Iran, Iraq, Bahrain and Azerbaijan, but they also have significant populations in Afghanistan, Pakistan and several other countries. The Hazaras generally stand out from other Afghans not only by virtue of their religion, but also quite often through their physical appearance. Many of them have Mongolian rather than Turkic or South Asian facial features. Largely due to their religious and physical differences, the Hazaras of Afghanistan have been persecuted for hundreds of years. General Dostum has consistently been, more than any other warlord, the Hazaras' strategic guardian. He has proved this by keeping Mazar e Sharif, on the northern edge of the Hazarajat, a secure place for Hazaras.

A nomadic segment of the Pushtun population known as the "Kochie" have traditionally competed with the Hazaras for grazing grounds, especially in the central plateau region, the Hazarjat. This has also created problems. The country's other ethnic groups have often been in harsh conflict with Hazaras as well, particularly the Tajiks. I would come to know more about how widespread this repression was at a later date. At times, it would even include Massoud and his allies.

Political parties representing all of these ethnic factions, splinter groups from within them, and varied religious devotions saturate Afghanistan. This makes it a land of a great many divisions. The country is a melting pot of political and religious ideology, often in heated struggle. The many differences celebrated by the various peoples of the nation makes them easy prey for foreign powers and such interference often shapes Afghanistan's history.

I have benefited from reading material to a degree, but an Afghan community Farzaneh and I located here in Toronto has given me a feel for what Afghans are really like. The gracious people of the community offered to help. They recently presented me with a mound of boxes full of clothing to either send or take back to refugees from their homeland. We received some envelopes with $5 donations that could have represented tomorrow's food. This was very touching to us, appreciated much more than a fat corporate donation would have been. Friends and I packed some boxes of goods as well, which included medicines donated to the Remote Communities Development Foundation. Because the cargo will take at least a month to get to any Central Asian destination, I have already sent it to Tajikistan.

Having made contact with the Afghan embassies in both Tashkent and Dushanbe was certainly a coup. The staff at the embassy in Dushanbe informed us that the refugee camps I have been seeking could indeed be found right there, in the country's capital. It was ironic to discover this from my own hometown after thousands of miles of travel failed to provide me with the information. Still, I welcomed the news. One of the embassy representatives also disclosed that Massoud occasionally visited the city, but that no one could predict when. The commander obviously kept his schedule to himself – a matter of survival.

I hope to leave in a few weeks. Despite the new information and contacts, it looks like the Massoud part of the equation will remain a gamble.

CHAPTER 5

*UZBEKISTAN to TALOQAN, NORTHERN AFGHANISTAN:
JANUARY 1998*

"Where did I put my baggage tags?"

This issue is causing me a bit of stress me as I enter the arrivals corridor of the Tashkent Airport. Unfortunately, losing things is not so uncommon with me. The closer I inch toward baggage pickup, the surer I become that my ticket, tags and boarding pass remain on the plane. To further erode my credibility, the handler in Bangkok who charged me for my thirty kilograms of excess weight offered no receipt. I dread the potential fiasco involved in attempting to claim my luggage without any proof of ownership. This place runs on suspicion and paranoia.

Suddenly I spot Zaid, my money-changing guide from the first time I passed through here. He remembers me. I briefly convey my dilemma as he nods in acknowledgment. He dashes away to grab a friend who performs various airport functions, including the lucrative foreign exchange. This fellow sticks with me throughout the tedium of foreign arrival procedure. He helps me collect my bags and personally assures the authorities that this small mountain of possessions really does belong to me. The payoff, as I found out last year, is the luxurious thirty three percent commission these hustlers skim off the dollars they expect you to convert. But it's a necessary transaction, and twice now I have benefited from their other services. I climb into a cab, feeling thankful to have escaped an uncomfortable delay in my proceedings at a fairly reasonable price. I find the baggage tags as soon as I get to my hotel.

The following day at the Tashkent Hotel, fatigue overwhelms me. I would rather not leave the hotel. I also have a pounding headache. This could be bad. Wasting a valuable day here would not be advisable. I maneuver someone else into getting me a traveller's visa for Tajikistan. The in-house travel agency that helped out so much last time once again comes to my aid. One of their representatives collects the necessary documentation from me and promises to return, permits in hand. I pay an extra fee for the service, but it's insignificant considering the trouble it spares me.

I checked in last night at 3:00 a.m., badly needing a wash. This was impossible because the water was turned off in the hotel. I woke up this morning feeling neither fresh nor well rested. The water was turned on and a nice long shower energized me a bit, but I have yet to eat. Today I will freely indulge in the cuisine of the land, but I have chosen to participate in the daytime fasting ritual of Ramadan once I get to Tajikistan. Most Uzbeks I meet adhere to a more European tradition during this special religious month, and it doesn't include the same abstinence from food. I will likely begin the fast in two days. I hope taking part in the ancient Muslim tradition will help to put me in closer touch with the people I hope to soon meet.

I continue to track the goods I forwarded two months ago to the Afghan embassy in Tajikistan. I sent them via a Russian airline but it looks like they would have gotten there quicker by boat. That is, if Tajikistan wasn't a landlocked country. Yet, today's fax exchange reveals that Russian New Years has forced another delay. Knowing how bureaucracy works, I hope a one-day holiday does not result in the shipment collecting another two weeks of dust. At least the articles have safely journeyed that far.

The afternoon's business moves along nicely, despite the fact that I wander outside only for a few seconds. The travel agent returns with my visa. Another helper purchases some new batteries for my camera. I still must find somewhere to eat, because the hotel only serves breakfast in the morning. Then I will turn in nice and early for tomorrow's sunrise departure. I'll be travelling to Kojund en route to Dushanbe.

This popular excursion across the border to Kojund comes with a guide who arranges a ride for us to the border. We will cross the border on foot and then find another driver for the remainder of the journey. The three of us make our way out of town early, without any hitches. We will be heading directly to the airport instead of the town because I hope to be on this afternoon's flight to Dushanbe. Falling snow delays our progress in elevated sections of the roadway, but we manage to stay on schedule. Our perfect timing doesn't matter once we get to the airport. Unstable weather conditions have grounded the flight. My guide will suddenly be of greater assistance than I expected, as we're left with quite a bit of time before the next departure, at 8:00 a.m. tomorrow.

I will eventually need somewhere to sleep, so we stop by a quaint European-style bed and breakfast I remember seeing last year. We stay just long enough to drop off my bags. An excursion to the local market will be interesting, so we go there first.

The name of this colourful gathering place is Panj Shanbe, which means fifth-day-of-the-week market. I assume it has evolved into a daily affair, with an expanded version of what one can see this afternoon presented every Thursday, the fifth day of their week. Dushanbe, they tell me, signifies second-day-of- the-week market, which is Monday to Tajiks. Because such a large city must have earned its name hundreds of years ago, I wonder if the meaning bears any relevance at all to the current market situation there. Yet, many Asian centers have risen from this humble starting point. Plenty of them still feature the wares of the region-at-large on one special day each week.

Lunch includes some local flatbread sold at the market. It's not unlike the rough bread that one finds locals eating throughout Middle East and Central Asia. We then take a trip to the region's hydroelectric dam. I hear that much of the power generated from the dam ends up in Uzbekistan. The matter is apparently a local irritation. It also shows how much influence Uzbekistan can at times exert over northern Tajikistan. At six o'clock, my guide suggests we head over to the home of a family who will not mind us joining them for the evening. The idea appeals to me. I would like to communicate with few local Tajiks while I can.

The family looks interested to meet someone from such a faraway place. Part of our discussion centers around how geography shapes the social and cultural alliances of their land more than arbitrary national borders do. They say the residents here in Kojund view Dushanbe, not far south as the crow flies, as a city in some other country. Many Uzbeks live here, but very few have made their way south to the capital city. More importantly, the towering mountains between make flying the only reasonable travel option. The average person can afford this luxury only rarely, if ever, so the cities don't have much of a relationship. In contrast, fairly smooth roads can take the Northern Tajiks across the border to the Uzbek cities of Bhukara and Samarqand. Both of these locales, historically, house very significant Tajik populations. Many of them have settled in so comfortably that they now call themselves Uzbeks.

With a little prompting on my part, the conversation moves onto politics. A border dispute has been causing friction between Tajikistan and Uzbekistan. Tajiks look upon some of the lands east of Termez as their own, even though the territory in question appears on maps as part of Uzbekistan. Further inflaming the dilemma, the Tajiks who live in the disputed lands do not feel adequately represented by the Uzbek government, considering their substantial numbers. The Uzbek hierarchy obviously finds these complaints somewhat threatening. The implications of the disputes tweak my interest.

Our host says Uzbek intelligence agents were recently discovered trying to infiltrate Tajikistan from Afghanistan. Their mandate was apparently to use whatever means necessary to destabilize the country's social/economic infrastructure. I assume that "whatever means necessary" could refer partly to drugs and guns, but I don't know how much the alleged plot involves the border disagreement. Although the plan obviously failed, the animosity between the neighboring countries appears to be growing.

I imagine infiltrating Tajikistan would not normally be so much of a challenge. This indicates to me that there might be some shuffling of national alliances. It's not likely Uzbek intelligence would be wandering around Afghanistan without some assistance from Northern Afghan intelligence, for instance. And yet, the Northern Afghans are traditionally linked more closely with Tajikistan than Uzbekistan. This could be a shifting.

We watch a few moments of television news just before I say goodbye. One report says a Russian delegation headed by the prime minister will also touch down in Dushanbe tomorrow. Interesting.

Russia struggles desperately these days to maintain strong political ties with former Soviet bloc countries such as Tajikistan and Uzbekistan. It needs them to maintain as wide a buffer zone as possible from the inevitable American incursion into the region. An impending invasion is obvious to the Russians. Outside of more domestic considerations, Russia too demands its right to the oil development that these Central Asian nations and their bodies of water are projected to yield. The country does not seem to be gaining any ground in this two-pronged battle. The tremendous wealth, oil exploitation technology and military might of its main rival make the US a more desirable partner in every way than the former communist superpower. The Americans therefore continue, bit by bit, to forge deeper bonds with

many countries formerly ruled by the Soviets. It's clearly a long-
term strategy. The nations include Uzbekistan, Tajikistan, Azerbaijan,
Turkmenistan, Kyrgyzstan, and Kazakhstan. The Americans are gaining
the upper hand in negotiations for the oil of the Caspian Sea Basin. I
believe this is part of the plan.

I am now on my way to Dushanbe. The weather is fine today,
so my plane speeds down the runway right on time. The aircraft
tentatively lifts off as I squeeze the armrests of my seat. Sparks fly from
the engine and land a little too close to the fuel tank for my liking.
This is not what I had in mind when I asked for a window seat. It
reminds me that the airline lost a flight full of passengers on the way
to United Arab Emirates, just a few weeks ago. The mass confusion
at the airport so early in the morning did not encourage me either.
Every miniscule administrative detail required me to line up at another
one of the shacks that characterize the airport. Still, as a foreigner I
avoided the worst of it. The authorities asked the departing locals an
intrusive quantity of questions. And Tajiks arriving from Dushanbe
were searched for contraband. I am not sure what accounts for the
airport's heavy security. Perhaps the Islamic Movement of Uzbekistan
once again comes into play. The Ferghana Valley, their home base, lies
close by. It not only straddles the borders of Tajikistan and Uzbekistan,
but Kyrgysztan as well. Calling the Ferghana a strategic location for
the radicals would be an understatement. Its valleys form a labyrinth
leading further north to Kazakhstan, and southward to Afghanistan,
now home of the IMU's ally, Osama bin-Laden. In any event, the
intense security measures at the airport in Kojund are unfortunately
what domestic travel entails in more than a few parts of the world.

The flight remains a rather unsettling affair, but a bird's eye view
of the Hindu Kush Mountain Range compensates. Once everyone is
safely on the tarmac and collecting their belongings, I can see that most
of them wear Russian fur hats. Mine is similar, but fleece, manufactured
from recycled plastic bottles.

An Afghan airport employee intercepts me before I make my
way out of the airport, and introduces himself as Haji Timor. This
is a pleasant surprise. Mr. Timor holds an honourary position in the
building, handling the section of the Dushanbe Airport dealing with
Afghan affairs. For twenty-five years he worked as the head duty officer
at the Kabul airport. He showed up for work every day, regardless
of how many times it was hit by bombs. Timur, an older man who

would become my friend, is practically legendary in his own right. He arranges my lift to the hotel and assures me someone named Mr. Mehdi will soon be in touch from the embassy. When we finally part ways for a few years, he says, "Next time we meet it will be in Kabul." I do not have a clue that his prophecy will come true.

Mohajeddin Mehdi is the first secretary of the Afghan embassy in Dushanbe.11 He visits me in my room the next day. He writes respected poetry, as did his father. Although writing poetry is common among Afghans, this artistic inclination tells me Mr. Mehdi is more than just a diplomat. He is also thoughtful enough to offer me a book of his poems. The depth of his passion for the spoken word comes close to the concern he feels for the well being of his countrymen.

Mr. Mehdi is a well-built, somewhat heavy man with a large nose. Someone has obviously briefed him about me. The secretary knows about the shipment of goods and my intention to help people in his native land. After I expand on these subjects, he answers a few questions. I also express my desire to meet Massoud, not an uncommon request but also not easily satisfied. A year or so after this encounter, Mr. Mehdi would make it possible for me to aid Afghan refugees in the settlements of Dushanbe. The RCDF would send nurses from Canada, equipped with donated medicines and bandages, to educate village nurses in basic health care training. Mr. Mehdi cleared the path of all bureaucratic obstacles, set the itinerary, and made all necessary arrangements. Right now, he makes a valuable contribution to my journey by placing me in touch with contacts who will help me fulfill my goals.

Amrullah Saleh, my next visitor, is a young man about twenty-three or twenty-four years old. He fills the room with energy. I have reached a point in my journey where I need to rely heavily upon others, as if I am to be led around like a blind man for a while. Hopefully, Amrullah is the prime candidate for my guide.

The young man would naturally want to take an accurate read on my sincerity level. There are security issues at stake here, and what does anyone here really know about my history or affiliations? When Amrullah tells me he will function as my liaison and interpreter in the coming days, I look forward to the pleasure of his company.

Amrullah obviously feels comfortable with me because the next day he returns with Mohammed Saleh Registani, a well-dressed, short and slim man with a more officious manner. Mr. Registani is the foreign military attaché for Massoud's Northern Alliance forces. If someone of his stature cares to meet me personally, I could be making some headway.

The plot unfolds at a pace exceeding my expectations, but I sit alone in my room waiting for Amrullah to call. I can't see the city or get any fresh air. I can't use the room phone to make overseas calls either, and I really should bring my family up to date. Only a cell phone will improve the situation. It will put me over budget, but will also solve many problems. I simply walk downstairs and rent one from the front desk.

Dushanbe holds almost 600,000 residents, a size I can get along with nicely. It's a garden city, really, surrounded by mountains. People here boast about the beautiful flowers blooming on the slopes in spring. The scenic views apparently compare favourably to those found in towns of the Swiss Alps. I don't expect to see many flowers in early January, but the park across the street from here is still very alluring. The trees and bushes glisten with ice and snow. A short walk takes me from an urban setting to a rural one, still inside the city. I walk past the trees and shrubs in my path to small farms, some with livestock and fruit trees, right up alongside urban dwellings and stately European-style architecture.

A chance encounter during one of my strolls ends up in the home of French national. The man has been here long enough to love this country and marry a Tajik woman. He seems to have an insider's perspective. His house is sort of a thatched roof affair, part hobby farm and part chalet. The Frenchman claims that Tajikistan experienced its own bona fide civil war from 1992 to 1996. Over 50,000 people died. Some of the Tajiks who fled still live in other countries such as Uzbekistan or Afghanistan. Throughout this period, rebel forces seeking to eliminate all remaining Soviet influence in the country tried to dethrone a post-Cold War government still living in the dark ages of Russian communist oppression. Many of the leaders of the opposition coalition wanted to replace the current regime with an Islamic state. Meanwhile, the organizers of the Imu, Juma Namangani and Tahir Yuldosh experiencing frustration with the lack of promised democracy in these emerging communist nations, found some commonality with the Islamic fundamentalist side of the Tajik civil war. Their common enemy was the old Stalinist guard. It was left filling the vacuum when these nations formed the Commonwealth of

Independent States. Both the communists and the Islamists rushed to fill this vacuum. Namangani and Yuldosh got involved and the struggle spilled into Afghanistan. Four years of sporadic battles ended only when the Tajikistan government gave the dissident warlords enough territory and power to override their broader concerns.

Amrullah calls the next morning to inform me that not only has Massoud just slipped into town, but he has also promised me an audience. Evidently, he came up from the south around the same time I flew in from Kojund. I wonder if he is here to meet with the visiting Russian delegation. It doesn't matter. The likelihood of our travels coinciding in such pinpoint fashion was extremely slim. Later in the day, January 16th, Mr. Registani's Mercedes Benz pulls up alongside the Hotel Tajikistan and I am on my way to fulfill an ardent ambition.

Our drive takes us to a less congested part of the city. Here, the vehicle edges into a driveway that ends out a safe distance from the road. We come to rest in between a modest single-floor dwelling and a barn. The entire property resembles a small, neglected urban farm. Several armed honchos, dressed in army fatigues, watch over the grounds from just inside the open-faced entrance of the barn, showing only marginal interest in us. They recognize Mr. Registani's car and a couple of its occupants.

The front room of the hideaway contains little more than a basic wooden table with chairs, resting on a dirt floor. The light is faint. A couple of men sit there, casually conversing in Persian. Amrullah introduces me to Massoud, who promptly presents Dr. Abdullah. He is the foreign minister for the Massoud's Northern Alliance, which does not involve much of Afghanistan at this point. The world would frequently see the doctor on international newscasts during the US air raids on Afghanistan in 2001. He would become the foreign minister in the new interim government for the entire country. In 1998, however, Dr. Abdullah performed his tasks in relative international obscurity.

Massoud's sleek, tanned face hides about half a dozen of his forty-five years rather well. A vein occasionally popping out of his right temple is the only facial feature that won't cooperate. As in almost all the photos I have run across, Massoud wears a soft, double-ribbed cap slightly dislodged from center position. Its bulky swirls rotate from the peak of his forehead to the base of his skull. Apparently, he always wore his "pakool" cap tilted, left to right. He told his people he would wear it straight the day he defeated the Taliban.

Massoud's uniform on this day consists of khaki tan pants and a loose fitting, equally non-descript cotton shirt. A lot of the local men seem to wear khaki or even camouflage combat clothing, intermixed with their shawal khameez. If the commander's wiry, perhaps five-foot-ten, frame offers any hint of ferocity, it would be that of a street fighter. Yet the thoughtfulness in his manner reveals a more evolved sense of discretion than one would normally find in such a person.

Massoud has not mastered English to the extent of some of his confidantes, but philosophical metaphors color his speech. I find it very appealing. This student of life is known to spend long hours with his statuesque Tajik nose buried in texts of Islamic poetry. I would discover that the tendency toward metaphor, although particularly pronounced in Massoud's speech, is not an exclusive practice. In this society where most live without electricity, let alone the questionable benefit of television, the sentiment of ancient poets can often provide a profound sense of comfort. Many readers go on to repeat the words of wisdom in their own conversations. The commander can draw from a French vocabulary with greater ease than English. He studied the language at an all-French high school. Massoud's ability to speak some of the language has helped him obtain valuable social and political aid from France.

As I awkwardly justify my request for the meeting, I would not describe Massoud's gaze as piercing, but I can tell that anything less than complete honesty on my behalf would be foolish.

Our exchange lasts about 45 minutes in all. I basically repeat the proposals heard by everyone else, ending with a suggestion to send Canadian training nurses into the Panjshir Valley. Although several worldly authors have already released books about Massoud, I present my sincere wish to write another. He nods, acceding to my request. I also hand the man two gifts. The first is a compass that he studies with enthusiasm before remarking it will help him locate his "quibla," or prayer direction. The second is a beautiful, multi pocketed winter jacket – top of the line. I would love to own it myself. Massoud examines it with a touch of amusement before tossing it into a corner. He says through Dr. Abdullah, who periodically interprets for both of us, that it will please one of his nephews. It's apparent the man cannot be easily impressed with material things – especially an item featuring a conspicuous designer logo. It's a lesson for me in the different social outlooks of our two diverse cultures.

I reflect on my meeting with Massoud during my walk through downtown Dushanbe the following day. I think I may have appeared a little awkward in the commander's company yesterday. What I really want to do now is finally cross that border some miles south of here. But whatever happens, I feel privileged just to have met the man. Then the phone rings. It's Amrullah. It sounds like good news. He says Massoud will fly homeward within forty-eight hours and welcomes me to join him. Am I interested?

I use the pause in my schedule to ring some friends and share the whirlwind of developments. One of them passes the word along to my wife, so she is the next person to phone. According to her, only a crazy person would fly into a war zone with the Taliban militia's worst enemy. I agree with her, as I usually do, but explain that I am going anyway – only for a few of days. At this point I do not realize it will be longer than this. I believe I am addressing my wife's concern. It will not turn out this way.

The final two things I need to do are return the cell phone and check some of my baggage at the hotel. Having brought along 30 kg of excess in the first place, a generous allowance will stay by my side.

When Mr. Registani's Mercedes stops by to get me this time, it is part of a six or seven-vehicle convoy full of Massoud's men, now dressed in civilian clothing. Intrigue fills the air. We ease into the flow of traffic for a bit, then erratically pull off into a maze of side streets and back alleys. I suspect the maneuvers are designed to expose any undesirables who might attempt to tail us. Soon we halt and some of us change cars. We then proceed through another obstacle course to the Afghan embassy, where a guard tells me to wait in the lobby. After a notable delay, one of the crew ushers me into a different automobile. The chameleon-like motorcade again merges with the regular stream of traffic. We navigate our way through one more maze before making a final vehicle transfer.

The clandestine ride ends at an airfield not far from the airport proper, but obviously servicing an elite clientele. Here sits a revved up helicopter, rather than the plane I have been told to expect. More intrigue. Once inside the noisy craft, Massoud motions for me to join him at the table, while Amrullah sits elsewhere. I guess my host wants to make sure I feel at ease. Amrullah tells a story about one of Massoud's guards who is not present at the moment. He was a Russian conscript captured by Massoud's militia during the war with the Red Army.

The unflattering glances of the guards in the helicopter make me feel I am little more than a luggage-laden Westerner in their eyes. Perhaps their commander will not allow them to impose a frisk-and-search on me, and it perturbs them that they cannot do their duty. It is indeed most gracious of Massoud to have spared me this inconvenience on both occasions now. I believe the man depends on a razor sharp intuition.

We roar over the Oxus River, locally known as the Amu Darya, in less than an hour. The river represents the border between Tajikistan and Afghanistan. It is clear to see that the architecture on the north side of river looks like part of the modern-day world, whereas the south side appears stuck in a past century, maybe before the dark ages. At the very moment we cross, the soldiers start flushing out weapons they had cleverly hidden in every corner of the chopper. I am certainly not an arms expert, but the selection would likely impress anyone sharing a fascination with weapons. It's practically an arsenal. These little trips into Dushanbe would appear to offer the guards the opportunity to do some luxury shopping. They would probably not just shop for guns, but also for other items not available in the Panjshir. And they might enjoy a couple of glasses of wine, or "sharab," during their stay, as they cannot access this at home either.

I cautiously attempt to pull out my camera for a couple of choice shots of the scenery below. Before I get it up to my face, one of them gives me a "don't even think about it" kind of look. I would not understand the full significance of the precaution for several years, after an assassination more devastating than most of us on board this helicopter could imagine.

At this point, I realize my life is in the care of a rebel army commander, at war in a land thousands of miles away from my home.

After cruising through Northern Afghan airspace for a short period of time, we begin to gradually descend. A sound like the crackling of lightning suddenly startles me. It's gunfire from down below!

CHAPTER 6

MASSOUD:
1980 to 1996

According to Amrullah, statistics compiled by the USSR showed that Massoud and his militias were responsible for close to two thirds of the Red Army casualties during the war. This figure would make Ahmed Shah an extremely vital cog in the Afghan resistance. He definitely received a lot of publicity. Part of this was because of regular broadcasts by the Russians that would report his death, only to have him turn up again the next day to cause them more grief. But although the nation considered itself victorious – and rightly so in many ways – at least a million and a half of its citizens lost their lives along the way.

The Afghan victory was a concerted effort on behalf of many different groups and ethnicities. No single group needed to hide their heads in shame that they did not participate and sacrifice to defeat the Red Army. The struggle against the Soviet "liberators" was homegrown, and fundamentalism set the direction. The CIA, Pakistan, Saudi Arabia, Egypt and France provided the means to train and equip the resistance in their efforts to bring about the collapse of the Soviet occupation.

The gritty men who faced the communist army in this war came to be known as "Mujahideen," or warriors fighting in the cause of Allah. It's a composite of the term "Jihad," or "Holy Struggle." They included a problematic cast of characters such as Wahhabiist Osama bin-Laden, the rich Saudi rebel; Mullah Mohammed Omar, the one-eyed, soon-to-be leader of the Taliban; the Pushtun Gulbuddin Hekmatyar, often a rival of Massoud; the Tajik Ismail Khan, eventually a powerful warlord in western Afghanistan; the Tajik Burhanuddin Rabbani, who worked on the planning end with his peers, Maulvi Yunis Khalis and Nabi Muhammadi; the Pushtun Abdul Haq, a brilliant guerilla warfare tactician; Maulvi Jalaluddin Haqqani, Taliban leader of the Southern Command, plus numerous others also of great significance. About 900 legitimate Afghan military commanders and their armies fought to varying degrees in the war. Seven major resistance parties had set up headquarters in Peshawar and surrounding areas, next to the madrassas (religious schools). Even before the full Soviet assault there was at least one serious attempt to coordinate their efforts, but it proved too difficult a task. It was ultimately individual resourcefulness that characterized the fight for independence against the Red Army. And all factions were well armed by one sponsor or another.

Another man who played a key role in the war was Abdullah Azzam, Osama bin-Laden's first contact in Peshawar. Some call him bin-Laden's mentor. Born in the West Bank, Azzam was an idealistic Arab who earned a PhD in Muslim studies at the Al-Azhar University in Cairo before continuing on to be an extremely influential leader of the Muslim Brotherhood, an Islamic organization founded in Egypt in 1928. Burhanuddin Rabbani and Gulbuddin Hekmatyar opened an Afghan chapter in 1969, to which Ahmed Shah Massoud was known to belong.

The brotherhood was founded by a young man named Hasan al-Banna and developed along the lines of the then recently formed Syrian Young Man's Muslim Association. Both these organizations sought to resist foreign domination and hoped to stop the spread of Western culture. The brotherhood particularly opposed the loose morals of the West and the "darkness of materialism". At the same time, it aimed to bring about a resurgence of the purest principles of the Qur'an. The organization was eventually driven underground, but it continued to hold momentous appeal.

The Muslim Brotherhood gained peak popularity in Arab countries such as Egypt, Syria, Sudan and others. The reknowned Palestinian resistance group in Gaza, the "Hamas", grew out this Egyptian organization. So did "Jamaat al-Islamiyya" and "Egyptian Islamic Jihad," Egypt's two largest Islamist militant groups. Both of them had important ties to al-Qaeda. Osama bin-Laden and Dr.Ayman al-Zawahri, the top two al-Qaeda masterminds, joined the Muslim Brotherhood in their early years.

When the Soviet Union invaded Afghanistan in 1979, Azzam issued a "fatwa", or an urgent call for defense of Muslim lands. This "fatwa" was a command for Jihad, one of the five basic tenets of the Islamic religion. Jihad is by its very nature spiritually obligatory. The only question involved is the legitimacy of the call to war itself. At the time, Azzam operated a small operation called "Mekhtab al-Khadimat", or "Services Office" from a small storefront building in Peshawar

Pakistan. Here, he organised housing and training coordinates for Arab guests arriving to fight in Afghanistan.[12] These recruiting efforts set a precedent for the eventual establishment of al-Qaeda.

Azzam's rallying cry drew the support of millions of Muslims far and wide, including that of Saudi Arabia's Grand Mufti, the highest religious scholar in the land. It also flooded Afghanistan with recruits from all directions. The ideological and paramilitary infrastructure that Azzam established for the growth of militant Islamist movements matured during the Afghan/Soviet War. It would continue to guide their development for decades.

Azzam continued to focus his efforts on the liberation of Afghanistan after the Soviet war. He felt that Massoud was the right man to support. Bin-Laden disagreed, favouring Hekmatyar instead. Some believe the difference of opinion contributed to Azzam and his son being blown up in a car bomb in 1989. Bin-Laden then took over his organization and transformed it into Al-Qaeda (the Base).[13]

It would become apparent in time that actions by American intelligence incited the birth of this worldwide militant Islamic network. Feeding weapons to the Mujahideen via Pakistan's ISI during the Soviet occupation was just the beginning. In the latter war years, volunteer fighters flocked to Afghanistan from a variety of countries such as Saudi Arabia, Yemen, Sudan, Egypt, Algeria and Somalia. In adherence with their religious belief, these men did not differentiate between Muslims living in one country and those living in another. They believed they were all part of the nation of Islam, which was under attack on Afghanistan soil. If another Muslim country was being invaded, then they had an obligation to defend it, as long as they were able. This was similar to the situation in Iraq today.

There were plenty of arms for all. By 1987, under Ronald Reagan's administration, such military support had reached an annual level of 65,000 tons of artillery. Some of the volunteers would be seen back in Algeria and Somalia not long after the Russians retreated. They were also spotted in Kashmir, Chechnya, Tajikistan, the Philippines and Bosnia-Herzegovina, where they again furthered the Muslim cause. Weapons from the overflow in Afghanistan also made their way to some of these lands.

It was quite possible that many who received arms from the US in the 1980s and early 1990s did not know who their benefactors really were. American intelligence could not be accused of the same naiveté.

They would come to claim that this new militant Islamic network was simply an unfortunate side effect of war. But the CIA would continue to use these hardened Muslim warriors to further its own agendas in the region, for years to come. Most of these men, the vast majority of them Arabs, were actually trained at CIA-sponsored camps in Pakistan, during the Russian invasion. The guerrilla training was combined with Islamic teachings. Some of the same schools would go on to train Taliban fighters, rebel leaders from Chechnya and the Balkans, and terrorists who would go on to Kashmir. According to Zbigniew Brzezinski, the CIA itself created the "international Islamic brigade."[14] And just about anyone's definition of an "international Islamic brigade" would include al-Qaeda.

In all, about 35,000 militant Muslims from forty different Islamic nations participated in the struggles of Afghanistan from 1982 to 1992. Tens of thousands more came to study at the madrassas, or religious schools, teaching radical Muslim fundamentalism. These schools were very important to the war effort and the CIA because they would produce more fighters for not only the conflict with the Soviets, but also for future battles involving Muslim peoples. Both the CIA and the ISI sought to transform the Afghan Jihad into a global confrontation pitting all Muslim states against the Soviet Union. They therefore actively encouraged this mass migration to Afghanistan and the madrassas on the other side of the border.[15]

General Zia-ul Haq, working hand-in-hand with the USA, was the Pakistan leader who helped to pave the way for the madrassas. The madrassas themselves were established by Wahhabi fundamentalists mostly from Saudi Arabia, with funding from their own country.[16] (. Most Arabs were members of a very strict and conservative branch of the Sunni Muslim religion called "Wahhabiism." It was the teachings of Wahhabiism that had inspired The Muslim Brotherhood. Wahhabiism was founded in Saudi Arabia in the 18th century. The sect had grown militant in recent years, partly due to the US military's presence in Saudi Arabia. This was sacrilege in the land of Mecca, the center of Islam.

Wahhabiist warriors not only set up numerous madrassas in Pakistan, but tens of thousands of them fought in the Afghan war against the Soviets. On top of guerilla training received at the hands of the CIA, a great deal of them would be taught al-Qaeda-style techniques, sometimes at the very same schools, after the war. This was, of course, before madrassas went on to a play a more obvious role in the burgeoning militant Islamic network. Even more questionable, a controversial "visa express" program was implemented for Saudis to come to the US for training. It circumvented immigration procedures and allowed unrestricted migration to the US.

The network of mobile Islamic warriors, as well as its support base, would indeed continue to grow. Today, more than fifteen years after the Afghan/Soviet war, the Muslim Brotherhood, an integral and very well-respected part of the movement, would likely win any election in Egypt quite comfortably. It also has a prominent presence in Syria.

Wahhabi interests actually won the election in Algeria, but the results were annulled by the country's military. The non-democratic governments of the region are the main reason these groups have not yet risen to political power in some of the countries where they have gained a great deal of popularity. And while most of these dictatorial governments operate with the blessing of the US, their tyrannical policies have very much given birth to extremist groups such as al-Qaeda and the Islamic Movement of Uzbekistan. In Uzbekistan, an extremely harsh dictator runs his country with the growing approval of the US.

The heroin trade stemming from poppy production in the "Golden Crescent", a fertile region encompassing parts of the Afghan-Pakistan borderlands, boomed from a minor concern before the Soviet war to the largest heroin operation in the world by the early to mid 1980s. This heroin supply quickly began to provide sixty percent of what police would soon attempt to confiscate on the streets of the USA. CIA funds and influence facilitated this production, while Pakistan's military administration was deeply involved. But it would be difficult to prove the degree of culpability of all the individuals. Lieutenant-General Fazle Haq, governor of North West Frontier Province, was only one of a number of high-ranking Pakistani officials and businessmen directly incriminated in the trade. The ISI, now a tremendously powerful operation with CIA backing and US military aid – reportedly 150,000 strong when one tallied all aspects of its operations – also played their dutiful role. At the very least, they offered protection to the Afghan leaders and local syndicates who surreptitiously operated hundreds of heroin laboratories in the Pakistan borderlands. The billions upon billions of dollars of heroin profit turned over during the Soviet War contributed significantly to the CIA's financing of the Mujahideen.[17]

According to Dr, Rajwali Shah Khattak, the Director of Pushtun Studies at the University of Peshawar, heroin played an extremely important role in the war. He would later comment, "The war against Russia was fought with drug money mostly... ... Mafias...patronized by US and other force."

The weapons American intelligence handed the Mujahideen did not come from the USA. Many of the best arrived from China. Many were purchased in Egypt. The Brits would make some money here as well, and Israel actually sold the CIA weapons confiscated from the Palestinians. Guns would arrive in Pakistan before making their way to camps in the borderlands that served as Mujahideen training headquarters. Although the CIA met with ISI personnel, they did not work directly with the Afghans in this exchange. The ISI supervised both distribution and training, sometimes complaining about the quality and type of weaponry received. (A lot of rusted-out duds arrived from Egypt.) Artillery and arms would be smuggled into Afghanistan via mountain passes and trails that separated the two countries on the modern day map. Because the mountains were well protected by Mujahideen fighters, the size of some of the caravans was staggering. They would include horses, camels, trucks, survival gear, tools, construction materials and other supplies useful to the Afghan resistance.[18]

Not only did the CIA pay for weaponry and training, but they also designed and engineered Tora Bora for the Mujahideen. To this day, Tora Bora, or "black dust" is the name of an extensive tunnel and cave complex, located between two mountain ridges of the White Mountains of eastern Afghanistan. It was built by extending natural caves into a massive, multi-storeyed encampment, perfectly suited for subterranean living and guerilla warfare. All of the cliffs and forests in the area made it difficult to access by land. Such conditions would eventually create a perfect lair for al-Qaeda operatives. US forces believed that Tora Bora was bin-Laden's last bastion before he disappeared not far from there in a valley near the town of Shahi Kot.

Throughout the early 1980's, the Soviets continued their attempts to depopulate locales with large civilian pools potentially available to the resistance forces. They were concerned about an increasingly cocky Panjshir militia with its ultimate designs on Kabul. Despite the mounting death toll in some valley areas, the determination of Massoud and his men in the Panjshir offensives of 1981 and 1982 is quite possibly what led the Russians to adjust their tactics. They would incorporate greater air presence for the remainder of the war.

Ahmed Shah Massoud and his armies had assumed authority over areas north of the Panjshir Valley, as well, by the end of 1981. The precious emeralds and lapis lazuli found in certain territories now under Massoud's command had begun to provide him with a significant source of funding. Geologists from France assisted him in this endeavour. The men not only spent time researching the emeralds in the valley, but they also provided Massoud with an opportunity brush up on his French. Again, the commander's grasp of the French language would help him significantly in his beneficial relationship with France.

Early in 1983, the commander signed a ceasefire treaty with the Soviets, applicable to his territory alone. The pact would give him time to reel in greater political support and offer a respite for his troops, but would also allow the Red Army unchallenged passage through the Panjshir Valley. The cloak and dagger agreement unfortunately did not meet with the approval of everyone privileged enough to know about it.

Massoud used this opportunity to bolster resistance fighters in other areas, such as Takhar province, with his troops. The ceasefire also granted Massoud an opportunity to revitalize his efforts to explore the mineral wealth at his disposal, especially the emeralds and lapis lazuli. French buyers seemed to have a particularly hearty appetite for the gemstones. The resulting finances strengthened the commander's forces dramatically in the weaponry department.

Just as the agreement with the Russians expired, Massoud formed a supervisory council designed to regulate resistance efforts stretching all the way from the Panjshir Valley to Badakhshan province, in the extreme northeast. This was a noteworthy gain, but by the spring of 1984, the communists hit the valley like a hurricane. The massive infiltration drove the commander into the mountains for a period. of time. It also created another serious refugee crisis. Many went to Pakistan.

Over the course of the ten–year war, about three to four million Afghans fled to Pakistan, creating a stressful situation for all concerned. I would come to see, during my own trips to Pakistan, that quite a number of the men found employment in the transportation industry, driving lorries. Most of the refugees had the freedom to come and go freely from the refugee camps, primarily in the wilds of what is known as North West Frontier Province. Shamshatoo Refugee Camp, north of Peshawar, was one. It fostered plenty of resistance activity, becoming the home of Gulbuddin Hekmatyar's Hizb-e-Islami Party. But the addition of so many new residents to North West Frontier Province over such a short period of time put tremendous strain on the area, especially the city of Peshawar. It wreaked havoc on the drinking water and sewage systems as well as other public utilities. The mass migration taxed the social infrastructure of rather significantly. Peshawar, known as a garden city, turned into a dust bowl during the war with the Soviets and for some time afterward.

This entire border area, with its Pushtun majority, was once a part of Afghanistan. It housed Mujahideen training centers and weapons supply depots in these years. Because many of the Afghan refugees preferred to fight for their homeland rather than hide, many would regroup here, equip themselves and return to the battlefields of Afghanistan. This amounted to a threatening situation for the Soviets. As a result, the Red Army carried out air raids on the Pakistan border towns of Miram Shah, Parichnar and Bannu, where many of the refugees lived. These were the cities bordering an area known as "Shawal" territory.

Such attacks targeted Mujahideen and their weapon caches more than civilian refugees, but the plan did not guarantee the refugees safety. The Shawal is a renowned stretch of land just west of Bannu and Miram Shah. It straddles the current Pakistan/Afghanistan border, sprawling almost as far west as Khost, on the Afghanistan side. Many direct descendants of the Holy Prophet Mohamed (PBUH – The capital letters often follow his name, meaning "peace be upon him") of the seventh century purportedly live in the area to this day. The steep, closely-knit hills and mountains combined with dense jungle make the Shawal impossible for an outsider to enter and navigate. The narrow valleys shooting off in various directions give it a maze-like quality. Its fortress-like characteristics make it an ideal refuge, for which purpose it has been used for centuries, including the duration of the Soviet/Afghan War. It has also been used as a smuggling route for decades. In later years, the unique natural phenomenon would be implemented to provide shelter and ambush posts for resistance forces fighting the US presence in Afghanistan. Reports would surface from time to time that al-Qaeda chiefs Osama bin-Laden and Dr. Zawahri continued to elude their US enemies by hiding somewhere inside the Shawal. The lesser-known Zawahri was the Egyptian eye surgeon who founded the Egyptian Islamic Jihad militant group. He would go on to be generally regarded as Osama bin-Laden's right hand man.

Aside from the Afghan refugees living in Pakistan, another one to one and a half million of them from the western provinces escaped to Iran. Although the Russians maintained a command post nearby in Herat, they apparently saw no activity around the Iranian refugee camps intimidating enough to bomb. The treatment of refugees in Iran was very different than in Pakistan. Many here were housed in camps surrounded by barbed wire while others were recruited to fight in the Iran–Iraq war. The most fortunate Afghans displaced by the Soviets were among the 100,000 or so who found homes in Europe and North America. But this was sadly a tiny percentage of the sprawling refugee migration out of the country.

The Russian offensive on the Panjshir Valley in the spring of 1984 included a sidebar to assassinate Ahmed Shah. It was not the first. The Afghan secret police, called KHAD, wanted the commander dead. KHAD was established in 1980 and run by an Afghan named Mohammad Najibullah, but the KGB controlled it. Najibullah, a Pushtun Afghan born in Kabul, had previously been a leading member of the Parcham Party, under Babrak Karmal, now the Afghan president. To solve the irritating problems Massoud was creating for Soviets, a friend of Najibullah, named Kamran, visited the commander in the Panjshir with the intention of catching him off guard and killing him. The man was apparently the captain of the Afghan national soccer team. After spending some time with Massoud, however, Kamran understood the commander's need to resist the Soviets and handed over the special muffled gun that Najibullah had given him for the assassination. He then requested asylum in Germany.[19]

The attempt on Massoud's life was only one of several plans in 1984 to silence Panjshiri resistance once and for all. To solidify their presence, the occupiers also built a trail of forts inside the valley wall. The bases proved to be far from secure. Ahmed Shah's men immediately blocked their lines of communication, then executed a synchronized attack on the posts. They hit Russian fuel convoys as well, using classic guerilla tactics, creating a disastrous fuel shortage for the Red Army and stranding reinforcements in Kabul.

To attack a Russian garrison, Massoud's men would use a basic but very effective technique. Before spraying the fortress with mortar fire from their rocket launchers, they would plant dense minefields around the entrances and exits – their whereabouts known only to the Mujahideen. After a brief period of bombing, they would charge in, carefully avoiding the mines. These very same mines would take care of any Soviet reinforcements that might be called in behind them. The number of ingenious strategies the commander could call upon at any given time frustrated his enemies. Most of the Red Army troops withdrew from the Panjshir by mid-June. After eight major assaults on the valley, the Soviets had achieved very little.

Some accounts claimed the Soviets employed up to 50,000 men in their onslaught against the Panjshir in 1984. *Time Magazine* would go on to report that the strength of the communist throng would have earned "the admiration of Genghis Khan." Yet, Massoud and his men eventually triumphed. The Soviet experience in Afghanistan was like the American fiasco in Vietnam. Neither the USSR nor the USA suffered a true military defeat, but they both lost a war of attrition.

Throughout the war, the Russians relied upon allied Afghan soldiers from the communist Kabul regime to help them wherever possible. The dirtiest work was given to them, in order to reduce Red Army losses. They fought effectively on the whole, but sustained three to four times the casualties of the Soviets. The central Afghan army was obviously the Soviet frontline. Its ranks were continually thinned by mass defections. Both young Afghan soldiers and Russian conscripts changed sides. Some moved into Massoud's camp.[20]

Mikhail Gorbachev ascended to power in 1985, quickly ordering even more troops into Afghanistan. He also mapped out certain forbidden zones. Only a year later, he would describe the Machiavellian endeavor as a bleeding wound, but he didn't call off the war effort. He was not yet ready to embark on the journey that would soon win him a Nobel Peace Prize for easing East-West tensions. Some whispered he also won a nice financial reward from American intelligence. Instead, Gorbachev replaced Babrak Karmal, the Afghan President, with Mohammad Najibullah, the head of KHAD. Najibullah had been responsible for many terrorist strikes against the Mujahideen in the tribal areas of Pakistan, from where the resistance sprang their campaigns, as well as their tactical headquarters of Peshawar. He had also ordered the deaths of 80,000 Afghan enemies-of-the-state in a relatively short period of time.[21] It was likely this type of efficiency that earned him the highest of Afghan promotions.

It took Gorbachev until 1988 to see the futility of the Red Army's mission in this rugged and rebellious Muslim nation. The Stinger Missiles from the CIA were regularly shooting down Russian planes and the Russian premier did not like it. He announced a withdrawal of troops to take place over a ten-month span, but the two factions would continue to scrap.

The Stinger Missiles that the CIA bestowed upon the Mujahideen in the late 1980s would come back to haunt the US military.. After the Russians left Afghanistan, some of them were suspected to have ended up in the hands of al-Qaeda. Hekmatyar and possibly other Mujahideen were thought to have sold some Stingers to the Iranians that were later used against the US.[22]

According to the US, this was in retaliation for an Iranian civilian airliner accidentally shot down by an American warship in the Persian Gulf in 1988 – accidentally according to them, anyway. The European-made A300 Airbus, carrying 290 passengers, was allegedly mistaken for an Iranian F14 fighter plane.[23]

The whereabouts of the unused Stinger Missiles from the Soviet War became such a concern that the CIA eventually initiated a recovery program to get them back in the early 1990s. They managed to buy back about 100 of the 2000 they had given to the Mujahideen, offering as much as $150,000 for a missile retailing for about $55 thousand. A great many have still not been accounted for.[24] An Afghan I briefly encountered was said to have been part of the recovery program. A source said the man had been detained by US forces in Afghanistan for failing to produce adequate results.

As northern armies forced the Soviets out of the key northern city of Taloqan, an historic city I would finally visit nine years later, one of Massoud's old adversaries once again entered the picture. Gulbuddin Hekmatyar, much like Ahmed Shah, had left his northern province of Konduz over a decade ago to pursue a college education in Kabul. Similar ideologies had brought the two men together in their failed attempt to destroy the Daoud Khan government. After the 1975 plot failed, however, Hekmatyar accused Massoud of divulging their plan to the enemy. Their relationship was further damaged some seven years later, shortly after Massoud signed his ceasefire with the Russians. Hekmatyar's forces captured and killed thirteen of the commander's top men.[25] The two military men neither liked nor trusted each other. It was not surprising then that nothing had changed in another five years when their forces combined to expel the communists from Taloqan. The two eminent commanders did not shake hands. They instead ended up waging combat for control of the city. Massoud eventually prevailed, but this would not keep Hekmatyar down for long. Long afterward, I would meet a pair of Hekmatyar's troops in the Panjshir. I could see the look of frustration on their faces, being forced to collaborate with their old adversary, Ahmed Shah Massoud, in their fight against the Taliban.

Gulbuddin Hekmatyar also maintained a relationship with Burhanuddin Rabbani, who would resurface shortly to become the president of Afghan government. Rabbani had formed an Islamic political alliance with Hekmatyar and a commander named Rasoul Sayyaf earlier in the Soviet war. Anyone in Afghan politics also knew plenty about the Pushtun warlord, Gulbuddin Hekmatyar, a man both physically and socially grand in stature. With his ISI support, more weapons from the CIA may have found their way to him than to any other military commander fighting the Russians. And although funding and supplies continued to find their way to him after the Red Army departed the country, Hekmatyar became the most identifiably anti-Western among all of Afghanistan's resistance leaders.

The Red Army's exodus from Afghanistan in 1988 and 1989 presented certain complications that a clever Massoud took full advantage of. Massoud controlled the Salang Tunnel, the only route leading northward through the mountains surrounding the Panjshir Valley. For his personal guarantee that the exhausted Soviet soldiers would pass safely through the tunnel, he negotiated a settlement of weapons and military control of other northern areas.[26]

The guns provided by the Russians would eventually help in ways the commander could not possibly have conceived of at the time.

Most of the Soviets were soon gone, but the surplus of weapons in the country created a crisis for the land and its people. The fact that the Americans and Russians were still feeding armaments to their favoured groups intensified the situation. Considering this dilemma plus an array of social and political quarrels once again rising to the forefront, no one who understands the country would have predicted a smooth transition to peace. The presence of a brutal Soviet puppet in the president's chair only added to the discord. At least six political parties representing ethnic Pushtun groups alone retained headquarters in the relative safety of Peshawar, Pakistan. Dozens of smaller minority groups also sought due consideration. To further cloud the circumstances, the CIA, Saudi Intelligence and ISI would oversee formation of a new Afghan government. Parties who had developed strong ties with Pakistan would be given a closer look. And Hekmatyar, the leader of the Hizb-e-Islami, had risen to become Pakistan's favorite choice for Afghan president.

Meanwhile, in a struggle that lasted almost half of 1989, eastern Mujahideen troops lost close to an additional 10,000 men in an unsuccessful attempt to win the city of Jalalabad back from Soviet-backed rebel forces under Najibullah's ultimate command.[27] Some of Najibullah's men initially surrendered when they saw the city surrounded, but these men were killed by Arab volunteers with a harsher agenda than the Afghan locals. The executions prompted a six-month defence of the city. In the end, the defeat at Jalalabad was the single most punishing one absorbed by any Mujahideen army during the lengthy Soviet siege of the country.

In 1990, the US and the Soviet Union finally agreed on something about Afghanistan. They decided Najibullah would continue to hold the throne until internationally supervised elections could be fairly held. Most Afghan leaders didn't care what the two manipulating superpowers thought.

Najibullah did not want to be caught napping when Kabul was burning. Although he had been a tyrant, he still believed he was doing what was best for Afghanistan. A power struggle would surely overrun the capital city in the not-too-distant future and Najibullah looked to minimize the havoc as his forces disintegrated. His first priority was that the national army serving the country for the last fifty years be preserved. The second was that an ethnic Pushtun, like himself, should take control upon his departure – at least at first. But neither of these wishes would ultimately manifest. Instead, both his government and military soon became seriously split, once again largely along Parcham Party and Khalq Party lines. Massoud had many Parcham sympathizers while the Khalqs generally favoured Hekmatyar. Even worse for Najibullah, his defence minister, Shahnawaz Tanai, was trying to usurp him. Hekmatyar's friends at the ISI were egging Tanai on.[28] Tanai failed and fled to Pakistan, but some of his forces left Najibullah for Hekmatyar's side.

Massoud was said to have eventually received word from somewhere within the Kabul power structure that he was free to take the reins of the administration in Kabul. He did not necessarily trust the offer, deciding to wait and watch instead. When Gulbuddin Hekmatyar received an invitation to take control, he set out from Peshawar, taking a route toward Kabul through Miram Shah. He gathered his forces together as he traveled. Past the "Shawal," they arrived at Khost City, the first city freed from Russian occupation. From there, they slowly made their way to Chara Asyiab, Hekmatyar's Afghan base, just south of Kabul.

Once in Chara Asyiab, Hekmatyar ordered two of his lieutenants to intercept Massoud's forces, on the other side of Kabul, if they attempted to charge the capital. Kashmir Khan, an allied commander was sent to Kabul, where government officials encouraged him to help himself to the armoury. Kashmir Khan and his men were also allowed to take control of the most important government ministries, on behalf of Gulbuddin Hekmatyar.

Hekmatyar proceeded to order Ustad Farid, one of his supreme commanders, to stave off Massoud and his forces at Charikar and Bagram Air Base. In the eyes of many Kabul urbanites, Hekmatyar and Farid were their last shield from the chaos Massoud and his northern hordes would bring to the capital. But Farid managed to keep Massoud's forces at bay for only two days. Massoud had just made a pact with General Dostum at Jabal Seraj, causing his ranks to swell.

Dostum, the powerful Uzbek general of the north, had primarily served Soviet interests during the Soviet war. His army was large, well fed and fierce. The new partnership would give Massoud the military might he needed to seize the capital and ward off Hekmatyar. He could hardly sit back while Hekmatyar's people took charge of the government ministries. The new alliance included Mahmud Baryalai, Babrak Karmal's brother. Karmal was the Soviet proxy who had officially presided over Afghanistan for most of the war. Other Afghans formerly associated with the Soviet regime, such as Najib Moammaddi, General Babajan, General Momen and General Nabi Azimi were also involved.

Meanwhile, Hekmatyar had started his march on Kabul. With Dostum and the others under his command, Massoud was able to temporarily push the Pushtun leader back to Chara Asyiab, where he was forced to wait for the next turn of events. He didn't have to wait long.

The situation exploded in April, when the armies of both Hekmatyar and Massoud fought their way through Kabul to the legislative buildings. At times, they battled each other to determine who would get there first. Massoud and his allied forces prevailed. Najibullah fled to the UN building, where he applied for asylum.

Throughout the 1970's and 1980's a bipolar political divide had existed in Afghan politics and the politics of the region. There were the great reformist communist ideologies such as Marxism and Leninism, and there were the Islamic parties. By the 1990s Afghans in general wanted little to do with communism, and the well-established Islamic parties clamored for control.

A seven party coalition, anxious to shift the country from a communist to Islamic state, signed a treaty called the Peshawar Accord as soon as Massoud and Rabbani took control of Kabul. It was announced on April 26, 1992. The agreement initiated a rotating presidency to precede general elections. This new amalgamated force of Afghan political parties, commanders, warlords and tribal chiefs agreed that Sibghatullah Mojaddidi would be the first president of a new Islamic Afghanistan. He was a Pushtun spiritual leader representing the Sufi faction. Mojaddidi would preside over the country for a two-month period and then Rabbani would take over for another four months after that. Hekmatyar, pressing for more power than the coalition would allow him, had abandoned the group a couple of years back and did not sign the pact. As the representatives of the seven parties celebrated their new partnership, Gulbuddin Hekmatyar was busy plotting to destroy it.

Two months later, in June of 1992, the presidency was awarded to Ahmed Shah's senior associate, Burhanuddin Rabbani. But the true seat of power, the position of defense minister, belonged to Massoud.

Hekmatyar wasted no time. He rocketed Kabul as soon as Rabbani assumed leadership. The errant blasts killed two thousand civilians, once again shocking the nation's capital. Massoud soon answered Hekmatyar's fire. Suddenly both sides were bringing destruction to Kabul and its people.

Hekmatyar's list of grievances featured the fact that General Dostum, Massoud's new ally, had fought with the Soviets during the war and Hekmatyar did not want communist interests included in the new Afghan government. Also of significant note was that Dostum's troops had helped decimate legions of Hekmatyar's Mujahideen in Jalalabad, only three years ago.

Hekmatyar continued to wage war on the new government. His efforts resulted in scores of fatalities and the return fire may have contributed equally to the death toll – but they did not win him any more support. In March of 1993, Hekmatyar finally decided to accept the prime minister's portfolio offered to him by Massoud and Rabbani when they first gained control of the government. The agreement was consummated in the Khanna Khabba in Mecca, the most holy location of Islam. But it would sadly last less than a year. The position of prime minister made Hekmatyar an underling to both Rabbani and Massoud, and he never really came to terms with it. Also, the fact that his two superiors were both of the Tajik minority, while he belonged to the Pushtun majority, may have disturbed Hekmatyar rather profoundly. Ethnic polarization was starting to set in. He resigned his post in January of 1994, then promptly resumed his efforts to overthrow them.

Negotiating with Ahmed Shah Massoud was something Hekmatyar viewed with disdain – especially Massoud in a defence minister role. He looked down on the man as a common military commander, certainly not a general of his own stature. Many Pushtuns held the belief that Massoud, the "great" Tajik military leader, was well overblown.

Hekmatyar's original grievances against General Dostum would soon seem to be little more than a ploy to discredit the new government and its army. He convinced the Uzbek to abandon Massoud's coalition and to collaborate with him instead, creating a massive enemy for Massoud to suppress. Even Mojaddidi, the Mujahideen leader who had served as president for two months before Rabbani, joined the expanding rebel force. The capital city, already awash in murder, torture, abduction, rape and every type of human rights abuse imaginable, would now also be ravaged by bombs ripping half of it apart. About fifty thousand of Kabul's citizens died in the process.

Some years later, I met an Afghan writer and journalist who showed me a copy of a letter that Hekmatyar wrote to Dostum around this time. I had seen other letters by Gulbuddin Hekmatyar, so I recognized his distinctive signature. His seal was also clearly visible. Although I did not get the opportunity to translate the dispatch into English, the journalist told me it had been written for the purpose of reconciliation. After Hekmatyar had complained so bitterly about Dostum's collaboration with Massoud, a serious effort at reconciliation was obviously required in order for Hekmatyar to earn the Uzbek general's favour. I consequently believe that the letter I saw played a role in Dostum's departure from Massoud's military alliance and his ensuing pact with Gulbuddin Hekmatyar's forces.

Dr. Rajwali Shah Khattak said the following about Hekmatyar's opposition to the new central government in Kabul: "Then the international Mafia worked on it...the international movement worked on it. So when Rabbani [and] the non-Pushtuns were brought into power they were not acceptable...some 18% Tajiks, Uzbeks, Turks, etc... considered Afghanistan their own country...and the Pushtun didn't like it."

Outside of Hekmatyar, another notable military commander who committed himself to Rabbani in these years was Rasoul Sayyaf. Sayyaf was the leader of the Ittihad-I-Islami Party. He was also a warlord of Paghman province, northwest of Kabul. To this day, a notorious freedom fighter/ terrorist group in the Philippines is named after Sayyaf. Sayyaf and Rabbani went to university together in Egypt. The Al-Azhar school in Cairo, home to the Muslim Brotherhood, was famous for producing Muslim leaders such as himself and Hekmatyar. Sayyaf's exposure here to students from many different countries offered him the opportunity to establish connections in Saudi Arabia. He would recruit many of his men from the country.

In February of 1993, Sayyaf and his men attempted to cross the Karta Seh district, a Kabul suburb to the east of the University of Kabul. They were heading northeast in the direction of a town called Afshar, at the foot of Afshar Mountain. The plan was to cut a path that would enable them to liaison with Massoud's troops in the center of the capital city. It was not an easy thing to do from this location, because of the sharp rising mountains that surrounded Kabul's western edges. The polytechnic that served as headquarters for the forces of the Hizb-e-Wahdat Party lay just to the north of the university, further complicating the situation. Some of the Hizb-e-Wahdat troops, under their leader, Abdul Ali Mazari, were doing their best to block Sayyaf's march. At a point when it looked like Mazari would effectively subdue Sayyaf's advances, Massoud sent support to the allied commander. The military reinforcement would prove to be far more than benign.

The Hizb-e-Wahdat Party represented Hazaras to a large extent. The forces of Mazari, the Hazaras' chairman of central command, had been routed by government troops not long before and this defeat had increased the animosity already existing between the two groups. Resentment now abounded between the Hazaras and the armed forces representing the Kabul regime.

Hazaras saturated the region of the greater capital city that Sayyaf's troops were attempting to cross. Once Massoud's men arrived to help them through, thousands of civilians in the districts nearby became trapped in the middle of the raucous linkup between the two militias and perished.

Accounts of exactly what happened varied considerably, but all of them were grisly. Some alleged mass beheadings and amputations. Others reported dozens of civilians being thrown down wells. Some described human limbs being fed to dogs. Women were also killed, or sexually assaulted and mutilated, while soldiers took others as booty.[29] Of the three groups involved in the conflict, none were innocent. As usual in such affairs, however, innocent civilians rather than soldiers paid the bulk of the price. It was a bloodbath that would not escape the attention of Amnesty International.

Although 1994 represented the most destructive phase of the clash, the desperate period between 1992 and 1996 left even Massoud helpless to exercise adequate control over his soldiers. The atrocious acts against civilians bothered the commander profoundly, but his efforts to overcome the opposition undermined any hesitation to advance. Uneducated and crazed warriors on all sides often fragmented from the main battalions along lines of ethnicity and sank into anarchy. The violence and degradation in Kabul were even more hideous than in Sarajevo.

The militant Islamic network the US created during the Soviet/Afghan war quickly served other useful purposes. Reports would surface that American intelligence was not only assisting rebel factions in Afghanistan's civil war but had also become involved in Yugoslavia's internal struggles. Hekmatyar – at least until recently – ran a guerilla training camp near Afghanistan's eastern border that was initially set up by the CIA and ISI during the Russian invasion.[30] And the US was helping to arm and train the Muslim forces of Bosnia-Herzegovina there, in direct contravention of the United Nations accords. American Special Forces also allegedly imported Afghan Mujahideen to join the fracas. This was part of an overall strategy to destabilize the Yugoslav government.[31] But unlike the situation in Yugoslavia, the world did not really take much notice of what was happening in Afghanistan.

One member of the Islamic brigade of freedom fighters who would eventually garner some international notoriety was David Hicks, a young Australian man who converted to Islam. Hicks fought in 1999 for the Kosovo Liberation Army (KLA) in Kosovo before joining the Pakistani army to further his Arabic studies. The CIA admitted they helped train the KLA weeks and months before NATO bombed Yugoslavia.[32] A Pravda article claimed "German document reveals secret CIA role" in the Kosovo Liberation Army.[33] Hicks was suspected of being a pawn of the CIA. He ended up in Afghanistan and was there when the US invaded. David Hicks was charged by the US for fighting alongside the Taliban.

If the democratic process still interested Massoud and Rabbani by mid 1994, it is doubtful many other Afghan politicians gave it much credence. Rabbani was still president only because the havoc had resulted in an eighteen-month extension to his original four-month term. Although many wanted him to step down, no one could rationally accuse him of holding onto his position illegally. The UN still recognized his government. But neither he nor Massoud found it possible to accomplish anything of value in the war zone of Kabul. This resulted in a lot of heavy-handed criticism from practically all directions. Ahmed Shah took the brunt of it. Many who had recently considered him a national hero now viewed Massoud as a man turned corrupt and tyrannical with a hunger for power.

There is no doubt Massoud's diplomatic abilities took a turn for the worse during a significant period of his term as defense minister. The only way for him to stifle the violence in Kabul would have been to unify the ethnic minority groups of the region. This would have forced Hekmatyar to the bargaining table. Maybe such a treaty was not possible given the situation's emotionally charged context, but Ahmed Shah's many critics during this period were certainly in no mood to grant him any concessions. In the end, accounts of these years would force me to admit that Massoud, as much I came to like him as a person, may not have been all that different from his adversaries on certain occasions.

Today, ten years or so after the civil war in Kabul, the struggle's implications for many civilians living there at the time bring to mind a story about the Holy Prophet Mohamed (PBUH), the founder of Islam. The Prophet Mohamed lived about 1,400 years ago.

After being banished to Medina for twenty years by the non-believers of Mecca, the Holy Prophet returned to Mecca with an army and emerged victorious after a lengthy Jihad. He then invited his Mujahideen to partake of yet another, larger struggle. The victors wondered why they would be commanded to go on with another battle when Mecca, the site of their efforts to protect Islam, had already been secured.

Prophet Mohammed told the soldiers that this greater struggle would be largely a battle with their own egos, as opposed to strictly physical warfare. He said that while they were dealing with the remaining "kafir," or unbelievers, they would be required to restrain themselves from harming or taking advantage of the Meccan civilians in any way. In these times, it was common for the victors to seize the women as well as the property of some of the conquered. However, the Holy Prophet said that the innocent would instead require and deserve protection, as they would be vulnerable.

During the fight for control of Kabul, Hekmatyar and Massoud owed the city residents a much more concerted effort to meet these particular challenges. This was especially true considering the innocent victims they left behind were not "kafir," but fellow Muslims. About 50,000 Kabul civilians were victims of this war, fought primarily among Afghan Mujahideen factions.

In June of 1996, the headstrong Gulbuddin Hekmatyar once again accepted the prime minister's seat in the central government led by Rabbani and Massoud. No other realistic choice remained. His high-powered Pakistan allies had been courting new patrons and the support of Prince Turki bin-Faisal, the head of Saudi intelligence, had virtually expired. Apparently, the prince was not only irked by Hekmatyar's ineptitude on the battlefield in Afghanistan, but also by his purported support of Saddam Hussein in the Gulf War. The CIA, too, no longer backed his cause in a significant manner. They had decided instead to offer their support to a new, radical fundamentalist movement. By the summer of 1996, this huge assembly of students and warriors had not only conquered a couple of key Afghan cities, but was also threatening to take Kabul. These hardcore Islamists were the Taliban.

Massoud.
Panjshir Valley, Feb. 1998

My host and our cook.
Panjshir Valley. Feb. 1998

Engineer Mirdad,
Panjshir Valley. Feb. 1998

Street Scenes, Bridge made from tank treads.
Panjshir Valley, Feb. 1998

Part of the inner circle of Massoud. Panjshir Valley, Feb. 1998

Trusted member of Massoud's executive council
Panjshir Valley, Feb. 1998

EID celebration and the end of Ramadan.
Panjshir Valley, Feb. 1998

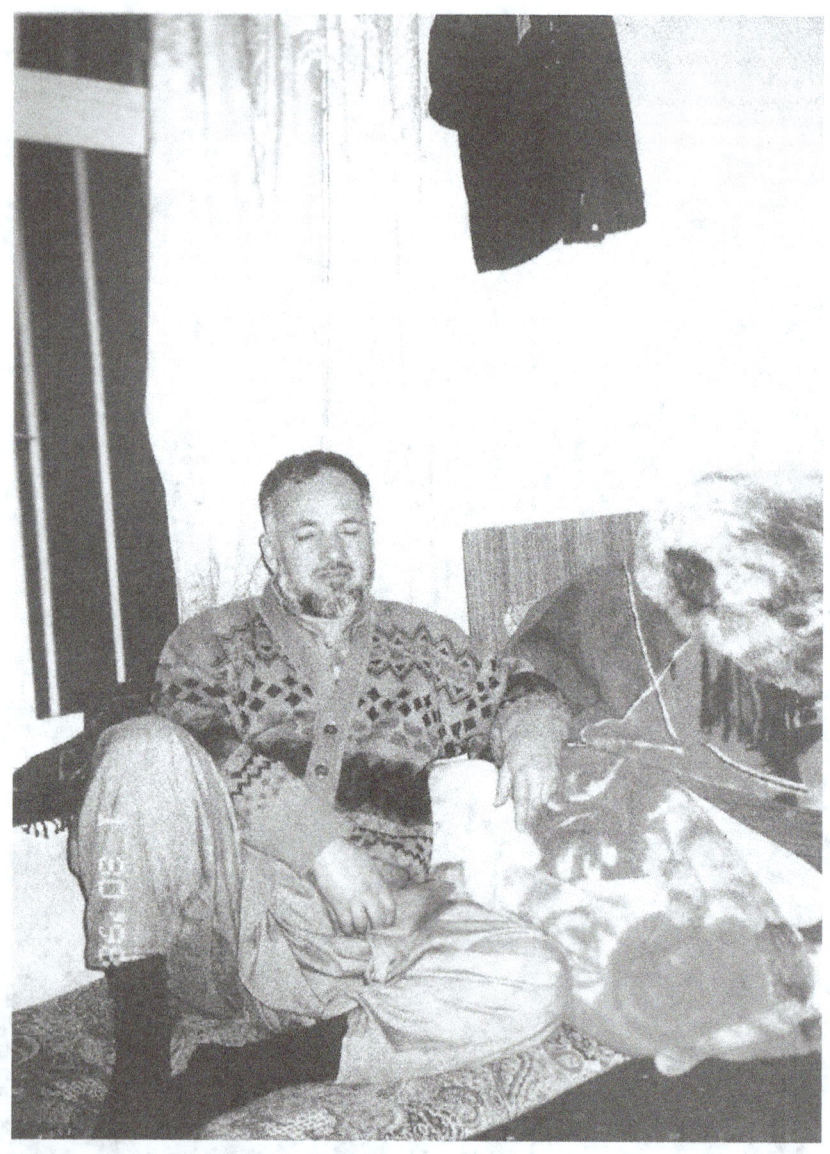

Engineer Ishaaq, very close confidant of Massoud.
Panjshir Valley, Feb. 1998

My 'home'.
Panjshir Valley. Feb. 1998

The children of Panjshir Valley. Feb. 1998

Russian Journalist with his vintage cameras.
Panjshir Valley, Feb. 1998

The Panjshir Valley. Feb. 1998

PART TWO

THE EMIRATE OF AFGHANISTAN

CHAPTER 7

TALOQAN, NORTHERN AFGHANISTAN:
JANUARY 18-22, 1998

Since the kohl of our insight is the dust of your doorway, Please tell us, where do we go from this threshold?

– Hafiz of Shiraz, one of Massoud's favorite poets, translated by Elizabeth T. Gary Jr.

Welcome to Taloqan, one of the largest among many rustic towns and villages in the rugged landscapes of Northern Afghanistan. It is also Commander Massoud's military command center. As soon as I saw the muddy, archaic landing field, the firearms everywhere, and the lack of any customs procedure, I knew my experience in this land would be far different than in any other.

Our chopper wasn't attacked by enemy fire, but, rather, greeted by gunshots welcoming a hero home. Although I did not expect the gunfire, my intuition prepared me for the possibility. I am trying to keep as alert as possible because I know not what to expect on a day-to-day basis. Every morning I rise and allow the day to unfold as it may.

We have come to rest in a large, flat grassy area, likely an athletic field of sorts. It's actually right inside the small city. The calls and chants of Massoud's supporters continue as we gather our belongings inside the helicopter. The boisterous greeting party, perhaps fifty strong, consists mostly of armed men and an overall tribal atmosphere. Massoud politely signals for me to disembark, but after one glance at the crowd, I step back and gesture him to exit ahead of me. It would be in bad form to walk out first into his applause. Finally, embraces and salutations are made, with Massoud attracting most of the attention and I, thankfully, almost none at all.

A driver drops Amrullah and me off at a walled compound. Upon entering, I see a wall on my left that shoots straight back to a boundary wall obscured from my view by another barrier. It's a semi-detached Flintstone-style abode with several units. Amrullah explains that the apartment we have just entered will serve as our quarters in Taloqan.

I view my new surroundings with a touch of awe, really. I have read so much about Massoud's exploits in Northern Afghanistan and it inspires me to finally get here.

Because we are now closer to sea level, modest shades of green have begun to compete with the dreary, muddy browns of a spring that obviously comes earlier here than in Canada. Maybe it's an all-year-round phenomenon, as January has not even ended yet. The spherical, snow-capped mountains lie somewhere in the distance, in a direction I believe to be south. Northern Afghans must consider the area a bit of an oasis. This stretch of fertility appears to be in sharp contrast to much of Afghanistan, which looks more like moonscape. Maybe two to three hundred thousand people live here, quite a few more than I expected. But populations tend to fluctuate dramatically in Afghanistan. I tend to think almost twenty years of conflict would have the same effect anywhere.

Comfortably seated in my temporary home, I see that it is part of a larger compound, divided into three or more separate dwellings. The entire building belongs to the governor of this province, Takhar, and he resides in a unit somewhere in back of mine. Staying in the house adjoining ours is none less than the UN-recognized president of Afghanistan, Burhanuddin Rabbani. Massoud has been something like a protégé to Rabbani for many years and still cares about him deeply.

The housemate I will dine with tonight is Haji Qadir, an influential Mujahideen commander who until recently governed the province of Nangarhar, on the Pakistan border. The affluent region of the country includes the city of Jalalabad. Not unlike Massoud and Rabbani, the Taliban forced Mr. Qadir to seek refuge further north when they overran Jalalabad a couple of years ago. It surprises me to be housed among such important Afghan dignitaries.

Just before dinner is served for Mr. Qadir, Amrullah and me, the commander steps in to join us. He not only places me in the company of extremely interesting individuals, but also stops by to make sure that all goes well. This reflects a considerate nature I was not aware of. We keep the conversation fairly light on this occasion, discussing for a while the political and economic relationship between Canada and the US. We joke that America doesn't control my homeland militarily because we basically surrender 80% of our economic control without much argument. Massoud possesses a delightful sense of humor. Every story he tells results in more laughter. Lighthearted moments such as these offered me no clue that within five years, two of the three men before me would be assassinated. The other would go on to be the Head of Intelligence for a new central government in the country.

As I pick away at any food on the table that looks like plant matter, it arouses curiousity. I must admit to my vegetarianism sometime soon, but do not want an irrelevant issue wasting precious conversation time tonight. I sense that Massoud finds me a little odd, anyway. It's not an altogether infrequent observation.

Amrullah and I enjoy a stroll around the city the next morning when we come across a mob circling a fellow who's been caught stealing some shoes. The shop owner tries to guard him until police arrive on the scene, but the rowdy bystanders become more vocal by the moment. It appears they might take the law into their own hands before the authorities make it. The man is terrified. Fortunately, the police march him off before the crowd loses total control. I hear later that they give the thief a stiff warning and a solid cuff up the side of his head before setting him free.

Pairs of women stand along the sides of the dirt roads in several places, draped in their burqas with full-face veils. Not an inch of flesh is exposed. Covering the eyes with a finely webbed mesh seems like stretching the modesty issue beyond health and safety considerations. Yet they are taking part in energetic conversations. I ask my companions how the women can tell each another apart on the street when their faces are so thoroughly hidden from view. The faded blue gowns don't differ much from one to the next. I pursue this line of thought, asking what identifies one lady from another. A torn hem or loose thread on the sleeve? He laughs and assures me they can figure it out.

The dress code for men is almost as monotonous as for women. Most of the males outside wear battle fatigues or the standard brown "shawal-kameez," which looks quite popular. The "shawal-kameez" is a very long and loose-fitting shirt combined with an extremely baggy, pajama-type bottom, tied at the waist. The humble garb illustrates a cultural belief in the importance of a modest appearance. Even jeans are rare. Those who own the blue denim trousers so common throughout much of the world are probably part of an elite who get the opportunity to travel once in a while.

Droves of police lounge around a circle in the middle of a bustling intersection, chatting away freely. They seemingly have no urgent business to pursue. The occasional ass-driven cart rolls on by, and I see a few horses, but no camels at all. Winter mud and snow still cover much of the roads, so few bicycles are visible either. I certainly don't expect to see anything resembling rush hour traffic. The odd beat-up car makes its way through the streets, but most folks walk to their destinations. In a few of the shops I enter (wooden huts brushing up against each other on either side), shivering merchants gather around tables with coal-burning fire pits in the center. They sell mostly practical items such as hats, shoes, jackets, sweaters, carpets, blankets and the like. Those dealing in food stack rows of canned goods on rickety shelves or on the floor, usually labeled in Russian, but sometimes Persian. The Persian-labeled foods are imported from Iran. We pass a shopkeeper scraping snow with the same type of antique wooden shovel I watched my grandfather use in Montreal in the 1950s. This was back when the milkman delivered glass bottles of milk to our door.

The rows of trees that intermittently line either side of the main avenue remind me a little of Dushanbe, but there are few other similarities between the two cities. Dushanbe, with its cobblestone streets is fundamentally European in appearance, while Taloqan is distinctly Asian, with few traces of Western influence. The haphazard buildings found here in Taloqan certainly bear no resemblance to the bold architectural designs found not too far north in Tajikistan's capital.

The quiet hours after tonight's dinner give me an opportunity to become more familiar with my housemate, Haji Qadir. His real name is Abdul. The name "Haji" can be used as a term of honor for a man who has performed the sacred Islamic pilgrimage of "Hajj." "Hajj" is trip to Mecca at a special time of year, to be endeavoured by all Muslims at least once in a lifetime. Haji and I talk about the political situation in Afghanistan and then Haji shares some of his personal experiences. He can converse quite freely in English, which helps him disclose some intimate details about Nangarhar, the province he governed.

Jalalabad, the capital city of Nangarhar, lies close to Peshawar, Pakistan. Its border location opens up trade possibilities for the city that most of the country does not enjoy. A lucrative exchange of goods with Peshawar is much easier for Jalalabad businessmen than for the merchants of Kabul, for instance. Sometimes the trade in either direction places Jalalabad businessmen in the coveted role of middleman.

Mr. Qadir made full use of these advantages when he lived in Jalalabad. Beyond legitimate trade materials, he would be hard pressed to deny his involvement in a controversial lumber smuggling operation. He also indirectly participated in a highly illegal gold smuggling business. The gold originated in Dubai, United Arab Emirates, and eventually wound up in Indian jewelry shops or safety deposit boxes. Some of it provided lavish wedding dowries. Such situations helped sustain and even increase the wealth of the province when Mr. Qadir ran it.

Several years later, while leafing through some research texts, I discovered that this Afghan politician had lived on a plush estate at the edge of some of the country's most fertile heroin-producing poppy fields. He had amassed very serious personal wealth, as well. Haji Qadir's family became one of the richest in Afghanistan, with its own fleet of planes called Khyber Airways. Haji claimed that the airline operated six flights a day to Dubai, United Arab Emirates. This must have been convenient with his brother, Abdul Haq, residing in the thriving Arab financial center.

Among the various businesses that the resourceful Mr. Qadir involved himself in, he used to import audio and video equipment, other luxury items, and practical goods such as refrigerators or commonly needed car parts. All of it would arrive at the seaport of Karachi, Pakistan for duty-free sale only in his country. Because Afghanistan is a landlocked nation, as well as an impoverished one, the Pakistan government had agreed to waive the duty on these items. But Haji Qadir's goods were not all sold domestically. The hundreds of thousands of televisions and other luxury items that landed in Afghanistan could simply not be used in a country where electricity was so scarce. Only the small percentage of people with enough money to purchase generators could take advantage of their cheap availability.

On the other hand, auto shops lined the roads at the edge of the Federally Administered Tribal Areas of Pakistan, on the outskirts of Peshawar. Here, cheaper car parts were under no risk of confiscation because the parts were often installed by roadside mechanics. This eliminated the chance of detection by the border service officials who ran the check-post nearby. Haji's merchandise would find its way to the tribal area non-duty market, known as the "barah." The market bought and sold the various consumer items that Haji Qadir dealt in, plus more. One way or another, goods purchased by the man consequently found their way back here to Peshawar, Pakistan, where a significantly better return was available. This type of market activity is part of the age-old free booty system of Afghanistan, which has always been a duty-free country bordered by many other potential markets

Haji Qadir went on to tell me about a famous international smuggler who he called Haji Baig. Baig, known much more widely as Haji Ayub, came from a large and well-armed tribe called the Afridis, in the Federally Administered Tribal Area (FATA), just across the border from Afghanistan. Afghans dispute which nation truly owns this land. Pakistan could not afford to provide facilities such as roads, schools and hospitals in FATA, its government was forced to offer a degree of autonomy to the region. Benizar Bhutto, the president of Pakistan at the time, was attempting to capture the smuggler to curry favour with the US, but finding the task difficult. The Afridis, aside from their weaponry, were probably 30,000 strong along the tribal border, and Ayub had many protecting him personally. It was said they even possessed Stinger Missiles as a defense against air attack, from Bhutto's air force in particular. Ayub apparently owned a fortress in Landi Kotal, Pakistan, not far from Jalalabad.[34]

Haji Ayub Afridi eventually came under a lot of pressure from Pakistani authorities. Haji Qadir told me he convinced the smuggler to fly to Dubai on Khyber Airways, where Mr. Ayub negotiated a deal to give himself directly to American officials. This made sure the Pakistan president would never receive credit from the US for turning their wanted man over to them. Bhutto lost that bargaining chip.

Osama bin-Laden came to Afghanistan in 1993 after being banished from his Saudi homeland and also Sudan. He eventually settled into Mr. Qadir's province of Nangarhar, operating terrorist training camps within its borders. At least on one occasion, he rented Mr. Qadir's private plane to fly some of the region's top leaders to Mecca for 'hajj".

Haji Qadir's family includes his hero brother, Commander Abdul Haq, celebrated protector of Kabul during the Soviet occupation. Enemy fire injured the man many times, but he always got up to fight another day. My housemate, Mr. Qadir, is part of a very proud and well-respected Afghan family.

A few years following my liaison with this very interesting Afghan, the US and their coalition - including some top men from Massoud's inner circle, the Shura-e-Nazar, - finally expelled the Taliban from

Kabul. Mr. Abdul Qadir, known as Haji by his friends, would once again rise to a position of political authority. He became one of the very few Pushtuns in the new Karzai interim government. Mr. Qadir would also, most unfortunately, become the second casualty of the administration, in an assassination that focused international attention on Afghanistan for two or three consecutive days. I took objection to the Western media referring to him as a former warlord, as if he were not more than that. But as far as warlords go, Abdul was pretty sophisticated and amazingly candid. It is obvious the press adjusts their perspective day by day, depending on what they have been fed. I have seen them turn their derogatory terms on Massoud as well, not long after showering the man with praise.

I hear Taliban planes bombing the outskirts of the city the next morning. I even see them in a while. Their wings dipping in unison as they pass overhead; then circling back again toward Taloqan The bombs whistle as they fall to the earth, before the inevitable explosion. Multiple anti-aircraft blasts echo somewhere in the distance.

Amrullah says a major Taliban objective in Taloqan is to eliminate Massoud. An air attack recently destroyed part of the bazaar next to the offices where he spends his days, so they obviously know where he works. I wonder how badly they want Rabbani? He is, after all, still the official president of the country. I'd bet that getting rid of Haji Qadir would be on the Taliban list of things to do. And they probably don't think much of the governor, either. This makes me wonder how safe I am. All three of these Taliban enemies are lodged in the compound with me. There's not much I can do about it, but at least there's no chance the circumstances can disturb my wife this time.

Rabbani and Massoud decide to discuss strategy with Mr. Qadir today, in our quarters. Their ill-humored armed guards confine Amrullah and I to our bedroom during the meeting. Some of them even sit on my bed while I squeeze into a corner, reading my Karen Armstrong book on Islam. They lighten up a bit when Amrullah starts to chat with them. The fact that the commander and the president plan what I assume to be both military and political strategies in this house brings a stark reality to characters I have studied in books and read about in international media reports. It feels strange, as though I am now living in another dimension.

Amrullah begins to show signs of boredom during his third day at my side while I scour the streets for points of interest. I am not sure what he'd rather be doing, but being so close to the northern front line, I can imagine any number of things more interesting than plodding along with me. He starts to beam whenever he gets an opportunity to hang out with his mates for a while at Massoud's office. I empathize with his situation, but he is following orders from the commander. I guess he is stuck with me. Hopefully Massoud finishes his work today and flies us into the Panjshir Valley tomorrow, which has been the plan from the start.

Like all devout Muslims, the men who surround me pray five times a day. Rabbani led them in worship even last night, during the meeting at the house. Only another ten days or so of Ramadan remain on this year's lunar calendar, so no one wants to miss any of the final opportunities to benefit from prayer during this "Holy" month. The fasting during the day continues to be an important part of their Ramadan ritual. After abstaining from food or drink for about fourteen hours, the men feast at dusk. They eat another hearty meal around 2:30 a.m. or so, after sleeping for a few hours. I, too, wish to respect the Islamic environment that surrounds me, so I refuse to eat until sundown as well, even though the servants periodically tempt me with snacks reserved for non-Muslim guests.

The governor does not spend much time in our unit, but he notices I resist the servants' offerings on a couple of occasions. He compliments me for honoring the Ramadan fasting ritual. I clumsily reply that with the way we stuff ourselves at dinner and in the middle of the night, it's not really much of a sacrifice for me. From his reaction, I realize he would have appreciated a slightly more subtle response. This was certainly not the only faux pas I would commit along my journey across these mountains and cultures.

One cannot easily navigate a helicopter through the lofty, narrow mountain pass that funnels down into the Panjshir Valley. It requires near perfect weather conditions. So when I wake to a blustery dawn, I can see we will not be flying today, regardless of the commander's schedule. I decide to use the opportunity to visit the local hospital. Seeing what kind of ailments and injuries most commonly afflict these people might help me assist them or others sometime in the future.

Above the front door of the infirmary, two signs catch my attention. The largest one names the hospital while the smaller portrays a circled painting of an AK47 with two red diagonal lines crossing over it. No machine guns allowed. I guess they don't mind rifles or pistols.

Afghanistan has the highest infant mortality rate in the world and one of the shortest life spans as well. This modest healing center nonetheless serves fourteen different districts, so it faces no shortage of patients. The facility relies primarily on generators for power. Many of the sick and injured here are children. The majority of them, especially those from the most needy families, fight pneumonia or other respiratory ailments. Malaria is also a common affliction. The hospital performs more types of surgery than I could have imagined and it reserves a separate building out back specifically for amputees. Very few of the ailing can afford to pay for medical care and no one tries to force them to. The doctors here engage primarily in a labor of love, while foreign aid finally plays a genuine role.

The ward we spend most of our time in caters to internal injuries. Some of the bed-ridden received their wounds from Taliban, while others stepped on landmines planted long ago by their own townsfolk. A car hit one man and a falling tree crushed the legs of another. The amiable surgeon who oversees our visit introduces me to two patients. One of them is a young male burn victim. After speaking briefly with the boy, I leave his father a small donation and move along to meet the second patient, a very brave woman.

The patient has gained some celebrity from a recent burglary incident at her home. She apparently subdued the perpetrators for half an hour, using a variety of weapons, including hand grenades. It probably sounds strange that one would store such destructive devices in their home, but with war devastating the nation for two decades, it is commonplace around here. Besides, surely it is no stranger than the Americans' obsession with their "right to bear arms". Afghans at least have an honest need for weapons right now. This is a place and time of war. The arms are acquired by the men and passed along to their wives, sisters and mothers with the prerequisite training. In any event, Amrullah claims this woman's stand accurately depicts the ferocity of Afghanistan's fairer sex when backed into a corner.

Amrullah and I continue our investigation, discovering that members of Medecins Sans Frontieres volunteer at this hospital. It's an interesting anecdote for me, although none work here at this time. On the way out, I notice another sign above the entrance saying BINGO, or Big International NGO. This Scandinavian outfit apparently helps with health care in the area. My Afghan guide shares a chuckle with me over a certain absurdity in both the name and its abbreviation.

We drive to a front line clinic after we leave the hospital. Near the clinic lies a very small refugee settlement. The refugees who live here came from Tajikistan. They apparently did not flow very well with the agreement the Tajik government made with the rebels to end the civil war in Tajikistan. The Russian-backed Tajik government, consequently, was on a collision course with these people. I would eventually hear that Russia expressed disapproval to Massoud for harbouring Tajiks who were considered enemies of their own government. Hekmatyar had shared sympathy for Tajik fundamentalists as well, conspicuously supplying fighting men and materials to assist the cause, as Hekmatyar also did with the Kashmir cause.

Later that evening, we sip tea and lounge about on cushions that surround the beautiful carpets adorning our house. Amrullah uses the time to share a few of his many insights into regional politics with me. He tells me that some of the commander's men refer to Massoud as "Commando." I have heard certain members of the inner circle call him "Emir Sahib," as well. "Emir" or "Amir" is an expression of considerable reverence referring to an independent Islamic ruler. It could be a commander or even a governor in some Islamic countries. To whom it can be properly used is often a matter of opinion and therefore sometimes a sensitive issue.

Amrullah reveals that although the Taliban lust after Massoud's blood, a more practical reason for their immediate interest is to keep the commander's forces at bay. They fear he will blockade the strategic neighboring city of Konduz, a crucial northern center now in their possession. Taliban profit nicely from an export tax on the heroin trade with Tajikistan. The enterprise contributes considerably to the Taliban treasury, despite the fact that much of the drug gets seized after crossing the border. The location of the city also provides the Taliban with the opportunity to barter with Tajik traders and the Russian military 201st Division for oil and other necessities.

Goods such as oil are smuggled to the Taliban across the Amu Darya, "darya" meaning river. The smugglers normally transport them from shore to shore via raft. This is the same river I looked out over from Termez Atta in Uzbekistan, about six months ago. Many Western maps refer to it by its ancient name, the Oxus River. The Amu's system derives from a dammed lake in the Pamir Mountains of eastern Tajikistan and provides most of the border between this country and Afghanistan. The dam itself sits on a fault line, creating a

potential risk for a great many inhabitants of both countries. The river
runs twenty five hundred kilometers west from Tajikistan, forming the
border between Afghanistan and Uzbekistan before emptying into the
Aral Sea.

It is unlikely that much smuggling will be taking place from
Uzbekistan, where the border looked effectively sealed when I was
there. But the Taliban can surely make good use of the bartering
option from Tajikistan, rafting across the river and southward into
Konduz. This is because of the difficulty transporting goods through
the Alliance-controlled territories surrounding Konduz province. The
commander has every intention to march on Konduz when granted a
reasonable opportunity.

Taliban, the first government in the history of Afghanistan to enjoy
approval from Pakistan, also holds possession of Herat, a northwestern
city near the Iranian border. Herat's location, right along the main
trade route between Iran and Turkmenistan, makes the city quite
a prize. Pakistan was kind enough to supply some of the offensive
needed for the Taliban to overrun this thriving center. They provided
the extra help in order to gain better access to trade with the Republic
of Turkmenistan, and to counteract the hovering influence of its
archenemy, Iran. Such animosity was nothing out of the ordinary;
Pakistan and Iran have long had an outstanding feud. Many citizens of
Herat, in fact, would applaud if Pakistan went to war with India, on
the other side of Pakistan. This would compel its troops to leave and
allow Herat's situation to run a more natural course.

Massoud would soon tell me that Pakistan, Saudi Arabia and their
friends erroneously thought they could destroy his homeland. I think
he meant that by supporting a Taliban rise to power, these nations
were trying to subjugate Afghanistan. This would be the natural
result, of course, when a struggling government is deeply indebted to
foreign interests. But to Massoud, who believes in a free and sovereign
Afghanistan, the direct or indirect domination of his country by others
must be fought regardless of how costly. "It has already cost us two
million lives. Protection of dignity claims blood," he would say.

I would never hear Massoud speak directly against the US. If
everyone else realized the American government was behind the
Taliban movement, he surely did too, but he also knew that throwing
around accusations would not improve his situation. It was much wiser
to hold his tongue and play the diplomatic game, which he did right

until the end. Nor would Massoud openly admit to receiving any type of foreign aid from Russia or Iran, although he would clearly defend his right to do so. The aid from India was even more controversial, but his forces needed all of the funds and armaments they could get their hands on. Most of the time, Massoud's personal army consisted of only 12,000 soldiers. The Taliban's was not only obviously much larger, but they also owned at least three fighter jets, of which I had already personally seen two in action. Massoud, on the other hand, possessed but ten helicopters, most of them old and refurbished.

With regard to Herat, the name of a province as well as the prosperous city, the commander considers methods to help its residents expel the Taliban. Numerous dissidents sought refuge in Iran when the new government took over. Massoud had considered it poor judgment that Herat's leader, Emir Ismail Khan, had disarmed the people rather than allow them to fight the Taliban. But now, if supplied with adequate weaponry, these refugees in Iran could return to help Alliance troops mount a serious threat against the common enemy. It would greatly enhance the operation's chance of success if the Northern Alliance could gain Khan's release from prison. They would either have to rescue him from detainment or exchange him for an important Taliban prisoner. The second option might be the more practical of the two, as Massoud already holds several such prisoners in custody. Mr. Khan, also a Tajik, earned his stripes for heroics during the lengthy confrontation with the Soviets. Before the Taliban finally overwhelmed his forces, he was one of the most preeminent military commanders in the country, presiding over several western provinces. Massoud could really use his help right now.

The ultimate goal is to win back Kabul, not at all an unrealistic aim in Amrullah's estimation. He says the Taliban defense lines to the north of the capital remain vulnerable because the city is supportive of Massoud. The commander freed Kabul's citizens from Soviet rule and an Afghan does not easily forget. One reason he hesitates to enter Kabul is the possibility of atrocities vengeance-obsessed soldiers have been known to commit. Such uncontrolled violence took place only six years ago and so Massoud is cautious not to let it happen again.

Some of the commanders under Massoud's ultimate command have been accused of operating in a less than dignified manner in the heat of battle. This mob mentality, devoid of personal responsibility, seems to be the case so often in war. These men, leaders in their own right, have only recently created a new alliance with Massoud in order to destroy their mutual enemy. They will also, of course, continue to pursue their own interests. The unique blend of ethnic and religious factions in each militia results in agendas that differ and often contradict each other. The heralded leader and hero of a soldier belonging to one ethnicity is a villain to a soldier belonging to another. This hampers any sort of master control. But even though most of the Pushtuns have now come under Taliban command one way or another, Massoud believes the ethnic minorities of the nation themselves could defeat the ever-growing enemy if united under a common banner. The various tribal chiefs and commanders representing these ethnic minorities are, unfortunately, often guided by a thirst for power rather than the good of the whole.

Allied forces in any war often hang together by the thinnest of threads. Such is the case with Massoud's coalition. Some of these allies do not wish to see Rabbani sitting in the president's seat for a second term, or possible perpetuity, with Ahmed Shah at his side. Rashid Dostum, perhaps the most enigmatic commander involved, thoroughly illustrates the point. The native Uzbek still directs a powerful and ruthless militia from the lands directly south of the Uzbek and Turkmenistan borders. In the 1980s, Dostum worked with the Soviets, to help them conquer Afghanistan. Early in the next decade, he aligned with Massoud and Rabbani to dispose of the leader the communists had left behind. Less than two years after that, he once again shifted allegiance and tried to overthrow the new government he had helped Massoud and Rabbani create. Although the three men have come together again, this time to oust the Taliban, Dostum remains an unpredictable character whose forces will move on his orders alone. Massoud must weigh many factors before making any advance on the capital city, including keeping an eye on his allies.

Most countries with any stake in Afghanistan still honor Rabbani's group as the official government of the nation. This is despite the fact that inconsistencies taint all of the alliances they forge. Uzbekistan would like to see Dostum in charge and so would many Hazaras. But first the Taliban must go. For this, the Uzbek general needs Massoud. Consequently, various powerful men fight together right now to earn an opportunity to install the type of leadership they each want to see in Kabul. Some of today's allies will certainly clash again somewhere down the road. Nothing is simple in Afghanistan.

Amrullah, who has worked for Massoud for two years now, renders the following comments about his leader: "He demands loyalty, but sees people on an equal level, not in hierarchical terms. His aura commands quietness, not through authority, but with respect. Massoud greatly appreciates poetry and is a very deep thinker. During the Soviet invasion, Massoud was considered the brightest star in the Afghan resistance. His positive image in his country and the world is not merely a coincidence. He has loved and served his country, struggling against several conspiracies instigated by foreign powers."

Indeed, Massoud has stayed with his people through tremendous hardship. For two decades he has lived with them, eaten with them, fought alongside them and prayed with them. He would gladly give his life for them. To many, including Amrullah, Massoud is symbolic of the great strength and resilience that is Afghanistan. His love of Islamic poetry revealed itself in 1996, when he retreated from Kabul. He took a library of two thousand books with him to the refugee camps in Peshawar, many of them the works of legendary poets. He did this to protect the books from potential harm.

Amrullah adds, "The commander knows a lot about classical poetry. He drinks knowledge and wants to speak with people from every walk of life. He always encourages young talent. I was amazed when one day he recited a line from an ancient Persian book and wanted me to interpret it. It was obvious he just wanted to check if I had a grasp of its meaning. Massoud is rarely far from a smile. He is shrewd, keen, and intelligent, has a good sense of humor and always shows respect for others. He is a remarkable commander who has devoted his life to his people with the prime objective of preserving the dignity of Afghanistan."

★   ★   ★

All factors for passage into the Panjshir finally fall into place the following morning. The skies are clear and we're ready to go. The men, all of them very religious, declare "Bismillah," which means "in the Name of God." This is an affirmation used at the commencement of an activity or event. But before the helicopter rises barely thirty feet into the air, smoke billows from the engine. Without delay, the pilot drops us right back down again. Better now than when half way there, I conclude. Still, the weather could prevent our departure tomorrow as well. It fortunately does not.

The roundup ritual begins again about twenty hours later, with Massoud and his Land Cruiser eventually pulling into the airfield well behind the rest of the motorcade. I rush back and forth, trying to load all my gear on board before he takes another good look at how much I travel with. I hear him quip over the whirl of the propeller, "Maybe you should have ordered another chopper for your luggage." I react with a forced grin while my face grows flushed.

As we gain altitude, the commander snoozes while I mull over the fact that the Taliban's jet bombers ruled this airspace only four days ago. I hope Massoud's well-documented network of spies keeps him accurately abreast of the enemy's daily flight schedule. The last thing I want to see is a couple of Taliban planes patrolling these skies today.

We begin climbing higher and higher in order to clear the mountain pass that leads into the valley – 4500 meters above sea level. These old Russian helicopters function better at lower altitudes, with more oxygen, and likewise struggle at heights where the air becomes thinner. Our flight verifies the principle, sputtering and dipping as we approach the pass. The atmosphere inside the aircraft gets tense. The five bodyguards gripe in agitated tones as they dart glances at my luggage and me. One of them is the fellow who gave me a stern reprimand with his facial expression when I tried to use my camera during our flight into Taloqan. I am not sure of the specifics being discussed by the guards, but it's obvious they wouldn't mind dropping a hundred pounds or so of the spoiled Westerner's possessions to help us make it through the pass. As they bicker amongst each other, the commander suddenly opens his eyes and lunges into the cockpit, pulling a surprised pilot out of his chair and replacing him at the helm.

Now, this is the Massoud I have heard about, a man whose talents shine best amidst chaos. He reminds me of a boy right now. To him this is an adventure, another challenge to embrace. I believe my host thrives in situations that require pressure-filled decisions and great courage. Not that our current dilemma presents as serious a threat as countless others he must have faced.

I have no idea to what degree Massoud's piloting skills help to push us through the gap, but soon we coast into the fabled Panjshir Valley, the famous stronghold of resistance against the Soviets. What a remarkable sight! The other face of the mountain hints at spring's rapid approach, but here we descend from the snowy peaks into a breathtaking winter wonderland.

So this is the land of his birth, the rugged beauty he has taken so many risks to protect. I suddenly feel I understand a little of the passion that dwells within Massoud. I want to know more.

CHAPTER 8

MASSOUD and the TALIBAN:
1994-1998

...There is a misunderstanding in the world community about the Pushtuns. Maybe [because of] mullahism or fundamentalism or the religious people tend to be dominating everything, so the real spirit of the Pushtun - very little is known. You will find out in the Pushtun areas of Afghanistan to what extent [they are] civilized, quite liberated.

> – Dr. Rajwali Shah Khattak,
> Director of Pushton Studies at
> Peshawar University

The Taliban movement grew primarily as a response to lawlessness that had gripped southeastern Afghanistan after the Soviet retreat. With warlords trying to restabilize their kingdoms, homeless refugees roaming back into the country, and a variety of displaced Mujahideen trying to carve out fortunes in the post-war era, the potential for trouble hovered over the land like hornets from a nest. A small group of Islamic students from a madrassa along the border in Pakistan would be the first members of a Taliban-dominated Afghanistan. Initially, the "Talibs," or students, were regarded as little more than convenient social functionaries in their villages. For income, some of them would have to rely entirely on the benevolence of the public they served. Many of them graduated to become Mullahs, or Islamic clergymen. Once the Taliban movement got under way, they almost leapfrogged the Mullahs in the prestige department, a truly profound transformation in Afghan society.

In the spring of 1994, about thirty Talibs saved two teenaged girls who had been abducted and sexually assaulted. These students were under the tutelage of Mullah Mohammed Omar of Singesar, a small village near Kandahar. The Taliban's popularity as an Islamic liberating force suddenly began to flourish. After a six-month period of intermittent growth, fifteen hundred of the puritans, including foreign recruits, marched on Kandahar. The Taliban claimed the city as theirs when the three-day melee had run its course. It was victory number one.

Most residents in this influential southern center appeared quite willing to trade some rights for the restoration of law and order. The Taliban moved quickly, banning female education, collecting weapons, punishing thieves and drug traffickers, and setting radical new laws designed to create a pure, Islamic state. Some punishments were extraordinary, but their measures brought order to the area. Taliban efficiently halted tyranny, such as highwaymen along the surrounding trade routes and robberies inside the city walls.

The Taliban practised a strain of the Sunni Muslim religion called Deobandi. It derived from northern India in the mid-19th century, in resistance to British colonial rule of the country. It then spread to Pakistan, where it became quite popular. Although the Deobandic interpretation of Islam was generally considered to be somewhat purist, the Taliban's version would come to be regarded by some Muslims as particularly authoritarian.

Perhaps the most noteworthy coup for the proud young radicals in their early days of law enforcement was their weapons confiscation program. En route to their victory in Kandahar, the Taliban had already captured a huge weapons supply depot belonging to the militia of Hekmatyar at its southern base in Spin Boldak. This meant they didn't need any more guns at the moment. But they did need men, and the program secured many new recruits who preferred joining them to surrendering weapons that had become so much a part of their lives. The Taliban quickly imposed their ideology upon all they encountered in the territories surrounding their base city, Kandahar. Many Afghans were hopeful that after twenty years of war this religious group of Mullahs and students might finally afford them some peace. They certainly didn't put up much of a fight in most areas. The Taliban owned the entire south of Afghanistan within four months of their first triumph, and along the way had welcomed thousands of new warriors into their army. Their numbers swelled to startling proportions even before the Afghans knew much about them.

Massoud suspected early on that the new revolutionary force had procured themselves some solid foreign backing. Helicopters, jets, tanks and a steady flow of sophisticated artillery were pouring into the Taliban camp. Hekmatyar's clumsy efforts to overpower Kabul were surely making him out to be somewhat of a failure in the eyes of his CIA benefactors. At the same time, reports out of Pakistan had probably suggested to US Intelligence that with the proper amount of help the Taliban could fill their needs. Anyone who cared to examine the big picture closely could see that the new idealists were not acting without some type of serious sponsorship.

But why might the U.S. interfere in the internal politics of Afghanistan? Partly because of their plans to build a pipeline across the nation. For an undertaking of this enormity to succeed, a government that could stabilize the land would have been imperative. Perhaps Rabbani and Massoud could have delivered this stability in time, if also financed and allowed to do their work. However, it appeared the Americans thought otherwise.

From their headquarters in Kandahar, the Taliban stretched northeast toward Kabul, and northwest approaching Herat. They took towns and provinces by force only if necessary; more often than not they bribed military commanders with wealth and power. The commitment and resources this new group appeared to possess were remarkable. By now, many of its officers were driving around the country in brand new Japanese pick-up trucks.

Everywhere the Taliban landed, their first edict was "Sharia" law, or at least their own interpretation of it. It has always been the supreme law of Islam. Women were suddenly banned from the workplace and barred from the classroom. One of the first things the Taliban did in Kabul was empty the hospitals of female employees. The principal surgeon at the time was a woman. Although informed she would be able to return to work soon, she never did. And women who did not already do so were immediately required to wear a burqa when outside their home (a robe that covers every inch of flesh except for the hands). This cost a small fortune in Afghan terms and most families could not afford one, so two or more households might share the same burqa. The law increased the difficulty involved in a woman getting out of the house. Taliban insisted a woman could not stray from her dwelling at all unless accompanied by her husband or a male escort from her immediate family. A Qur'anic injunction against women making excessive noise with their shoes while walking in public was also enforced. They were not allowed to talk loudly outside, either. These types of behaviour were deemed to attract unnecessary attention from men. No makeup, sheer stockings, high heels, bright colors or even short-styled haircuts were allowed, and those who ignored these commands could be whipped or worse.

The Taliban eventually settled in and formed a government. Their top priority was ensuring the observance and implementation of their "Sharia" law. The "Ministry for the Preservation of Virtue and Suppression of Vice," a small army consisting mostly of young Islamic students, wandered the streets of Kabul, waiting for infractions. Sometimes they would use broken car antennas on perpetrators. The Ministry had set the official punishment for a woman exposing her face in public to twenty-nine lashes. For a more serious crime, like adultery, the accused could be stoned to death or buried alive. Male doctors were not allowed to examine the opposite sex, leading to an urgent healthcare crisis. Under such edicts, females would become a burden on their own society. Many girls could be bought as future brides, at an embarrassingly young age. The suicide rate among Afghan females began to escalate quickly.

Homosexuality was also outlawed by the Taliban, although usually not treated with anywhere near the same severity as female transgressions. The male version of the nation's dress code required men to grow a beard of at least several inches and wear the traditional robes, as opposed to Western garb. All games, sport, or other forms of leisure and entertainment were banned, even in one's own home, as were cigarettes. Some of the edicts were just an exaggeration of social norms in the region. For instance, the banning of cigarettes was not peculiar in Taliban areas, as Massoud had banned them in the Panjshir Valley as well. The purist Taliban lawmakers also expected men to pray five times a day at the mosque. Leaving doors unlocked was compulsory as a testament to the security that the Taliban's version of Islamic law had brought. Punishments to either gender for many of the worst crimes in Taliban society were carried out in public, sometimes in former soccer stadiums, with tens of thousands forced to watch. Shootings, hangings, beatings, the hacking off of limbs, could all be witnessed as part of a lavish exhibition to deter criminal activity. It was this showmanship that finally earned the Taliban some Western media attention.

In September of 1995, less than a year after settling into Kandahar, the Taliban conquered Herat. The victory followed a lengthy seesaw battle with Ismail Khan's forces along the well-traveled road between Herat and Kandahar. The Taliban had already taken Hekmatyar's key position, in Chara Asyiab, but could not withstand Massoud's counter-attack. This temporary defeat made the victory in Herat, Afghanistan's second largest city, an even more vital gain.

Prior to the Taliban capture of Herat, the Massoud/Rabbani camp generally felt that supporting their new enemies was an effective way of disarming Hekmatyar and breaking the stalemate at least for the moment. The government forces believed they could deal with the Taliban later. No one had any idea the movement would grow exponentially. But some months before the Taliban swarmed the capital city, some of their top men held a meeting with Massoud. They were of course hoping that the commander would decide to concede power to them without bloodshed. Massoud refused, but when he left the meeting, he admitted that he now had a serious fight on his hands.

Many of Hekmatyar's men defected to the Taliban when he lost Chara Asyiab. The new enemy had become an even greater threat to his political ambitions than Rabbani and Massoud, so Hekmatyar accepted the prime minister's office for the second time in the summer of 1996. But it would prove to be too late. The rivals merged armies in an attempt to save Kabul, but after four years of depleting each other's resources, they could neither develop the cohesion, nor muster the strength. Not even the combined forces of Rabbani, Massoud, Sayyaf, Khalili, Dostum and Hekmatyar could prevent the inevitable.

The Taliban blitzed Jalalabad on September 5, 1996, chasing Haji Qadir across the border into Pakistan with little resistance from his troops. Then on September 27, one day after forcing Massoud and Rabbani out of Kabul, the Taliban swept into the capital city. Aside from a handful of dissenting provinces to the north, Afghanistan was now the Taliban's to do with as they pleased.

When the Taliban seized Kabul, a US State Department spokesperson named Glyn Davies claimed that her government did not object to the fundamentalists' efforts to force "Islamic law" on the country. A US Senator, Hank Brown, commented that at least now one political group in Afghanistan looked capable of developing a government in its capital city.[35] Also around this time, a US diplomat said Afghanistan would become an American oil colony, with huge dividends for the West. He recognized there would be no democracy and that women would be legally persecuted, but stated the US could live with this.[36] One who couldn't was Madeline Albright, then US Secretary of State. She would call the Taliban human rights abuses "despicable." But even more American representatives did not seem to mind them. Zalmay Khalilzad, a former official of the Reagan and

Bush Sr. administrations, was a particularly influential one. This man, an Afghan expatriate now working for US oil interests, was one of a group of White House advisers very much involved in the lucrative business. He recommended the US government throw its enthusiastic support behind the Taliban. Assessments such as his would lead to a Taliban delegation soon visiting Texas, to listen carefully to the latest American pipeline proposal.

The founding father of the Taliban, Mullah Mohammed Omar, referred to his rapidly expanding army as a peacekeeping force appointed by God and the people. Many Afghans found it difficult to buy into the self-righteous party line. This so-called peacekeeping force had showered the capital city with hundreds of deadly rocket blasts in the year before they took it.[37] Restrictive laws practically turned women into prisoners inside their own homes. The public executions, amputations and floggings looked more like the work of fanatics. To their credit, they had been a particularly well-disciplined group while infiltrating most of the land. They had generally avoided the rape, torture and mass murder seen in Kabul relatively recently. But the level of sophistication evident in the Taliban's military strategy also invited suspicion. Who had taught them such effective battle tactics? And where had all of the money for the artillery come from? The radicals had left a trail of unanswered questions behind them.

Before the Taliban settled into the charred remnants of Kabul, they paid a visit to Dr. Najibullah, who had taken sanctuary at the UN enclave. He had apparently turned down Massoud's offer to help him escape because he feared retaliation against himself outside of the compound. He would regret the decision. The Taliban tortured and mutilated him before shooting both him and his brother to death. The men were left hanging by their necks, for all to see. Interestingly, Najibullah, in his final interview before slipping into seclusion, had warned the world about the turmoil that would prevail if Islamic fundamentalism ever swept the country.

An Afghan official would later explain to me why the two siblings were together at the time the Taliban entered Kabul and killed them. Apparently, Najibullah had sent for his brother because he believed that when the Taliban marched in the king would come back and give them both very agreeable ministerial postings. This deception was passed on down from high places, likely the CIA or some other similar organization. Najibullah's brother, who had not been in Afghanistan for years, came back to Kabul from the safety of a Western country to meet his untimely end only days after arriving in Kabul.

The enemy pursued Ahmed Shah from Kabul all the way back to his home ground, laying claim to more territory along the way. The commander blamed the loss of the capital city on Hekmatyar's half-hearted effort to flank his government troops. He singled out Haji Qadir as well, for giving up Jalalabad without an adequate resistance. Nonetheless, a reinvigorated allied force soon pushed the invaders almost all the way back to Kabul. But five trying years would pass before any of these men would penetrate the Taliban troops guarding the capital.

When Massoud and his once strong militia reached the Panjshir Valley, just over half his men remained. Many had died or defected to the Taliban, while others simply deserted. He probably realized to some extent that superior military strategy, more than manpower, had checkmated him in Kabul. In any event, he most definitely knew that his troops were in for a lengthy and desperate struggle now. The commander told those who stayed that if they wished to continue fighting alongside him, they might as well consider themselves dead men.[38] Matching the new enemy's numbers would probably be impossible, regardless of what alliances he could slap together. Although the Taliban would soon offer Massoud a role in determining their new government structure, he did not trust their vision for his country. Ahmed Shah would instead continue to fight for his vision of a more moderate and autonomous Afghanistan.

It took little time for Massoud to issue a tactical response to his defeat in Kabul. Before 1996 expired, Karim Khallili,, the head of the Hizb-e-Wahdat party, signed up with the Alliance. The party largely represented the Hazara and Shi'a minority of the land. This man, like Dostum, had once sided against Massoud, but the dire situation. required a drastic measure. Dostum had been back with Massoud for a while now, but Hekmatyar refused to join in. He stated a rather empty-hearted conviction that he would wage an independent war against their mutual enemy. It would take the heads of this new power-sharing body until May of 1997 to prepare their response, when they set up offices in the northern confines of Mazar e Sharif.[39] At the same time, the enemy pressed on, hoping for the perfect moment to march into the city. It was now the largest metropolis in the country still shielding itself from a Taliban takeover.

Bringing Mazar e Sharif under control was a crucial operation for the Taliban in more than one regard. From there they could cut off Massoud's supply lines running from Tajikistan down to the Panjshir Valley, draining some of the stamina from the commander's defense efforts. It would also lure many of Massoud's southern troops further northward, keeping an Alliance return to Kabul at bay. Either side had strong fronts in both regions.

The Taliban took their cue to infiltrate Mazar e Sharif from the defection of one of Dostum's prominent generals, Abdul "Malik" Pehlawan. Although his loyalty probably shifted to the Taliban around the beginning of May, the plan's completion would require a few more weeks. A feud had recently broken out between Malik and Ismail Khan, who had been crowding Malik's territory since returning to Afghanistan from a 1995 escape into Iran. Malik was also upset with General Dostum at the time. He had accused his direct superior of recently ordering the assassination of his older brother, Lt. General Rasool Pehlawan. By consorting with the Taliban, the disgruntled Alliance general hoped to rid himself of two powerful rivals while gaining more territory for himself. A sizeable cash bribe may have helped him justify the traitorous behaviour. It was customary.

For a brief moment, it looked like Malik's defection might facilitate his wish for greater glory. He successfully disarmed the militias of Dostum and the loyal commanders under him. A great many of the officers, including Dostum, fled into Uzbekistan. When the Uzbek general crossed into the city of Termez, he apparently had to empty his pockets and walk across the bridge without a vehicle or any possessions. Had Malik been there as well, the sight would no doubt have pleased him. Things were working according to plan. But when General Malik Pehlawan invited the Taliban into Mazar e Sharif on May 24, 1997, absolutely no one, including himself, could have predicted what would take place.

Back in 1995, the Hazara ethnics of the nation had placed their support largely behind a man named Abdul Ali Mazari. He was Karim Khalili's predecessor as leader of the Hizb-e-Wahdat party. The Taliban had invited him to join their campaign against Massoud, and although he accepted, some of his troops rebelled. The Taliban had held Mazari responsible and killed him. It was an incident the Hazaras in Mazar e Sharif, their urban stronghold, would not have forgotten in the brief two years that had passed. They were definitely in no mood to listen to Taliban promises. When the Taliban Foreign Minister attempted to plead reason with the city's occupants, the Hazara civilians began to fire. Even the women pulled triggers.

With a string of victories against remarkably docile opponents, the rebelliousness took the Taliban by surprise. They were certainly not prepared for what happened next, although it is not without precedent in Afghan affairs. General Malik, their coveted defector, suddenly had a change of heart. Fearing the severity of resistance that would bear down on his forces if he persisted in this betrayal of the city, Malik suddenly enjoined his men to kill his Taliban collaborators. Out of nowhere, the confident invaders were suddenly outmatched. Many who did not die on the city streets soon found themselves in prison without much of a fight. Many others ran for their lives. Among the slaughtered were many Pushtun functionaries who had not come to fight, but to set up the new civil administration.

Taliban deaths and captures from the victory in Mazar e Sharif that May surpassed three thousand. The commander had never allowed the execution of prisoners, according to his brother, Afghanistan's ambassador to Britain. This, however, did not prevent thousands from perishing within the ethnic melting pot of the ancient city over the next few days.

Following the slaughter in Mazar e Sharif, Massoud led some of his men to positions along the Taliban route homeward, blocking a withdrawal from the north. Some of his troops stationed slightly north of Kabul in the Shomali Plains ambushed the Taliban reinforcements on their way to aid their brothers. The maneuvers were perhaps the best choice possible considering the situation. With General Dostum out of the country, however, Ahmed Shah's forces would be overtaxed. Two weeks later, about 2000 of the trapped Taliban troops escaped the Alliance in a town called Puli–Kumri, about halfway between Mazar e Sharif and Kabul. They rushed directly northward to another major city, Konduz. Here they melded with sympathetic Pushtun leaders who formerly followed the now invisible Gulbuddin Hekmatyar. The Northern Alliance, still known as the United Front, had never been able to make serious inroads in Kunduz city themselves because of its huge Pushtun population.

Kunduz, although an important acquisition for the Taliban at the time, was not such a difficult coup for them. The city was basically a big island of Pushtuns amidst a sea of Tajiks. In an effort at ethnic integration, an earlier king of the country had moved groups of them up from the south to settle in Kunduz and also in certain Hazara regions. Hekmatyar's family roots in the province of Kunduz could be attributed to the same forced migration. It made the city of Kunduz unique amongst cities in the nation, but especially in the north. The metropolis of Herat, for instance could claim a thirty percent Pushtun population, but most of them didn't even speak the language. On the other hand, the majority of Kunduz was clearly Pushtun. The common ethnicity made many of the city's inhabitants much more sympathetic toward the Taliban than the Afghans of most northern locales, generally dominated by other ethnic groups.

The after-effects of the Alliance victory in the north would be felt throughout the course of 1997. When news of the debacle spread, Taliban soldiers from provinces to the west and south of Mazar e Sharif began to disperse. They had already established a foothold in these areas, but now feared a broader revolt. Massoud's reaction was to cave in part of the Salang Tunnel, the only practical route that could lead the frightened men to the safety of the south. I would see nature do a very similar thing to the tunnel less than a year later, when visiting the Panjshir Valley.

These developments unfortunately halted the Taliban advance only until September. At this time, the Taliban who had found safe haven way up in Konduz captured a major Northern Alliance supply base and started making some headway of their own. Konduz made an effective strategic stronghold for the Taliban. It was not only a Taliban island in the middle of Northern Alliance territory, but also its location opened up trade possibilities with smugglers from Tajikistan. The presence of the Taliban in a city so close to areas regulated by Massoud threatened all resistance in the area – especially because Kunduz was Pushtun, and therefore generally more sympathetic to the Taliban.

Massoud continued to make progress further south, having recaptured Parwan province from the enemy in July. Concerned with the latest Taliban advances in the far north, he also appealed to General Dostum, still in Uzbekistan. Dostum returned to a temporary truce with Malik before pushing the antagonists back from their newest strongholds. But the peace between Massoud's northern partners would not last for long. By November, their forces once again began to fight amongst each other, resulting in Malik leaving the country this time. The inability of Ahmed Shah's coalition commanders to maintain a semblance of unity in their fight against the Taliban would present him considerable difficulties for the duration of this war.

After he returned to Afghanistan in September of 1997, Dostum announced the discovery of mass graves hiding thousands of Taliban corpses. He claimed they had been prisoners who were captured in Mazar e Sharif and then slaughtered by Pehlawan.[40]

Massoud attempted to use the Taliban defeat in Mazar e Sharif to his best advantage in the last seven months of 1997. Disturbing casualty reports accompanied his efforts. Sources would claim that up to 20,000 Pushtun civilians disappeared by the end of the year in areas the Taliban had abandoned. Although this was never properly investigated or verified, it would seem as though minority ethnics who had resisted the Taliban had taken the opportunity to punish many Pushtuns who had not.

Some ruthless ethnic cleansing took place in Mazar e Sharif after the Taliban dispersed. Malik and some Shi'a leaders might have delivered orders facilitating the killing, but it is not a matter of record. By the end of the following summer, their enemy would storm the city once again and exact plenty of revenge.

Dr. Rajwali Shah Khattak had his own view about Mazar e Sharif. He commented, "...genocide in Mazar e Sharif...killed innocent people...not with Taliban they were innocent Pushtun speaking people...terrifying them...driving them out from the northern area."

Mullah Mohammad Omar, the reclusive Taliban boss, made an unprecedented trip from Kandahar to Kabul in early June of 1997. He usually refused to leave Kandahar, feeling less vulnerable in the south, where his charges ruled everywhere by now. In Kabul, Omar appealed to the masses for support and assured them of an all-pervading conquest for Islam in their country. He also issued an impassioned plea for foreign help that drew 10,000 new Pakistani recruits. According to Massoud, the foreigners in the Taliban army eventually accounted for about forty percent of the whole.

As 1997 wore on, Commander Massoud's troops remained fairly intact, while those of the once formidable Malik/Dostum partnership had at least partially scattered from the internecine squabbling of their leaders. Ahmed Shah now certainly reigned supreme amongst the military commanders in the resistance. The loyalty Massoud had earned in many circles easily exceeded that of Rabbani, who was now more a figurehead than ever before. Instead of alienating leaders with whom he had frequently not seen eye-to-eye, Massoud now sought to broker a more widespread resistance. The newest coalition included Malik and Hekmatyar. However, Malik never really trusted the agreement, and a largely power-drained Hekmatyar once again quickly walked away from a cooperative effort. By the end of 1997, the four principles participating in the newly declared coalition, the "United National Islamic Front For the Salvation of Afghanistan," would be Massoud, Rabbani, Dostum, and Karim Khalili. This was the patchy military tapestry upon which I first set foot in Afghanistan, about two and a half weeks later.

CHAPTER 9

THE PANJSHIR VALLEY, AFGHANISTAN:
JANUARY 22-27, 1998

The need for Wahy (revelation):
Every Muslim knows that Allah Almighty has sent man into this world
as a matter of test, and in return for his being obliged with certain duties the
whole universe has been placed at his service. For this reason, once he is in the
world he must do two things:
　　1. He should make the best use of this world, and things created in it.
　　2. While using this world to his advantage, he should keep the injunctions
of Allah Almighty in sight and do nothing that goes against His Will or
Pleasure.

> – Ma'ariful Qur'an
> By Maulana Mufti Muhammad Shafi
> Volume 1 (Surah Al-Fatihah, Al-Baqarah),
> page 1 introduction

The man who grants me lodging in the Panjshir Valley is Massoud's Head of Military Intelligence. He owns a sturdy two-story structure, much nicer than the governor's residence back in Taloqan, which left me with few impressions beyond the meticulously hand-woven rugs. I guess you could refer to it as a guesthouse, since the commander's guests seem to board here. The well-known BBC journalist, Sandy Gall, stayed in this very same home back in the early 1980's when he traveled through Soviet-occupied Afghanistan for his first book about Massoud and the country. Most of the same men Sandy Gall encountered turn up at the house now, including the cook and other staff members.

At the guesthouse, I can doze or read in my very own room with a wood stove. In a village dominated by basic stone dwellings, I would think that few enjoy such luxuries. We're situated on the outskirts of a little town named Bazarak. It's probably not much different than several others in the seventy-mile-long valley, except that the man who spearheads the Panjshir's population of about 200,000 resides in this village. I can't immediately determine who lives in the guesthouse outside of my main host, but I believe two of his brothers as well, plus three sons split somehow among the three gentlemen. Amrullah shifts to part time duty now while visiting his nearby mother.

Massoud's residence in this hamlet is his family quarters, housing his wife and children. The commander, however, maintains a variety of secure dwellings in the northern areas controlled by his forces. The circumstances of his vocation require the man to keep moving from one location to another, although not as much as in the past. During the Russian occupation Massoud would often move to higher ground in the middle of the night, seldom staying in one place for more than a few hours. Nowadays, the moves are not so spontaneous, but he still acts on intuition.

The southernmost point of the diagonal Panjshir Valley lies about thirty miles north of Kabul, and Bazarak looks to be quite a bit further northeast from there. Impressive peaks of the Hindu Kush pinch the scrubby, dwarf-treed strip of lowland on either side of the Panjshir, where the villagers have assembled their homes here in the delta. I ask if I can go for a jaunt into the foothills, to take in some of the alluring scenery. The boys are told to accompany me and not just to honour custom. The men of the house say certain areas still hide land mines left over from the Soviet incursion and the boys know where they are. I don't ask who planted the little explosives, some no larger than the boys' hands. I imagine the locals buried plenty, in an effort to thwart the Soviets. Unfortunately, what seemed like a stroke of ingenuity at the time created the possibility of innocent civilians being maimed even decades later. The mines have been replaced with small explosives called IEGs, or roadside bombs. Here in Afghanistan they seemed to be frequently planted in bicycles, and most often detonated by remote control. But they can be disguised in any variety of ways and are not necessarily set off from a distance.

The old mines still buried in the Panjshir Valley aren't the only mementos reminding all of the gruesome battles fought here back in the 1980s. Resourceful villagers built the pedestrian bridge we just crossed, with scrap metal from military hardware left behind by the communists. Beat up tanks, helicopter shells and other assorted flotsam remains strewn about. It has been Massoud's edict to leave the debris as monuments to the brave war effort.

On the other side of the bridge, we cross a frozen pond, guiding us closer to the mountains. Children who have probably never owned skates or even seen hockey sticks slip and slide in their boots, thoroughly enjoying the moment's frolic. The scene takes me back to the winters I spent as a child skating or playing hockey on ponds near Ottawa. A young boy jabs the finishing touches into a snowman, obviously pleased with his creation. Within ten minutes, I begin to work my way up one of the grand wintry slopes of the valley.

It bothers me when I learn that the cute little pile of wood sitting by the stove back in my room was sliced from healthy cherry trees. With the lack of decent timber, the folk here are forced to resort to such extremes, but probably only for the elderly, sick and privileged few. This week's privileged few includes a guest from one of the world's most wasteful countries. It is ever so ironic that I lobby against unsustainable logging practices back home.

Two friends of the commander stop by the house to see me after dinner the following night. The first is a traditional medicine practitioner familiar with plants indigenous to the Panjshir. I mention that I am interested in traditional medicines and like to include them in the health care curriculum for RCDF. He gives me his address, which ends not with "Afghanistan," but "Panjshir Stronghold." The herbalist reminds me of a story told by Massoud upon our first encounter, at his hideout in Dushanbe. Some years ago, after listening to complaints about chest pains, the man handed Ahmed Shah an herbal preparation to place under his tongue. Massoud soon started to protest a new discomfort in his mouth. The herbalist urged him to stay with the procedure until the pain subsided. When Massoud's anguish rose even higher, the same recommendation was again made, resulting in greater and greater pain. The man finally asked Massoud if his chest pains were bothering him anymore and Massoud replied that he couldn't tell because his mouth was on fire. The humorous little anecdote was very much appreciated on the afternoon I first met the commander.

The second guest of the evening is introduced to me as Engineer Mir Dad. I have learned in my journeys that many developing nations are casual with their prerequisites for titles such as "engineer" or "doctor." Mir Dad, however, possesses genuine credentials. I have brought several large bottles of multivitamins for local children who may be undernourished and Mir Dad offers to distribute them.

Mir Dad proceeds to tell me how the Taliban intentionally demolished an ancient aqueduct system in the city of Charikar, close to the southern end of the Panjshir, north of Kabul. The shortsighted bit of destruction was undertaken in an attempt to depopulate the area, undermining its citizens' ability to revolt. One can only guess how long the residents could have resisted had they mounted their most strident effort, but they didn't. Massoud had cautioned against it, for their own safety. Now, with the aqueducts laid to waste, many citizens of Charikar naturally wish they had fought the Taliban.

I take some laundry down to the river the next morning and learn how well- adjusted Northern Afghans have become to surviving the icy winters without fuel to heat their homes. While a valet delivers me warm water each day for at least a partial wash, some of the more courageous villagers submerge themselves chest high in the frigid outdoor stream. I submerge only my arms. Yet After forty-five seconds of scrubbing garments, they grow numb and red, sparking with pins and needles. Regardless of how many petty inconveniences I may have been exposed to in the course of my travels, I am so fragile compared to these people we may as well have come from different planets. They are as tough as nails and I can't help but respect it.

The month-long ritual of Ramadan expires soon and the holiday of Eid Mubarak follows on its heels. It's a three-day period of feasting and socializing: the official end of the fast. I would enjoy the festivities, for sure, but because staying here indefinitely was not a possibility I had planned for, I should prepare to depart before the celebrations sweep all other considerations aside for a few more days. The call of duty to family and business has started to prey on my conscience. However, I have still not interviewed the commander as thoroughly as I would like to. We have not yet sat down to anything resembling an official one-on-one. So when the recently elusive Amrullah shows up this evening to report that my host will summon me tomorrow afternoon, the news brings relief. I greatly appreciate the fact Amrullah would have time for me at all. It's a rare opportunity for him to be with his family, especially at this most special time of year.

Amrullah also mentions that in the morning a small group will be visiting the front lines near Kabul, and he can reserve a car seat for me should I so desire. It's an enticing proposition. It does not seem entirely ethical, though, to play voyeur to a group of men willing to lay down their lives for principles they deeply value. I also do not want to be an unnecessary obstruction on the front line just to satisfy my ego. And so I decline the privilege.

Another excursion, available to foreigners in particular, is a trip to see a prison full of Pakistani inmates, captured from within the ranks of Taliban. It is understandably important for the Alliance to spread word abroad that their neighbor plays an active role in this civil war and that the commander prefers to imprison rather than kill his captives. As to Pakistan's complicity in the affair, seeing Pakistani prisoners won't change my thoughts, but I find it notable how Massoud obviously understands the media machine. Since I also believe that ogling men through bars degrades everyone involved, I turn down this generous offer as well. Besides, I want to make sure nothing gets in the way of tomorrow afternoon's meeting with Massoud.

The next morning, some local boys show me a few new things: first, an alternate method of crossing the river. Over a particularly narrow section, just far enough from the bridge to assist villagers living further along the bank, a cable runs about twenty feet above water level. It's attached to a post on either side. From the cable hangs a basket just right for one adult, but from which four or five children can dangle like monkeys. First of all, one of the kids has to bravely traverse the cable hand over hand to retrieve the basket from the other side. It looks like a wilderness ride one might find at a Western amusement park, except there are no electronic alligators snapping their jaws below. Of course, there are no safety harnesses either. And no one would want to lose their grip on that rusty cable with the freezing water raging below.

A popular sport on the river is grenade fishing. Enterprising young sportsmen lean over the bridge railing and drop their explosives, either randomly or after spotting a school of fish. This would be considered reckless in many places, but it's mainly due to the lack of an environmentally friendlier way to get food here. It's certainly not the type of willful environmental carelessness so often seen back home. With all the knowledge in the world available for decades now in the Western World, we still allow our governments to permit and even subsidize the decimation of our own natural resources. And this includes not only our water, but also most of our ancient rainforests, and many species of creatures as well.

I take a half-hour stroll into the village center before noon. Along the way, the boys treat me to an exhibition of snowball fighting with biblical-style slingshots, reminiscent of David and Goliath days. It's obvious that in the right hands these unassuming playthings could knock a man right off his feet, even with just a lump of snow. I remember hearing something about weapons such as these being used effectively against Soviet soldiers. Unlike our modern version, they have a circular trajectory. The boys fire from one hilltop and squarely hit their targets on the next one over. The range and accuracy, already remarkable, would be increased with a heavier object. Imagine what kind of damage could be done with a ball bearing.

We reach a large dirt field with a dozen or so men on horseback, playing a vigorous game of some kind. Afghans call the sport "buzkashi." It's a very aggressive and competitive sport with few rules to restrict the competitors' behaviour. The riders basically compete to pull or carry the headless carcass of a goat or calf to the scoring zone. While doing so, they are allowed to obstruct each other in a variety of ways, including using their riding crops on other players. I would imagine the sanctimonious Taliban would be hard pressed to ridicule this age-old Afghan sport. Perhaps the horsemen derive some special gratification from this leisurely activity, knowing that neither time nor politics have been able to change it one iota.

★   ★   ★

Around 2:00 p.m., my driver drops me off at the edge of a mountain where I need to climb a fairly steep path in order to get to my next encounter. At the end of the trail, or at least its first stage, lies the headquarters of Engineer Ishaq, perhaps Massoud's most valued consultant. One could consider this more senior member of the hierarchy something like Minister of External Affairs without portfolio.

When I reach the plateau, I pull back the canvas entrance flap serving as the doorway of what appears to be an office. The room has a modest design to it and seems to have been constructed rather hastily. Its ceiling is canvass, like the top of a tent. The mountain face serves as the room's back wall. I feel as though I have just entered Ali Baba's cave- that is, with a modern twist: the cave is full of modern-day electronics gear.

Some of the paraphernalia here hints at Engineer Ishaq's role as a communication's expert for Massoud. It all operates off of a very noisy generator, which rattles away in the background without interruption. The limitations of my fifty-dollar tape deck aside, the clatter from the generator assures that my interview with the man will be far short of broadcast quality. The place is nice and warm, courtesy of a wood stove lying in the center of the room. After being inside for a few minutes, the room reminds me of the inside of a special teepee where a group of aboriginal leaders might congregate for a tribal council.

The engineer shows me his state-of-the-art computer, of which he has a right to be proud. Who would expect to see such a computer here, on the edge of a barely accessible mountain wilderness? The unit is connected to a satellite phone for internet access. It obviously keeps him up to date with world events because the next time I see him he wants to know what I make of the Bill Clinton and Monica Lewinsky affair. As for this afternoon, I assume he has been informed that I hope to speak to him about other matters.

Engineer Ishaq and Massoud go way back, to Kabul 1971, when Ahmed Shah's focus on a college education was so suddenly diverted to the art of overthrowing an unpopular government. Ishaq's respect and affection for his long-term comrade makes itself apparent from the start. They not only attended Kabul Polytechnic at the same time, but also hid together somewhere deep in these mountains following their failed attempt to destroy Daoud Khan's government. Engineer Ishaq claims that while Ahmed Shah continued his military career, he himself quietly reverted back to his studies and to the printing and distribution of Jamait-i-Islami doctrine.

With great patience, Engineer Ishaq goes on to enlighten me on Massoud's policies and points of view until all of my inquiries are satisfied. Amrullah had provided basically the same service the previous night. Allow me to piece together a bit of what I learn from these gentlemen during the two meetings, along with some of my own observations:

According to the engineer, the Panjshir Valley, meaning valley of five lions, received its name from an ancient tale surrounding the legendary Afghan king and conqueror of India, Sultan Mahmud Ghaznavi. Ghaznavi, although Turkish by descent, was born and brought up in Ghazni, Afghanistan, a town that has been widely adopted as the man's last name. This heralded figure was a much-favoured subject of the great poet, Rumi. Apparently the king ordered a dam to be built somewhere around here near the beginning of the second millennium, when he ruled his kingdom. As he coordinated his work force and sought out material, five holy men from the area intervened and offered to do the job themselves quickly. Ghazni was so impressed when they completed the dam overnight, he called the men lions in disguise. This is, of course, according to ancient legend.

As for present day Afghanistan, both Engineer Ishaq and Amrullah stress how the country needs to reclaim its natural geographic birthright as a corridor for trade between the East and West. It seems as though every time the nation makes a bit of progress another conflict breaks out to sabotage the momentum. The land appears to be smitten by Murphy's Law: if something bad can possibly happen, it will. In the end, because an unstable nation does not make a reliable business partner, the opportunity for international agreements or economic gain is continually stymied.

Afghanistan prides itself in having perpetuated amicable relations with China, who Amrullah believes will one day commercially dominate Central Asia. Chinese engineers are currently helping with a regional power generation project in the Panjshir. Some say Chinese aid dates back to the 1950s, during King Zahir's reign, before any other country extended a hand in friendship. They apparently convinced the Shah of Iran to befriend Afghanistan as well. Further support was shown when they placed sanctions on Gorbachev's government until he removed Soviet troops from the land. To this day, the Chinese send foreign aid packages for Afghan refugees in Pakistan and Iran, with little fanfare or expectation of reciprocation. Sadly though, like other prospective benefactors, China refuses to pump meaningful funds into a consistently weak Afghan central government.

Engineer Ishaq insists Massoud realizes the necessity of maintaining good relations with Pakistan, even though it offers tacit support to the Taliban movement. This is especially true because the ties that China shares with Pakistan eclipse those it has nurtured with Afghanistan. So, regardless of how much Pakistan's policies might aggravate Afghans, serious protest runs them the risk of falling into disfavor with the "Land of the Dragon" – amongst other countries.

Aside from Pakistan and China, Afghanistan also has relationships with four other bordering nations to consider. All of these will require at least some degree of appeasement or creative maintenance. A strong Afghan government must work hard, both domestically and internationally, to undergo a transformation that will earn it even the minimum requirements in education, health care, utilities, transportation and media. Such advancements are necessary to rescue the country from hopeless dysfunction. With the third lowest literacy rate in the world, it unfortunately has a long and difficult road ahead. The external forces promoting violence in the land certainly do not help matters.

Central Asian oil is currently a major catalyst shaping foreign relations within much of the hemisphere. Turkmenistan, Kazakhstan and Azerbaijan in particular hold untold fortunes. American interests have aggressively pursued this resource for some years now. To gain the upper hand in the complex process of owning the rights and transporting it to the marketplace, British Petroleum would merge with Amoco this very year to form BP Amoco, the largest oil consortium in the world. The move would provide the US and England with a solid motive for aligning their political objectives in the area. But oil interests from other countries, as well, have postured themselves to gain from the precious industrial oasis of Central Asia.

Russia, which governed Turkmenistan until the fall of the Iron Curtain, has had pipelines running from the country for years, albeit aging and poorly maintained. Billions of dollars from France, Italy, Belgium, Iran, China, and Argentina are also on the table. Although plenty of oil exists in the region for all to share, the foreign interests involved are competing with fierce determination to limit their competitor's gains. The US, for instance, would love to phase out the Russians from any Caspian Sea oil or gas consortium.

The US plan is starting to sound like a revival of the "Great Game" played out by Russia and Britannia for much of the nineteenth century. Both countries sought to control the area between Turkmenistan and the Pakistan portion of the country then known as British India. Afghanistan was, and still is, the heartland of this region. British meddling went back to 1839 when they stormed the capital. The Emir of Afghanistan, Dost Mohammed, was apparently too friendly with the Russians, so the Brits replaced him with their colonial puppet, former King Shah Sujah. According to an article in an 1862 edition of Harper's magazine, "The ruler of the independent state of Cabool was 'desired' to form no alliance with the Czar. His reply to this modest demand was unsatisfactory, and the English undertook to depose him and place Shah Soojah, a creature of their own, upon the throne."[41]

This was a face-off not unlike Daoud Khan's legendary stand against the Russians one hundred years later.

During the tenure of the Rabbani-Massoud government, one could hardly find any US citizens living in the Afghan capital. Amrullah says that according to reliable sources, there are more than 200 of them now, in 1998. A number of prominent American ex-diplomats have set up offices in Kabul and Kandahar, claiming to be engaging in research and furnishing official assessment reports. They are more likely devising infrastructure and paving the way for oil companies such as American-based UNOCAL. The former US Ambassador to Turkmenistan now works for this group, as does another diplomat in residence, Charles Santos. Santos is a former member of the UN's special commission to Afghanistan. Both have involved themselves in mysterious activities inside the country and surrounding areas. Santos has been sighted several times in fairly dangerous sections of Afghanistan. Some believe that at least a dozen of these secretive characters are laying foundations not only in Afghanistan, but also in Islamabad, Pakistan.

★   ★   ★

Another interesting American figure at home in these parts is former US Special Ambassador to Somalia, Robert Oakley. Oakley led the US military intervention in Somalia back in 1992, deceivingly named Operation Restore Hope. This man delivered a clear message when he made the Conoco headquarters in Mogadishu the American command post and de facto embassy. ConocoPhillips is a huge integrated energy company involved in oil exploration and refining. Somalia possesses more than enough oil wealth to interest the US. It is also strategically located on the Horn of Africa, one of the few deep-water pivot points for international shipping lanes. The Horn of Africa controls access to the Red Sea and the Suez Canal. For a variety of reasons, the Pentagon would love to build a permanent base in Somalia.

When political meddling in African affairs blew up in his face, Oakley migrated to Islamabad, Pakistan. It would seem likely he was favourably disposed towards a Taliban rise to power. Oakley's wife, Phyllis, was believed to have spent some time in Kandahar, Afghanistan, some years back. This is now Mullah Omar's territory, the Taliban's headquarters. Phyllis Oakley was the State Department's Afghanistan

Desk Office from 1982 to 1985. From 1989 until mid-1991, she was on loan to USAID, working with the Afghanistan Cross-Border Humanitarian Assistance Program in Islamabad, Pakistan.[42] But finding tangible results from the project would not be easy. The Humanitarian Assistance Program was Mrs. Oakley's official posting, but USAID has synchronized with "reconstruction infrastructures" all around the oil world for decades.

UNOCAL and Argentina's BRIDAS are the top two contenders vying for a chance to construct a more than 1000-mile pipeline. It will stretch from the Caspian Sea in Turkmenistan, through Afghanistan and down into the friendly port of Gwadar on the shores of the Arabian Sea in Pakistan. The pipeline's northern reaches are ultimately projected to connect with the proposed Baku-Ceyhan pipeline, linking Central Asia with Turkey via the Caspian, Black and Mediterranean seas. This is UNOCAL'S first concern. The proposed Turkmenistan/Afghanistan/Pakistan (TAP) pipeline could be more easily routed through Iran instead of Afghanistan, but the Americans consider the option unsafe. And rightly so, for them. Afghanistan not only lies at the base of the oil rich nations of Central Asia, but it also skirts American rivals Iran, Russia and China. It could provide cover for additional American military bases in the region and also give them "strategic depth" in Central Asia. The new bases would line up nicely with others already in place throughout Central Asia, Eastern Europe and the Middle East, creating a lengthy buffer zone from the competition. The Russians, Chinese, Iranians and also Afghans are all aware of the plan. And they know from history that when imperialist intruders set up camp, they do not like to leave.

Having Afghanistan under their thumbs could bring the US much closer to goals they set for themselves earlier in the decade in a classified document called Defense Planning Guidance. Defense Planning Guidance is a Pentagon policy statement completed in 1992 under the guidance of Paul Wolfowitz and his underling at the time, Zalmay Khalizad. Khalilzad would later play an important role in the development of an American Afghanistan.

The Defense Planning Guidance states that USA's political and military mission in the post-cold-war era will be to make sure it permits no rival superpower to emerge in Western Europe, Asia or the lands of the former Soviet Union - especially lands of the former Soviet Union, some of them teeming with oil. It lists "Convincing potential competitors that they need not aspire to a greater role or pursue a more aggressive posture to protect their legitimate interests" as part of the mission. The 46-page document goes on to say the US "must sufficiently account for the interests of the advanced industrial nations to discourage them from challenging our leadership or seeking to overturn the established political and economic order." When a concerned, anonymous official leaked the document to the New York Times, the newspaper claimed it made the case for a world dominated by one superpower with "sufficient military might to deter any nation or group of nations from challenging American primacy."[43]

Oil is the means to world domination that the US seeks. And the superpower continues to make strides in this department. The point where the world's remaining oil reserves are on a downside curve is known as "Peak oil". Peak oil means oil becomes more difficult to recover, rendering it less and less accessible. It is also when oil companies will have to rely on more challenging oil reserves such as the Athabasca Tar Sands in Northern Alberta, Canada. Crude oil demands far more refinement than the "sweet oil" found in Iraq and the Caspian. It is a competitively sought after prize.

We are projected to reach "Peak Oil" in late 2004. It will make the resource an increasingly valuable commodity as reserves wane and the demand of an exploding human population increases. This is particularly the case with countries such as India and China, whose technology for economic boom depends on oil, even if the West tries to find alternative energy sources for itself. "Peak oil" will also make those in charge of the resource arguably the most powerful men on the planet.[44]

Just a short time ago, UNOCAL, the American oil company, formed a consortium with five other countries to facilitate the TAP project. It now operates within an alliance called Centgas, which includes Delta Oil, a Saudi oil giant allegedly run by two families with links to Osama bin-Laden. Meanwhile, the two companies hold the majority in the consortium. Within a day or so of the signing of this partnership, the government of Turkmenistan, also a contributor, announced a mega-dollars oil services deal with Halliburton, USA. Halliburton is the massive construction and oil services corporation run by Dick Cheney.

Part of this mosaic is The Carlyle Group, a massively successful Washington-based private equity firm. Its billions of dollars in investments includes not only the trade of military equipment and "weapons of war", but for over five years provided mercenary and security training as well, through a subsidiary, Vinnell Corp. George Bush Sr. has for years been a top advisor and often front man for the Carlyle Group. Certain bin-Laden family members and members of the Saudi royal family are clients of the elite Carlyle Investment Group.[45] They are a one-stop full service company from weapons to mercenaries.

★   ★   ★

Amrullah says the Americans' interest in his country is encouraging. But Massoud's group is also of the opinion that the US should not disregard any of the parties involved in the current conflict, because it is sometimes difficult to predict what will happen in Afghanistan. The Americans should consequently try to maintain contact with both sides of the equation. It goes without saying that Ahmed Shah would prefer the US to choose its business partners more carefully in the future. The White House has shown the Rabbani/Massoud government almost no recognition, even though the UN fully acknowledges it.

Instead of receiving American recognition, some of Massoud's people have recently accessed a "situation report" written by a US citizen living in Afghanistan. The report expresses hope that the Taliban will soon conquer the remainder of the land, facilitating the installation of the pipeline and other goals sought by American corporate interests.

The ISI, who hold similar hopes for the Taliban, represent an arm of the Pakistani people's interest to protect their country from being destroyed by its neighbours. Afghanistan is a threat, Iran is as well, and India, whose population and resources are eight times that of Pakistan is in a constant state of war with the nation. The two countries have already fought three major wars. There is no demarcation of a border between the two Kashmir provinces; one in India and one in Pakistan. Instead the dividing line is called "line of control." So in the context of the dangers presented by Pakistan's neighbours, the ISI is much appreciated by the country's public. Numerous bombings in Karachi and other Pakistan cities are thought to have been perpetrated by RAW, India's equivalent to the ISI.

Ishaq says Rabbani and Massoud realize that no single political or ethnic group could succeed at governing Afghanistan on its own. A broad based government will absolutely be required. Major considerations must be afforded the Pushtuns, who are unlikely to settle for a regime too top-heavy with minority ethnics. Massoud even hesitates to enter the capital city until attracting an adequate number of Pushtuns into his ranks. When he and Rabbani agree the time has come, Massoud will take Kabul by force. Their administration will include not only United Front leaders in positions of authority, but also members of other prominent political parties, in order to show their endorsement of an equally shared power structure. An election or grand assembly of fair representation known as a Loya Jurga will be the next step. Finally, Afghans will be able to select their own new president in a free election.

In the words of Amrullah, "Despite the fact that Massoud does not enjoy the same power as he did before 1992, he is still going strong and will eventually rescue his country. There are always prayers for him, asking God to prolong his life so that he may have time to achieve his objectives."

★　　★　　★

A man walks through the burlap entranceway of Engineer Ishaq's cabin about fifteen minutes after the interview with my new Afghan acquaintance has finished. He says the commander will see me now.

Massoud's office is another two to three hundred meters farther up the same mountain path, but after a sharp right turn. It looks similarly rustic, but somewhat larger and better lit. It definitely has a more spacious appearance. Instead of an array of electronic gear, Massoud makes use of a desk, currently piled high with business papers. He sits there working away when we walk in.

Amrullah is inside, expecting me. He informs me about etiquette here inside the office, as the commander appears to be busy. The relationship I share here with Amrullah in this capacity is a formal one. He displays as much warmth and good-humour as circumstances allow, but protocol ultimately controls our interaction, as it should.

Besides the two of us, several other men also stand around the one large room. A couple of them are likely guards. Their casual manner masks their underlying vigilance. These gentlemen appear to lurk in shadows created by daylight that filters through a window from the waning sun.

Massoud tries to keep interviews as brief as he can. I have no trouble respecting the policy. Despite limiting this particular public relations exercise to fifteen minutes, he probably cannot really afford to spare the time. It has consequently been more efficient for me to gain new knowledge from members of his fraternity. But the commander has provided me with ample opportunity to get my questions answered. Unfortunately, or fortunately, as the case may be, the questions I prepared for today's interview are no longer valid because Engineer Ishaq has already addressed them.

Massoud usually directs the conversation in a soft and measured direction whenever in my company. I get the impression he prefers to acquire information rather than depart it. Like other cutting-edge personalities I have briefly met, he never misses an opportunity to delve deeper into a fact or opinion that comes his way, before stating his own point of view. Perhaps this inquisitiveness reflects a desire to make guests feel at home, but I doubt exclusively. He does command politeness. Despite the fact that the man doesn't wear his power on his sleeve, Massoud will shoot you a pretty humbling look if he deems your conversation inappropriate.

The commander is ready to speak to me before long. The two of us sit on chairs in the room he uses as an office, while Amrullah stands close by. I don't think I have seen Massoud when he didn't appear overworked, but his fatigue seems especially pronounced this afternoon. This chronic condition stems partly from the fact that he is so generous with his time, constantly extending himself beyond all reasonable limits. Even Massoud's impressive endurance must have a breaking point. This afternoon, none of us have eaten since before dawn, and the hunger doesn't leave anyone in the group with energy to spare, with twilight now approaching. At least I slept for six hours or so last night. Massoud probably caught no more than two or three hours rest, which I hear is his standard allotment. Being in the company of such a famous person gives me a boost of adrenaline, as well. From the commander's point of view, this must be another public relations endurance test. He could be dealing with many other matters of extreme importance. But he keeps a poker face.

Because our meeting is at Massoud's office, it takes on a more formal tone than other gatherings. Amrullah opens with an official announcement of the required protocol. The three of us then proceed with some preliminary small talk. Massoud is polite, as always, indulging in touches of humour. Today, however, his humour has a more biting edge to it. I gauge this from his overall manner more than from his Persian words or Amrullah's English translation. Although he doesn't exactly show impatience, there can be no mistaking it: the commander is displaying some signs of strain. I will soon feel I am forcing him to suffer through one interview too many.

As the interview develops, my few unprepared questions receive brisk treatment. I slowly, and somewhat nervously, try to work the talk into the direction of Massoud's relationship with Rabbani. I finally ask the commander, in a rambling manner, how the two men continue to get along after some very trying years. Since at least 1991, they have made an endless stream of stressful decisions together, while under fire from their enemies. These decisions not only affect hundreds of thousands of Afghans, but they also face the close scrutiny of Afghan politicians, warlords and military officers. This must burden him tremendously.

I can immediately see my probe has hit a nerve. Massoud's body stiffens. I don't know if my wordiness has contributed to the reaction, or if the question is simply a little too informal for his liking. It becomes apparent this will be more of a one-way exchange. After being momentarily taken aback, he flashes a look of ire. He retorts, "Why don't you go and ask Rabbani?"

An uncomfortable period of silence follows the reprimand, but then Massoud begins to talk again. I finally work up enough nerve to ask the commander another question. He basically ignores it. He continues to speak, more heatedly this time. He laments the involvement of the ISI and Pakistani militia in the grim civil war he has been fighting for too long without positive results. Massoud gets more animated by the moment, even angry. He finally states emphatically that his message for me is to "tell the West!" He wants the West to put pressure on Pakistan to stop interfering in Afghan internal affairs. Before it is too late!

Being an outsider, I wouldn't argue the point even if it were not totally rude to do so.

Massoud's reaction to my question about him and Rabbani, along with his overall dour mood today, leads me to believe that some friction has developed in his camp. This unfortunately must remain a theory for a while; any attempt to verify it with Amrullah or others could alienate me from the men with whom I desire to build a trust. But research I compile years later divulges that opposing views damage the men's relationship around the time of my trip to the Panjshir.

Badakhshan province in the extreme northeast of Afghanistan is Rabbani's stronghold, while Massoud's beloved Panjshir Valley is located between Badakhshan and the encroaching Taliban front. Geography alone determines that the two men's interests sometimes collide. Massoud's control over the wealth of the eastern mines, as barter for weapons and helicopters, is another potential trouble area. It includes the world famous lapis lazuli, found in Rabbani's territory. Still, other issues are also at stake. And I believe the two men have started to disagree on one or more of them. Perhaps Massoud has begun to eclipse Professor Rabbani. The rift developing is one from which the partnership of Rabbani and Massoud may have never fully recovered.

CHAPTER 10

THE PANJSHIR VALLEY to BANGKOK, THAILAND:
JAN 28–FEB 3, 1998

There's no difference between one's killing and making decisions that will send others to kill. It's exactly the same thing, or even worse.

– Golda Meir

The youthful exuberance of the girls makes me yearn for my own young ones, seemingly light years away. I sheepishly click a photo of them. I am aware that the Taliban could lay a sound beating on me just for pulling out my camera, never mind photographing a female of any age.

Amrullah comes to get me early the next morning. Before an afternoon that will carry us to a variety of sites further up the valley, I would like to indulge Mir Dad's open invitation to knock on the door of his home.

I soon discover Engineer Mir Dad's house contains a traditional heated table very much like the one I saw in the shop back in Taloqan. It's a circular bench surrounding a wood stove, with a trench dug into the floor, to place our feet. This keeps everyone as close as possible to the heat emanating from the stove. We all cover our laps with a portion of the tablecloth, or "dastarkhan," which keeps the entire lower portion of the body extremely warm. The three of us sit around for a while chatting and drinking tea, while Mir Dad throws a log onto the stove every once in a while. The occasion has a very down–home, comforting feeling to it.

It worries me a bit when I suddenly see the vitamins I have given Mir Dad to distribute are sitting on his kitchen shelves. Then I realize rural Afghans probably wouldn't live in the same kind of panicked rush that so many people do back home – me for one. I'm sure he will hand them out just like he promised to, as soon as he gets a chance. He seems like a good man.

We begin our journey up the valley in about another hour. The dirt road gets more pockmarked the farther we drive, and this slows our pace considerably. We pass a group of men on horseback, returning from a game of "buzkashi." The car has difficulty passing them. We travel northeast, maybe thirty kilometers; it is difficult to tell with our speed fluctuating between slow and really slow.

The Panjshir hospital lies close to what seems like the end of the navigable portion of the road. To go any further would require a four-by-four or donkey. The modest facility is nestled in a scenic vista where the valley narrows around the raging river. Part of it connects with the rock face of a mountain. The Panjshir Valley is strikingly narrow in a great many places. The cliffs shoot up thousands of feet on either side of you, in a dazzling fashion.

A sterile and stark atmosphere pervades the hospital when we arrive, so we don't stay long. Other than some malaria patients and a few souls stranded by debilitating ailments and injuries, all of the sick have made a special trip home. They all want to spend Eid with their families if possible. It's the most joyous celebration of the year for people of their faith. I would imagine many rural Canadian hospitals take on a similarly sparse appearance at Christmas time.

Next, we stop at a very engaging munitions depot. The depot hides beneath a natural outcropping of rock hanging right off the side of a mountain. There are a couple of other similar but smaller rock configurations, functioning as part of the depot as well (the Soviets also built a trail of forts into the sides of Panjshir valley walls). Up top lies a plateau where Soviet soldiers used to play volleyball in their leisure hours. It was also their signal center, from where they communicated with their men on the ground to allow access to the munitions depot.

One of the guards here is the tall man who scowled at me in the helicopter. The scene is submerged in twilight, making it hard to recognize him at first. I find the rock formations and the purpose they serve fascinating. The depot even has a chopper area nearby. Amrullah tells me a story describing how members of the Panjshir militia, back when communist forces controlled the storehouse, tortured an enemy soldier until he confessed the signal codes needed for entry. Massoud's men scaled the pinnacle formation and grabbed the Russian lookout sentry at the volleyball plateau. Once inside the depot, Massoud's men looted the facility for three days straight, in a morale-boosting triumph for the home side. The arsenal before me now has found its way into. Massoud's possession through more conventional means. I definitely do not attempt to pull out my camera in this circumstance.

Shortly after we leave, Amrullah points out a flattened mountaintop reminiscent of topography in the Grand Canyon. He claims that while stationed on this plateau, the Red Army used to keep watch on the valley, playing volleyball in their leisure hours. At this point, we see the guard from the munitions depot firing snowballs out of a slingshot for practice. I take the opportunity to give him a t-shirt displaying the words "FREE AFGHANISTAN" on it. The soldier has probably earned it many times over. It seems to put a little smile on his face.

Amrullah then directs my attention towards an historic artifact called "the wall of the infidels," left behind by a pagan tribe that once lived in the Panjshir. Members of this nomadic group, the "Kalash" people, still roam in an eastern quarter of Afghanistan known as Nuristan. The Kalash in Afghanistan have all been converted to Islam over the years and are now better known as Nuristanis. Most of those who have retained their original faith live over the border in Pakistan, in beautiful valleys of the Hindu Kush Mountain Range near the city of Chitral. They are a peaceful and spiritual people with a religion largely based on nature. Many Muslims see them as "kafir," or infidels, because they have not adopted Islam. Some believe the Kalash to be descendants of the army of Alexander the Great, which passed through the area around 325 B.C. Others believe they have remained in the same mountain valleys of Pakistan for three to four thousand years.

The story of the nomadic Kalash of Afghanistan reminds me that throughout history many roving peoples have called this country their home. Most of them have developed their restless nature to avoid persecution, sometimes from inside their country, but often from without. Afghanistan has provided a place of refuge for many, but the Shi'a Muslims of the land, mostly Hazaras, have felt persecuted for centuries.

One of the guests at our house tonight is a soldier from Massoud's forces. He comments that at least Russia fought its own war in Afghanistan, while the Americans slyly use the Taliban to do their dirty work for them. American complicity would certainly not be out of character. They have orchestrated many such coups in Central and South Americas, as well as distressed nations elsewhere. However, the fact that almost everyone in Afghanistan takes American involvement in the country for granted, while few North Americans know anything at all about these covert operations, is a noteworthy observation. On one hand, most Westerners believe that people in underdeveloped foreign lands are brainwashed by the propaganda of their own repressive regimes. On the other, most of us swallow every manner of misinformation and disinformation fed to us by our own governments, without suspecting we too might be getting programmed. Considering this fundamental reality, it would not surprise me three years later when the son of Colin Powell, USA's Secretary of State, became the head honcho of the FCC, America's media watchdog.

Rahimullah Yusufzai is a world famous BBC journalist and executive editor of the highly respected Pakistan newspaper, *The News International*. In his view, "Journalists cannot really report the truth; they are at the mercy of the people who control the news and are only able to tell the side of the news the spokespeople give them." Regardless of what degree the American government has been involved in supporting Taliban's rise to power, the media machine will continue to keep people in the dark.

American history books reveal little truth about the country's lengthy record of bullying. Between the years of 1898 and 1934, the US invaded Honduras seven times, Nicaragua five times, Colombia, Cuba and the Dominican Republic each four times, Mexico three times, Panama and Haiti both twice and Guatemala once. Over and over again, US Marines and their superiors would turn democratically run countries into dictatorships and then call the dictatorships democracies designed to liberate the masses.[46]

After the Second World War, Greece was one of the first stops on a never-ending railroad of invasions. Korea was next. In 1954 they orchestrated a coup in Guatemala.[47] The signature the Americans left at each station was tens of thousands dead bodies, sometimes hundreds of thousands. In Korea it was four and a half million.[48] The US also left military bases behind like mice droppings. By September of 2001, the US Defense Department would admit to having at least 725 military bases outside of the country, on all continents except Antarctica.[49]

The recently created CIA soon proved they were not the passive statistics collectors that the American government had led its public to believe. With the French departing from Indochina in 1954, the Central Intelligence Agency saw an opportunity and quickly went to work. They designated their puppet first, a semi-crazed anti-communist Christian from the south, named Ngo Dinh Diem. After all kinds of unexplained violence and an extremely controversial election, he became the president of South Vietnam. His reign consisted largely of murdering communist sympathizers, with CIA help.

Diem's rampant violence against Buddhists eventually began to add to the communist momentum in the country, so he was assassinated, with the American nod.[50] His death, however, did nothing to stem the communist tide, so the Americans stepped in with a solution that would have fit nicely in Adolph Hitler's portfolio. They blanketed Vietnam with seven million tons of bombs and four hundred thousand tons of napalm over a ten-year period.[51]

Also in the 1960s, the Americans practically obliterated Laos with secret bombing attacks. It was perhaps the poorest country on earth at the time. The bombing coincided with a minor social revolution in the land, but in reality had nothing to do with the war going on in Viet Nam.[52] And it was American phosphorus and cluster bombs, napalm and dump bombs that drove the Cambodian public into the massacring hands of Pol Pot's Khmer Rouge in 1975. The six hundred thousand or so Cambodians the Americans killed with their air raids on the neutral country provided a foundation for the fanatical regime responsible for up to two million more deaths.[53] I had the opportunity to work with healthcare training in northeastern Laos some time ago. It allowed me a firsthand view of some of the difficulties these people still regularly faced due to the American violence in the not-so-distant past.

Most continents of the globe have received their share of US largesse. In 1965, for example, the US also backed the Suharto military coup in Indonesia, leading to the death of another seven hundred thousand. In 1973, the CIA supported a violent military coup against the twice democratically elected president of Chile, Salvatore Allende. Allende, detested by the US because he was a Marxist, was replaced by Augusto Pinochet, a sadistic military dictator who instituted a police state that became an ongoing nightmare for the people of his country. In 1983, the American dragon belched fire on the tiny island of Grenada. Then it was on to bombing Libya. The pattern of death and destruction went on and on.

In the 1980s and 1990s, the CIA spent a lot of time and money creating guerilla armies and death squads around the world. The US used these forces to overthrow governments that would not cooperate with their agenda. Naturally, grassroots rebel movements sprang up where peasants' complaints about American-backed dictatorial regimes were not taken seriously. Speaking out against such oppression has cost hundreds of thousands of lives in Central American countries like Nicaragua, El Salvador and Guatemala. South American soil bears even more bloodstains than Central America, from courageous peasants who dared to rebel.

John Negroponte, one of the United States' foremost diplomats, is an American who was at times in the middle of the atrocities committed in Central America. While working as the ambassador to Honduras in the 1980s, he helped coordinate US covert aid to the Contra death squads of Nicaragua and also helped to fortify a death squad backed by the CIA in Honduras. He has been widely accused of supporting and covering up human rights abuses galore, as well as lying to congress about it. Negroponte's fine work in Central America earned him a lot of accolades from his White House bosses. He would go on to be appointed the American ambassador to the UN in 2001, and then the US ambassador to a very volatile Iraq only a few years later.

The counter-insurgency wars oppressing the peoples of Latin America have featured extraordinarily gruesome mass murders of civilians. Many of the worst have been committed by bought-and-paid-for men of war trained at the School of the Americas in Fort Benning, Georgia, USA. Here, Latin American military officers were trained in murderous intimidation techniques to better repel uprisings in their own countries. After more than fifty years and a controversial name change, this American institution continues to highlight the world's most effective methods of torture and terror garnered from intelligence agencies around the globe. It is more like an international school of assassins.

The methodology of the USA's so-called counter-insurgency wars has not changed to this day, but now people in countries such as Colombia, Mexico, the Philippines and Peru are being killed for the "War on Drugs."[54]

It seems that when genuine opportunity for a peacekeeping mission lies before them, the US does not bother to respond unless a substantial economic gain is also at stake. Take, for instance, the genocide in Rwanda in 1994. Eight hundred thousand Rwandans were slaughtered in a period of one hundred days. The most advanced technological country in the world, the USA, certainly could not claim a lack of information or enough response time. The killing took more than three months to accomplish. The US government chose not to respond to this horrifying emergency in a poor foreign land because they saw nothing could be gained by doing so. Some have even alleged American involvement in training a number of the Hutu killers, and that a CIA-related torture facility exists in Kigali, the country's capital.[55]

Of course, a great many other poor foreign countries have interested the US aplenty. One can find a multitude of examples where they have created havoc in such nations. When the thin veil of concealment is lifted from almost any coup d'etat in the modern world, one will likely find at least some American involvement. The fact that the US now appears to be backing the Taliban's rise to power in Afghanistan should shock no one who knows anything about US foreign policy.

★   ★   ★

I sleep lightly on this night, waking to the hum of prayer at 4:30 in the morning. Getting home is immediately foremost on my mind. I need to do all of the groundwork as soon as possible today if I want to be able to leave the valley sometime within the next forty-eight hours. A Russian film crew has been in town for a couple of days and I don't want my departure plans to collide with theirs. It doesn't take me more than an hour to find out that booking one of the much-in-demand choppers will likely entail some patience. The bird most commonly reserved for shuttle service between here and Dushanbe left last night to collect a shipment of medicine. This is targeted for Panjshir children, presently in the throes of an epidemic claiming some of their young lives.

Widespread disease is regrettably nothing new around here. Regardless of the helicopter's schedule, the cloud cover tells me that I will not be homeward bound today.

The young masters of the house will instead once again accommodate my desire for a hike through the surrounding wilderness. I have started to feel a bit like an uncle to them. This afternoon's trek is special because it might be the last time we enjoy our little ritual together. Each trip unearths a variety of treasures from the notorious standoff by their elders in the 1980s. The rust-permeated shells, bullets, canteens and assorted relics cease to amuse any but the youngest of the valley, but I relish each one as though it were a genuine archeological find.

Today, while foraging in a grove not far from the well-beaten path, we spot the skeletal remains of a human being. Dogs must have dug up the corpse sometime recently. The macabre discovery enthuses even the boys, who have known nothing but war their whole lives. I wonder if he was Russian or Afghan. On the way back, we run into a traveling minstrel with a lean and clumsy-looking string instrument slung over his shoulder, its giraffe-like neck shooting skyward. I have yet to attend a performance, but I encountered one of these fascinating fellows in the mountains of Nepal some years back. This was on the same trip I witnessed the fascinating Shivarati festival. Villagers explain that these men wander from town to town, recounting legendary tales and singing ballads for whatever payment the audience donates.

I decide to call upon Amrullah bright and early the next morning, to get the latest word on the Panjshir flight schedule. Snow unfortunately starts to fall even before I locate him. This type of weather will hardly allow us to fly through the mountain pass. Next, I find out that the Russian journalists have already booked the first helicopter heading north, which might set me back another day or more.

I suggest we catch up with the Russians and try to strike a deal. We do. One of them has so many cameras slung around his shoulder that he reminds me of a golfer with a club for every type of shot. The most noticeable to me is an antique Mamiya camera, worth a fortune. Another of the gentlemen has a Hasselblad, also a prized possession. The three jocular professionals, one of whom works for a magazine something like the Russian equivalent of *Newsweek,* tell us that the troubled skies have altered their plans. They now hope to negotiate a ride north toward the Uzbek border. With all their equipment, though, they cannot fit me in – "Sorry Meester." I suppose I could try to outbid them (vehicles are scarce here), but although such haggling might be considered fair in many places and circumstances, it doesn't feel right in this situation. The taxi turns up while we talk by the side of the road. I watch as they bribe the fellow with a voluptuous leather jacket and a variety of paper currencies for their drive through hazardous territory in poor weather.

The Salang tunnel is a famed section of Afghanistan's primary north-south transport artery. It was built with Soviet technology and money in the early 1960s. The tunnel saves days of travel over sometimes impassable mountain passes and cuts right through the range that sweeps west from the foot of the Panjshir. From here, right now, it could catapult the Russians into the spring-like weather not too far west of the valley, in Puli-Kumri. Unfortunately, things don't work out for them as planned. I find out tomorrow that an avalanche blocks the entrance to the tunnel and strands them an uncomfortable distance from anywhere. They will be back, sleepless and haggard.

While the Russians start out on their journey, I take a walk around my neighbourhood, occasionally waving at villagers I pass. The situation doesn't call for Arctic footwear, but some wear only sandals to help insulate their socked feet from the rising sheet of snow. This doesn't surprise me, as some hunters use only sandals fortified with rags. I've seen them marching with this humble footwear through the ever deepening snow, heading for the five-thousand-meter cliffs on either side of the valley corridor. I suspect a few crates of complimentary hiking boots would be cause for celebration in the Panjshir. Regarding care packages, I wonder what has happened to my long lost cargo of donated clothing. It's probably sitting in Dushanbe by now.

Everywhere I go I notice the seedy remnants of once-functional dwellings, gutted years ago by Soviet bombs. Not only do these dismal sights ornament the slopes of the valley, but assorted rubble also litters the otherwise scenic confines. The Panjshiris reuse all the waste material they possibly can, as most human communities will naturally do. But with so little money to go around, a more extensive waste management program can't possibly figure into community planning. I prefer this intermittent mess, anyway, to the sight of vulgar corporate advertising wherever I look.

A little farther along the road, one family operates a wheat farm, now dormant with the winter freeze. I have not noticed any livestock ranches. One can find few, if any, anywhere around here. Most families raise goats in their yards to provide milk, yogurt and meat. Most of the rice for sale here is grown in Pakistan. And it is no small feat getting it past the front line or over the mountains to the Panjshir. In Afghanistan, unless farming efforts help to manufacture opium or heroin, there will likely be no help from a financier.

A neighbor closer to home waves me into his residence to join his family in a bowl of "kishmish," a festive dessert made with rice and raisins. Ramadan ended last night and Eid has begun. In Muslim realms, the fanfare of Eid Mubarak bears a certain similarity to that of the Christmas season, so everyone is celebrating. All of the members of this household have donned their finest apparel and carry on in an appropriately merry fashion.

With Eid in full swing now, a small gathering takes place at the guesthouse tonight. Engineer Ishaq drops by before dark and will stay for dinner. A few other people join us for the dinner as well, mostly family of my host. Massoud arrives a bit later, but he wanders off to another corner of the house where members of the Russian film crew will interview him. It seems that this duty-bound being just can't find a break in his schedule. The commander has invited the Russians into the valley to shoot a documentary and perhaps write an article about the Panjshir. In the words of Rahimullah Yusufzai, "Massoud had a few helicopters. He flew people all the time: journalists, generals, into the Panjshir, Taloqan, Badakhshan...... he knew how important is the media to the country." Professor Rajwali Shah Khattak claimed that on the other hand, "the Taliban were very suspicious of foreign press."

Just like every other instance when I have dined with a group, we will consume our meal over a tablecloth, or "dastarkhan," that is spread in front of us on the rug of the dining area floor. It is similar to a "longie," a cloth East Indians might wrap around their waist. Dinner is not quite ready yet, so Ishaq and I enjoy some discussion first. The smell of food cooking in the kitchen is especially delightful tonight. If I am correct, the aroma tells me that this particular meal contains no meat. The prospect pleases me, but I know that these men, like most others everywhere, will not forfeit the animal in their cuisine without good reason. It also must be difficult to find vegetables here in the winter. I probe Ishaq about the wonderful scent wafting out of the kitchen and he evasively replies that the cook probably just didn't bother to prepare any meat tonight. I press the engineer for further details after eating and he confesses in a roundabout manner that the vegetarian dinner was scheduled out of respect for me. This is quite an honor.

Pushtuns live by a code of honor known as Pushtunwali. Amongst a variety of more complex rules and regulations, this doctrine demands an individual to feed, house and protect anyone who asks for sanctuary. In some circumstances, one might even be required to hand out money or house a former enemy. Although the creed derived from tribal Pushtun culture, other ethnic groups in the land have adopted a similar version of the practice. The bottom line is that Afghans are extremely gracious and hospitable hosts.

Engineer Ishaq knows I will be going home soon, so after supper he wants me to share some of my impressions of his country. I respond in very favourable terms, of course, as I have indeed enjoyed myself immensely. What a privilege just to be brought here with Massoud. I explain that it has honestly affected me deeply. I also confide in him some slightly personal details, such as the moments of embarrassment I have experienced while loading my mounds of luggage onto the helicopters. The commander's guards, for one, seemed to think the volume of material possessions was inappropriate. The bulk did not escape Massoud's attention either. The engineer nods and smiles empathetically, which is just about all I can really hope for. I also expect him to keep the matter strictly between the two of us.

Massoud finally joins us in my room, as weary as usual. He responds to a couple of questions from the engineer about the progress of the film crew, before seating himself on the edge of my bed. Next, Massoud asks the engineer, in Persian, if I enjoyed the meal and if I am being well looked after. Something to this effect, anyway. The finer details in Mr. Ishaq's reply will remain a mystery to me, but he soon appears to be talking about my luggage problems. I had really hoped he wouldn't go there, so to speak.

Trying to flow with the spirit of camaraderie developing between the two of us, I give the engineer a playful punch in the arm. This knocks him off balance and sends him sprawling onto his side. He looks a little shocked as he pushes himself back up and I clumsily try to help. I feel awkward. It's embarrassing. Massoud does not look at me; his eyes are on his flailing friend. I believe Massoud was beginning to nod off before the sound of Ishaq hitting the floor gave him a little jolt. He gave more attention to this than I have seen people around here give to the sound of shells going off in the distance. Yet, somehow the commander absorbed most of what Ishaq had said to him.

After a few breaths to refocus his train of thought, Massoud philosophizes, "I believe when a man travels so far from home, he should be allowed to take a few things with him." The philosophy doesn't fully validate the quantity of possessions I travel with, but it is charitable sentiment nonetheless.

Engineer Ishaq gradually withdraws from the conversation, preparing to translate for me. I begin a question in Persian and Massoud shows some excitement until Engineer Ishaq informs him that these are the only words I know in his mother tongue. In Massoud's eyes, I can see his enthusiasm dissipate. Then the commander inquires how long I have abstained from eating meat. He would like to know if my diet stems from an affinity to Buddhist philosophy. Wishing to pursue another line of conversation, I reply that it's been so long I can hardly remember what originally brought about the conversion. He next asks if my wife indulges in the same culinary quirk. I answer in the negative, but then he wonders about potential crises arising at mealtime. My spouse cooks with talent and efficiency, I say, and this successfully redirects the conversation.

Knowing this is our final get-together, Massoud asks if my voyage has met my expectations. I enthusiastically explain for a short while just how much it has. I am delighted to spend these last moments with Ahmed Shah Massoud. Anything he cares to express will interest me very much.

Massoud argues that despite all of the struggles, ethnic differences and bloodshed disrupting his country for decades, almost every Afghan believes in a single, unified Afghanistan governed by Afghans. They do not wish to see their country partitioned in any way, shape or form. This obviously includes the Taliban. Massoud also believes the conflict marring the nation today cannot possibly find a military solution. But other nations must stop interfering or the fracas will needlessly continue. The prospect of Afghanistan dividing along ethnic lines has at times loomed over the country. According to Dr. Rajwali Shah Khattak, "[With] the communist in Mazar e Sharif and other parts...... the situation looked as if Afghanistan would be divided into three or four parts at that time."

With the pattern of civil strife so well established inside Afghanistan, a ceasefire will now likely require commitment from the international community. Massoud would welcome it. He has already asked for it, but in the form of political pressure only, not with the deployment of troops. Massoud has always believed that without the ongoing support of Pakistan, the Taliban would not survive for long. The commander says United Front intelligence reports indicate that over twenty-eight thousand Pakistani citizens, including paramilitary personnel and military advisers, are part of Taliban occupation forces in assorted areas of Afghanistan. The Taliban also receive military logistics, fuel and arms from the neighbouring country.

Engineer Ishaq explains that in the commander's view, even if the Taliban eventually prevailed entirely, many Afghans would still not accept their repressive regime. Nor would the bordering countries feel secure with such a brutal and extreme leadership in Afghanistan. The only possible solution for the nation lies in a long-awaited democratic government. To achieve it, Massoud claims to have remained open to negotiating with his enemy. He might even agree to share an interim government with the Taliban to put an end to the fighting. But he feels the country must hold a general election soon after. It is Massoud's aim to see women cast their ballots alongside the men. And to ensure the voting is conducted in a legitimate manner, he says it should take place under the watchful eyes of the UN. He wants a "six–plus–two" cartel, comprising six neighboring republics plus the US and Russia, to supervise the election as well. Perhaps the transitional government could include the former king, Zahir Shah.

Right now, most of the extremely poor in Afghanistan, especially in Kabul, are non–Pustuns, like Massoud. Massoud claims the Taliban has expended great effort to create difficulties for these people, hoping they will leave Afghanistan. He says that about half the budget of Osama bin–Laden's organization goes toward buying houses from these poverty-ridden unfortunates, hurrying along their departures.[56] According to the commander, Mr. bin–Laden is compounding the country's problems by importing fanatical Saudi fighters for duty on the front lines alongside Taliban and Pakistani soldiers. He lures them with a call to "Jihad," or "Holy War" waged by his hospitable hosts with the flowing black turbans.

Massoud believes in equality between men and women, but realizes he cannot change Afghan culture on his own. He acknowledges the nation's cultural environment suffocates women, but says have never suffered as much as under Taliban rule. Amongst the many restrictions on women's rights, their inability to work, especially in the field of education, has hurt Afghanistan. The result has been that girls are not even allowed to pursue a formal education in the vast majority of the nation. The commander nevertheless still dreams of a university for women in the Panjshir Valley. The Panjshir has only two high schools for girls, while the young men enjoy ten. This in itself shows the tendency to favor males in an educational system difficult to find financing for. And such decisions come from too deep within the fabric of Afghan society for any sudden or dramatic change. Massoud expresses his desire to increase learning opportunities for girls, especially at the higher levels, as almost no college in the country will accept them today.

Summing things up, Massoud says the US should apply the necessary political and economic pressures on Pakistan to make them withdraw from this civil war. With the unwelcome advantage-seekers out of the way, Massoud maintains confidence that Afghanistan would, bit by bit, finally be able to sort out its own internal strife.

Diplomacy constrains the commander's offering tonight. This is unfortunate in a way because I would appreciate knowing who he believes to be behind Pakistan's support of the Taliban. The hand behind the hand, so to speak.

A dozen hours later, I once again encounter the Russians, now rebounding from their misfortune at the Salang Tunnel. They tell me the next chopper out of the Panjshir is theirs, while Amrullah assures me they have been misinformed. Part of the problem is that these gentlemen need to get to Mazar e Sharif, while I must head back up to Dushanbe in order to get home. So where do we go from here? I'm not sure, but when Amrullah reassures me I'll be on that helicopter, I set the matter aside.

Tomorrow, the skies look inviting and the competition continues. Amrullah knocks on my door at dawn, and within twenty minutes we reach the unassuming heliport. A chopper waits, being poked and prodded by either a mechanic or one of the pilots, but I do not step inside. We respectfully stand about fifty meters away. I want to make sure I follow the appropriate procedure.

After about forty-five minutes, the Russians pull up in an antiquated auto and hop on board without thinking twice about etiquette. These guys can be rather gauche at times. Amrullah then consults the pilot, who explains that he will be making a series of stops accommodating everyone. Perhaps this is the fairest way things could have ended for all concerned. We will deposit them in Puli-Kumri, a town where they can resume their work before moving on to Mazar e Sharif. The helicopter will then continue on to Taloqan, before leaving the country for Dushanbe. That will be my final stop.

The Russians pull out their cameras after we rise about a hundred feet and start snapping photos of everything in sight. This is off-limits, according to my understanding. Off-limits or not, the absence of the commander and his bodyguards now makes rules easier to break. These men practice the learned aggression of paparazzi, but probably need to in order to keep their jobs.

As we sail over Massoud's cozy, but non-palatial estate, they shoot film with a movie camera as well. I take only one picture of Bazarak, trying to continue respecting the rules. I passed the compound several times on foot and in cars, but as much as I wanted to, would never have dared take a single picture. Soon the town of Bazarak and the balance of the valley fade in the distance, as a clear sky guides us through the pass without controversy. All the while, I sense a mysterious, yet familiar, rumble welling up from deep within me. It's the sensation of separating myself from an experience that has touched my heart deeply. I wonder what fate lies in store for Massoud and some of the interesting men I have been privileged to get to know in these last few weeks. The future of many Afghan children may well depend on the decisions of these people.

I bid a fond adieu to my fellow travelers in the Russian film crew once we get to Puli-Kumri. The town is less than a day's drive from the wintry Panjshir, and only a few kilometers as the bird flies. Yet the temperature and scenery seem similar to a tropical country. The journalists will be heading from here to the Mazar e Sharif airport and then flying to Iran. From there, they will finally go home. I enjoyed meeting them. Our humorous little rivalry back in the Panjshir meant nothing at all. If their presence in these lands did not potentially benefit the Northern Afghans, then Massoud would not have invited them in the first place. These men, too, live in a country plagued with concerns. I would not be made aware of any such trend until 2002, but the life span in Russia would soon dip to fifty-five years.[57]

The same chopper that originally lifted me into the country, along with Massoud and his men, delivered the three of us from the valley as well. Its primary function makes itself very apparent when we begin our next stopover, back in Taloqan. Within minutes, Afghan natives desperate to flee their war-torn nation cram the passenger compartment to full capacity. There is a sense of urgency in these departures that I am unaware of at the time. Teloqan would fall to the Taliban only a short time later. Ostensibly, the Afghans are going to visit relatives in Tajikistan. But, in practice, the helicopter will deposit the refugees in Dushanbe, for further dispersal. Women now begin to shed their burqas. Some of them flash painted fingernails and have even applied make-up, rebelling against the imposed traditions of their native land.

The high-spirited Amrullah, who will remain by my side until I've cleared all bureaucratic hurdles, tells me that many of these refugees-in-waiting hold doctored passports. I think perhaps all of them. They will shortly attempt to fan out into a variety of countries where relatives offer sanctuary. He states that he, too, once relied on one of these phony documents, forging its seal personally with a carved potato and ink. This enabled him to enter Turkmenistan when the Taliban overran his country.

All of this information fascinates me, but it also leaves me wondering if the immigration officers who tend to such matters at the Dushanbe Airport will be fooled so easily. Well, we shall see soon enough. First of all we need to get there. We are currently experiencing a delay to determine who needs to vacate the overcrowded vessel so that the rest of us can achieve a lift-off. The seats are hotly contested. While Afghan authorities rectify the matter, Amrullah introduces me to the son of Mir Dad, one of the first friends of Massoud I conversed with back in Bazarak. This young man hopes to pursue a better life in Moscow.

Before long, we're sky bound, but the helicopter complains bitterly about its excessive burden. The engine sounds as though it growls a non-stop succession of four letter words in some crass alien language. I've flown in many machines and through a variety of semi-emergencies and I construe the situation as unsafe. When I mention it to Amrullah, he replies, "Don't worry; this guy is our best pilot. He has survived more crashes than anyone else." Experience can be an effective teacher, but this bit of information fails to reassure me.

Our expert pilot brings us safely down in Dushanbe and a crew of no-nonsense immigration officials immediately hops on-board. They don't concern me too much, thanks to the conscientious work of Mr. Lee, the travel agent working at my usual Tashkent hotel. He made sure I didn't leave Uzbekistan without a double-entry visa for Tajikistan. It should eliminate some of the potential confusion. Having left Tajikistan as a non-entity on a diplomatic flight, my passport would appear to indicate I've been inside the country all along. Yet, here I am, magically seeking re-entry.

The Russian law enforcers scrutinize the credentials of everyone on the helicopter. After the twenty-minute ordeal, the authorities approve my papers, one using a sharp-sounding word like "tdak" and the other saying "tummum." Both words basically mean "okay," but the former is Russian with the latter being more commonly used in the Arab world. No one else's papers, including Amrullah's, are readily accepted. Their fate hangs somewhere in limbo. Despite the vote of confidence I have received from the officials, no one motions me out onto the tarmac. The procedure is far from over.

We continue to wait for another forty-five minutes inside the claustrophobic cabin. The Afghans grow increasingly unnerved at the prospect of being ordered right back home again. Some of try to calm themselves by lighting up cigarettes, making the air even thicker. Then the Afghan Ambassador to Tajikistan pops his head inside the chopper, before leaving us for another uncomfortable period of time. He is obviously hashing the matter out with those it may concern. He finally returns with the good news: everyone can carry on. I sense a bribe, and possibly a large one, but I'm happy for my travel mates. I offer some cautious congratulations as we approach customs.

The Tajik-controlled customs should not present any problem for me. I think differently when my particular luggage inspector finds some detailed maps of the surrounding area, tucked away in the side pocket of one of my bags. His eyebrows start to furrow. Thank God Amrullah cannot only speak on my behalf, but can also tell a creative tale without flinching. I am a famous Canadian geologist studying rock formations in the region, so why wouldn't I own a few maps? The inspector accepts the colourful explanation without question and we're both through. On to Hotel Tajikistan.

I rent a cell phone at reception immediately, just like three weeks ago. Because they can't activate it for another hour or so, I jog across the familiar neighborhood park to get to the telephone center. My wife is probably beside herself with worry. I told her I'd be out of touch for five days or so, and it's been over two weeks incommunicado. Just as I reach the front doors, the new phone rings and out of the blue I hear my wife speaking. I did not expect the hotel to rent me the same device and number as before.

My beloved has been in Bangkok, visiting friends and relatives for the duration of my expedition. She waited about a week after I informed her I was flying into Afghanistan before anxiety set in. Since then, she has continued to dial this number, belonging to a disengaged electronic instrument hiding in a desk drawer. I told her not to, but in the midst of her panic it seemed the only lifeline she had left to me. In the last couple of days she has hinted to our six year-old daughter that Daddy might have met with a bad end. She pledged, in a traditional Thai ceremony, to try this number one final time, and here we stand. It's a challenging conversation.

A quick phone call to Mr. Lee arranges a reservation for me on tomorrow's flight to Kojund and a taxi from there to Tashkent. The pressure is off me now, so Amrullah proposes that we stop by the home of Mr. Registani, the man who organized my first rendezvous with the commander. This will enable my liaison to unload some messages, while I can extend an appreciative hello and goodbye to Registani, Massoud's military attaché in Dushanbe. He has been very helpful to me, truly a gentleman.

During our brief meeting, Registani accepts a telephone call and speaks in English, something he would not normally do without requesting an interpreter. This causes Amrullah and I to look at one another with curiousity. It must be something of a truly significant nature. I overhear the words "Assistant Ambassador" and I realize that because he chooses to speak English, the voice of the party on the other end probably belongs to the Assistant American Ambassador to Tajikistan.

This call is seemingly part of a budding relationship with America. Massoud has received support from a variety of countries, but up until this point no interest from the US apparently exists. So, in a sense, I believe that on this night I glimpse a shift in their political paradigm.

Less than forty eight hours later, my plane cruises over the awe-inspiring Hindu Kush and Himalayan mountain ranges, the tallest peaks in the world. The unrelenting majesty is the finest scenery I have ever seen from a jet window. My camera now unfortunately belongs to the driver of one of the many cabs I have taken in the last twelve hours. I must have left it on a taxi floor while unloading my gear. I would have preferred being able to capture the view on film, but without the camera to distract me, I can enjoy the experience more fully.

For the last week, I have been studying these immense mountains from the ground, as they surrounded me. The panorama from this juxtaposition is much more complete. We sail over the majestic peaks of Tajikistan, Afghanistan, China, Pakistan, Kashmir, India and Nepal. I see where the Himalayan, the Hindu Kush, the Karakoram, and the Tia Shan mountain ranges all merge, at the "Pamir Knot" plateau. I have seen these mountains from a several different angles over the years, but this view is as fulfilling as any. The jet eventually makes an abrupt turn south, leaving the magnificent phenomena behind. I am left spellbound.

★   ★   ★

My second day in Thailand, I turned on CNN to catch corporate America's version of recent world events. It was the morning of February 5, 1998. The top story described a massive earthquake yesterday in Northern Afghanistan. A tremor measuring 6.1 on the Richter scale ushered in a three to four hour succession of jolts, from its epicenter just outside Taloqan. I was stunned. This was the same Taloqan where I had stayed with the governor only two weeks ago. The same place where my helicopter took on twenty refugees just a few days back. The newscast divulged no facts on Taloqan damage, but the report said the quake destroyed more than four thousand homes in one neighboring town alone.

As soon as I possibly could, I arranged for six hundred kilos of Thai noodles to be sent to the Afghan Ambassador in Tashkent, for forwarding to Taloqan. I reasoned that it was light, transportable food with nutrition.

Words could not have conveyed the mystifying jumbo of emotion distracting me over the next few days. I knew that in all likelihood Massoud had not been directly affected. Although Taloqan was his northern military headquarters, he had probably not returned there yet from the Panjshir. My understanding was that Haji Qadir had flown into Panjshir the same day I left, and Rabbani had likely gone back to his home for Eid. They had probably missed the quake. However, the governor and the many other people I had met there might not have fared so well. I found myself anxious about the patients and workers in the hospital, among others. Only experiencing the devastation firsthand could have cut sharper.

PART THREE

A MURDER AND ITS WAKE

CHAPTER 11

TORONTO and AFGHANISTAN:
FALL, 1998 – SUMMER, 2001

Were the Soviet Union to sink tomorrow under the waters of the ocean, the American military-industrial establishment would have to go on, substantially unchanged, until some other adversary could be invented. Anything else would be an unacceptable shock to the American economy.

– George Kennan,
former US Diplomat, 1987

I opened a letter from the Afghan embassy in Dushanbe only days after flying home. It informed me that my supplies, donated months ago, had not only found their way to earthquake victims, but had also beaten the influx of international aid to the devastated region. They would amount to a pittance compared to the relief that would soon be required. Just three months later, in May of 1998, an even more severe quake rocked the very same area, resulting in a death toll soaring far beyond that of the first.

I met up again with Amrullah in Buffalo, New York, later that month. He was part of a Northern Alliance delegation invited to speak at a UN–sponsored conference discussing the world drug problem. A little hypocritical, I thought, for the US to host such a conference considering its own reputed CIA complicity in the drug trade. But before we talked politics, Amrullah told me that my large shipment of noodles to earthquake victims had been very much appreciated by all. He also remarked that the packets of spicy sauce were quite nauseating. Everyone threw them out. The little anecdote got us both laughing.

Amrullah predicted that the sands of change were now shifting. He said the catalyst had been in December of 1997 when female law students at the University of California at Berkeley staged their anti-Taliban protest. It was a sign of the times. The countless edicts issued against women by the new Afghan administration had already whipped up anger within human rights groups abroad, and increasing numbers of activists now grew impatient with the lack of response from the White House. Contracts from powerful oil corporations remained at the feet of the Taliban, and the completion of a deal could consolidate the Muslim purists' hold on the country.

The main thrust behind the women's rally was that not only men, but also qualified Afghan women, should be allowed to earn wages from the construction of the pipeline. But the Taliban were not allowing Afghan females to enroll in the engineer-training program offered by the US. This was far from the protesters' only complaint, though. Most of them absolutely deplored the Taliban.

The fundamentalists running the bulk of Afghanistan had grown pretty cocky by 1998. At one point in the year, they forced down a UN plane carrying Tajik heads of state on the way to Pakistan. But flaunting their power was starting to result in bad press. They did not realize until too late that such behaviour was bad international public relations and would ultimately result in undesirable consequences.

UNOCAL pulled out of the pipeline consortium in December of that year. The US government's concern about the growing outcry from American women probably did factor into the decision somewhat. The change of heart, however, was provoked even more by incidents that had occurred several months earlier.[58] Osama bin-Laden had decided to cast his vote about the pipeline back in August. He bombed the American embassies in both Kenya and Tanzania, resulting in hundreds of deaths and thousands of injuries. Major attacks against Americans had already taken place in 1995 and 1996 in Saudi Arabia, Osama's homeland. Bin-Laden would later argue the embassies in Kenya and Tanzania were only hot beds of CIA spies.

The US retaliated against the August embassy bombings only two weeks after they were perpetrated. They whistled satellite-guided Cruise Missiles into four bin-Laden terrorist training camps in Afghanistan and what was reputedly a chemical plant in the Sudan. The response emphasized the White House's stance with predictable machismo. But there was surprisingly little follow-up undertaken by Clinton for at least another year.

The Taliban finally captured the northeastern Afghan city of Mazar e Sharif only one day after the attacks on the US embassies in Africa. They slaughtered as many as five thousand people along the way, an extremely vengeful conquest. They also killed nine Iranian diplomats, according to Iran. The Taliban found the charge humorous. They claimed the nine men were involved in a weapons smuggling operation from Iran.

Pakistan's ISI played a definite role in the Taliban victory in northern Afghan city. There was even an intercept on record of an ISI officer saying, "My boys and I are riding into Mazar-i-Sharif."[59]

This second battle for control of Mazar e Sharif may have been nastier than the first. After storming the city with an army 5000 strong, the Taliban apparently shot hundreds of inhabitants at random before engaging in door-to-door searches, hunting in particular for Hazara males. Many were shot point-blank in the face or testicles, or had their throats slit. Other Hazaras, with some Tajiks and Uzbeks for good measure, were sent to prisons where the Pushtun prisoners had been released to make room for them. The overflow became so serious that many of the incarcerated were transferred to other cities in stifling metal cargo containers. Hundreds died inside them even before reaching their destinations. Patients were dragged out of hospitals and killed. The new Talib governor ordered the Hazara bodies to be left in the streets for days, until dogs had filled their bellies. As the days went by, the Shi'a Muslim mosques where Hazaras had once worshipped were seized and painted white for the Pushtun Sunnis.

More than just Afghan Talibs were likely involved in these transgressions. Foreign "volunteers" had joined the Taliban in throngs. These volunteers were often carry-overs from the jihad against the Russians, and some would later amalgamate with al-Qaeda. Either way, the slaughter in Mazar e Sharif represented a significant culling of the Hazara community.

This obvious effort to eliminate and dehumanize Hazaras was partly due to religious differences but also to avenge the overwhelming defeat suffered by the Taliban in the same city one year earlier. (Most Hazaras were Shi'as, but not all). And the agitated fundamentalists who ran the vast majority of the country were not through yet. Only weeks after their bloodletting in Mazar e Sharif, the Taliban invaded the mostly-Hazara province of Bamian, killing the citizens who were too elderly and weak to have fled with all the others to the deprivation of the highlands. They carried on, blowing up two huge, ancient Buddha statues carved into the rock outside of town. The irreverence netted the religious fanatics some very nasty press all around the world.[60]

The Taliban made no effort to hide their distaste for Hazaras and other Shi'a Muslims of the country, whom they did not consider Muslim at all. This time they gave the Shi'as three choices: converting to their Taliban Sunni Muslim faith, leaving the country, or dying.[61]

As these alarming news items made their way through to me in

Toronto, I was busy finalizing plans to send two Canadian nurses into the Afghan refugee settlements of Dushanbe. The two professionals would impart health care knowledge and techniques that were difficult for the Afghan women to access either in their own country or in their temporary Tajikistan base. The program is better known by NGOs as "train the trainers." I preferred to hold the workshop right in the Panjshir Valley, but the journey into Afghanistan would have been too difficult to accommodate, not to mention dangerous. Still, with Mr. Mehdi from the Afghan embassy in Dushanbe looking after all the local preparations, everything worked out better than we dared hope. His son, another very helpful sort, acted as interpreter. This was not an easy function to perform in a complex transfer of information. In a way, the training session completed phase one of my quest, as obscure and indefinable as the next phase seemed to me at the time.

The next couple of years in Afghanistan brought a series of military, diplomatic and terrorist tugs of war. A number of countries on the periphery tuned in carefully to the developments for their own safety. Iran, already an Alliance supporter, was infuriated by the loss of nine of their diplomats in the Taliban attack on Mazar e Sharif. Reports suggested that only some coaxing by the US defused air strikes planned to avenge their deaths. The Iranian government amassed 150,000 troops along the Afghan border to the west and southwest of Herat, to show the Taliban their displeasure.

As the Taliban appropriated more Alliance territory in the north, the Kremlin also threatened to bomb them, but the final orders were never given (Russia was ironically now an ally of Massoud). Uzbekistan had already signed an agreement with Kazakhstan, Tajikistan and Kyrgyzstan, binding the four former Soviet republics together in defense if the Taliban attacked any one of them. Pakistan, despite a change of leadership in October of 1999, continued to contribute fundamentalist Muslim fighters to the Taliban cause. The UN still refused to officially acknowledge or condemn Pakistan's role in the civil war, while the US administration worried more about bin-Laden's next potential attack against them than the rising death toll in Afghanistan.

The UN's reluctance to speak out against Pakistan's involvement in the civil war was a hard pill for Massoud to swallow. In an interview with the *Times of London* in 2000, he would state: "We have provided so far for the UN the name of Pakistani units here and their numbers; which division and regiment they come from and their position in

Afghanistan; the commanders; the names of those killed; the place and time their bodies were recovered; and details of the convoys bringing in ammunition and arms. A day before the convoy arrivals we give the number plates, as the munitions are usually brought in as humanitarian assistance. Recently we gave them the details of two convoys which brought in 15 tanks." And yet the proxy game continued unabated in Massoud's view.[62]

In November of 1998, the US staked a $5 million reward for information leading to the arrest of Osama bin-Laden. They followed this up with trade sanctions against Afghanistan in July of 1999. Despite the Cruise Missiles that had been fired upon bin-Laden's training camps a year earlier, the schools continued to churn out "volunteers" who eagerly awaited their first assignments. It took a few months for the next round of attacks to come, but in November of 1999, bombs hit a variety of US and UN buildings in Islamabad, Pakistan.

It would later be reported by CBC Radio and the *National Post* that a Canadian citizen operated one of these al-Qaeda training camps. "Secret intelligence documents" released by the Canadian government divulged that a twenty-two-year-old named Abdullah Khadr allegedly ran a training camp in Afghanistan.

His father, Ahmed Khadr, had been arrested in 1995, after accusations of involvement in the bombing of the Egyptian embassy in Islamabad. The Prime Minister of Canada, Jean Chrétien, successfully petitioned for his release in 1996, in an unusual intervention during an official visit to Islamabad. The entire family, including two brothers of Abdullah Khadr, was said to have ties to al-Qaeda and Osama bin-Laden.[63]

A few weeks after the November 1999 bombings of the US and UN buildings in Islamabad, UN stepped in with their own sanctions against the Taliban.[64] This resulted in retaliatory attacks on UN offices in five different Afghan cities. The show of strength won the banished bin-Laden a surge of support. The Taliban meanwhile stood firm in their aim to garner diplomatic recognition as the official government of Afghanistan. In all likelihood, they would have won it in spite of their pitiful human rights record, had they handed over their high profile guest. But instead of giving up bin-Laden, the Taliban offered to destroy all of the nation's poppy fields. It was not a fair trade in the eyes of the UN.

A reporter who lived in Nangarhar Province around that time later told me that the Taliban's decision to destroy the poppy fields, especially in that particular province, was a major factor in the Taliban downfall.

In March of 1999, the United States introduced its Silk Road Strategy Act (SRS), a counterpart to the fledgling political alliance of GUUAM (Georgia, Uzbekistan, Ukraine, Azerbaijan and Moldova). The Silk Road mandate was to support the economic and political independence of nations in the Commonwealth of Independent States (CIS) – these were countries formerly in the Soviet Union as well as other countries that lay along the old Silk Road, from Armenia to Uzbekistan. It was also designed to keep the former Soviet republics from establishing economic, political and defence ties with China, Iran, Turkey and Iraq.[65] Physically, the Silk Road was a resource–rich corridor running east to west buffering both China and Russia and linking the Caspian and Black Seas with the Mediterranean – a geopolitical prize. US assistance came in the form of NATO peacekeepers, backed up by the establishment of additional American military bases. The scheme showed the US had economic and military designs for Central Asia and the South Caucasus well before 9/11.

Two members of GUUAM, Azerbaijan and Georgia, link the oil–rich Caspian Sea to the Black Sea. The Black Sea's northwestern shores joined with both the Ukraine and Moldova, providing a natural passage westward. Not surprisingly, the inauguration of an oil pipeline called the Baku-Supsa surfaced shortly following NATO'S involvement. The conduit would use a route running through Georgia and ending in the Ukraine. Here, the oil could connect with the pre-existing pipeline that moved through Slokia, Hungary and the Czech Republic. The clever plan would circumvent the Russian lines as well as those proposed by the Iranians.

The addition of GUUAM to NATO provided more than an ideal infrastructure for westbound pipeline routes out of the Caspian Basin – especially considering the lengthy border Ukraine shared with Russia, which would allow the US to continue a military buildup right on Russia's doorstep. The Silk Road Strategy Act and GUUAM revealed premeditated aggression, but they were still just preliminary steps in a much broader plan that would soon usher the country into a bottomless war.

★   ★   ★

I focused on more domestic concerns for most of 1999, but made sure Farzaneh maintained periodic contact with Ahmed Vali Massoud, the commander's brother. This man, the longstanding Afghan Ambassador to Britain, had not yet crossed my path, but willingly remitted regular updates. Most of the recent ones, unfortunately, continued to progress in a distressing direction. The Taliban had seized Massoud's supply base on the fringes of Taloqan only days after celebrating their victory in Mazar e Sharif. After a series of setbacks and sometimes-effective counter-attacks, Ahmed Shah then lost the strategically crucial Bagram Air Base, lying between Kabul and the Panjshir Valley. This defeat alone cost the always vastly outnumbered resistance about a thousand lives. Then, as Massoud retreated homeward to regroup, the Taliban perpetrated the nearby agricultural lands of the Shomali Plain, not far from the air base. Here they killed resident Tajik farmers indiscriminately, burned villages and lay to waste precious arable land. This resulted in a quarter of a million or so more refugees.

Massoud slipped back into the initial battle zone under the cover of darkness. He immediately reclaimed the town of Charikar and surrounded Bagram Air Base within forty-eight hours. About a thousand of his enemies died in the two-week-long carnage, many of them "volunteers" from Pakistan and a number of other countries. But although victories such as this frequently tipped a regional balance of power, the shift was usually temporary. With regiments of imported soldiers at their disposal, the Taliban possessed the ability to replenish their numbers and forge ahead much more quickly than the Alliance.

On the diplomatic front, the US and Russia stitched together a loose group of "six plus two" nations, including themselves and all of Afghanistan's bordering countries. This would include Pakistan, Uzbekistan, Tajikistan, Iran, Turkmenistan and China. They would oversee peace negotiations for the troubled nation. Quite a few meetings convened over a four-year period, occasionally with representatives from both the Alliance and Taliban present. But regardless of how much progress prevailed in the boardroom, the quarrel in the real world usually resumed without much delay. Talks would finally peter out in the summer of 2001, when the Taliban Foreign Minister didn't bother to show up for a session in Berlin. The reasons were obvious. Not only had his government been asked to share power and extradite bin-Laden, but the UN had once again granted Afghanistan's seat in its assembly to Rabbani. The Taliban saw the forums as one-sided, and decidedly pulled out. With mainstream American publications printing articles on the villainy of the self-proclaimed government and the heroism of Massoud's men, the Taliban's limited credibility was now disappearing rapidly. Yet, with an unwavering conviction that God was on their side, the Taliban would not change a single thing.

In the summer of 2000, Massoud left the Panjshir to solicit the help of General Rashid Dostum once again, and also General Ismail Khan. They were both frequent allies of sorts. Dostum, the sometimes-friend-sometimes-foe Uzbek, had been in Turkey for a while, and Khan, the former leader of Herat, had finally escaped from his Taliban prison cell. Massoud helped him reach Iran safely. Although no accord with Dostum would be trouble free, the trio of warriors could capitalize on a recruitment pool extending along most of the country's northern perimeter. The three cautiously agreed to work together again, but the Taliban struck at the heart of Taloqan before they could restructure and inflict any damage of their own.

The commander finally surrendered the territorial capital of Taloqan to the Taliban on September 5, 2000. It was a clash that lasted thirty-three days and ran up a fatality toll of 300 on the Alliance end. Despite describing the retreat as temporary and strategic, and insisting that his forces had killed two thousand of the attackers, it was the most humbling setback since the loss of Kabul in 1996. The Northern Alliance now controlled as little as five percent of the country.

As I read reports, I tried to imagine Taloqan after the Taliban took over. When a town falls in war, the victors always seek out the best structures to house their administration. Defeated leaders are usually long gone by this time. It was consequently very likely the Taliban had moved into the compound I stayed in with the governor, Haji Qadir and Rabbani. On the other hand, it could have been reduced to rubble, but this would have probably been by accident.

In the same month the Taliban captured Taloqan, a politically sponsored template called Project for the New American Century was formed. In its own words, the PNAC was a "blueprint for maintaining global US preeminence, precluding the rise of a great power rival, and shaping the international security order in line with American principles and interests." The report, commissioned by future Vice President Dick Cheney, future Defense Secretary Donald Rumsfeld, future Deputy Defense Secretary Paul Wolfowitz, Florida governor Jeb Bush, and future Vice President Cheney's Chief of Staff Lewis Libby, was written for these heads of the George W. Bush camp even before the 2000 Presidential election. It stated: "The United States has for decades sought to play a more permanent role in Gulf regional security. While the unresolved conflict with Iraq provides the immediate justification, the need for a substantial American force presence in the Gulf transcends the issue of the regime of Saddam Hussein."The report went on to say that this "American Grand Strategy" must be advanced "as far into the future as possible." It also encouraged the U.S."to fight and decisively win multiple major theatre wars...as a core mission."

The core document, entitled a "Global Pax Americana" went one step further than Brzezinski had in his book, *The Grand Chessboard*. It urged the control of space through a new "US Space Forces"; the political control of the internet; and the undermining of any surge in political power of any country, even a close ally. The proposal also recommended regime changes in China, North Korea, Libya, Syria, Iran and other nations. It even went so far as to suggest that advanced biological warfare capable of targeting specific genotypes could be a politically useful tool.[66]

This blueprint strongly suggested that George W. Bush's cabinet had made the decision to unleash an attack on Iraq even before taking their oaths, whether or not Saddam Hussein was in power and with or without any legitimate threat. Very interestingly, the report echoed consternation that none of this was likely to happen anytime soon unless a "catastrophic and catalyzing event" was to transpire - "like a new Pearl Harbor"[67] -. A British Member of Parliament would comment about these findings, "This is a blueprint for US world domination -- a new world order of their making."[68]

Any plan for "maintaining global US preeminence" would undoubtedly be enhanced by majority control of the oil reserves of Central Asia and the Middle East. Afghanistan was a natural gas pipeline route, as well as a perfect location for military bases from which to police the countries of the Baku–Ceyhan route. It could be argued that the conquest of this country was a necessity for the US in their desire to carry out the grand ambitions proposed in the Project for a New American Century.

★　　★　　★

If the loss of Taloqan deflated Massoud, none but those closest to him could sense it. The commander stayed his course, buoyed by the return of Ismail Khan and an oath from his Alliance members to subdue their mutual opponent before confronting their own differences of opinion. At least outwardly, he remained composed and optimistic. He reasoned that in the year 2000, the Alliance had faced a shortage of finances and weaponry, which left several fronts in the north without sufficient support. This had allowed the Taliban to storm the northeast. However, by the time 2001 arrived, he had acquired a new arsenal of helicopters, tanks and assorted artillery from Russia, his backers to the north. Recent yields from the bountiful lapis lazuli and emerald mines probably factored into the quality of the armaments.

The commander had also recently received a supply of Afghan money, called Afghanis. Rabbani had printed a quantity back when the two of them ruled Kabul, and Dostum had printed some around the same time as well. Massoud ordered the printing of the more recent shipment himself, which arrived via Tajikistan. It was likely manufactured with the help of his Russian contacts. The Afghanis were not worth much, but they succeeded in devaluing the currency being pressed by the Taliban in Sweden. Since the Taliban controlled most of the land's foreign funds by this time, the Alliance needed to use any method they could to destabilize this fiscal grip on the country.

Many reports from these years pegged Massoud as a focus of CIA lobbyists. Teams of agents sporadically visited the Panjshir Valley, providing the commander with funds and intelligence equipment capable of intercepting Taliban radio transmissions. The CIA hoped the gear would help produce vital information about Osama bin-Laden's plans and whereabouts. After a while, the operatives left Massoud with a device that could photograph Taliban movements from long distances. Ahmed Shah obviously put the hundreds of thousands of American dollars to good use, but would have preferred some military aid of more practical value than just the high-tech surveillance equipment. The CIA professed a genuine desire to provide it, but alas, the White House could not offer any type of assistance that might substantially influence the outcome of a civil war. Or so they said.[69]

It is possible that their sometimes-awkward relationship with the Alliance procured the CIA some usable information, but it did nothing to stem the terrorist tide if this was their goal. As for Massoud, getting so close to the CIA could have left him vulnerable to them. The commander may have been an ally of sorts for a while, but most of his interests were not compatible with theirs. Such was the way of Afghanistan.

On October 12, 2000, two suicide bombers tore a huge hole in the American Naval Destroyer, USS Cole, as it refueled in Aden Harbor, Yemen. Osama bin-Laden would later claim responsibility. Seventeen American military personnel died, in addition to the massive damage inflicted upon the vessel. This drove the US hierarchy into a renewed furor over the impudent Arab with too much money.

The UN tightened restrictions on the Taliban only two months later, at the urging of the US and Russia. These sanctions, amongst other reprimands, prohibited any of their officials from escaping the country.

The White House's good friends in the Saudi Royal family, who were detested by Osama, paid out massive sums to radicals throughout most of the 1990s. These payments allegedly bought the royal family amnesty from al-Qaeda attacks. This money contributed greatly to Osama's training camp and terrorist operations. The bin-Laden family, although officially estranged from their rebel son, also sent him plenty of funds. What this meant was that some of the US government's closest friends were financing terrorist attacks against them while their mutual business continued uninterrupted. And it was hard to believe American intelligence agencies did not know something about it.[70]

The terrorist attacks of 1995, 1996, 1998 and 2000 all bore a distinct Saudi Arabian stamp. The nationality of most of the terrorists made it apparent that the land of bin-Laden's birth had offered itself up as the mastermind's main recruiting ground. Yet, the US did little to investigate Saudi involvement. Former CIA agent Robert Baer would come to call the Americans' apparent lack of interest in Saudi affairs a "conspiracy of silence" because of mutual business interests. He believes that it led to 9/11.[71]

Things took an alarming twist in Saudi Arabia. The Saudis were practicing a strange form of jurisprudence. At one point, a Canadian man, William Sampson, was unjustly held and sentenced to death for allegedly killing other foreigners. There were other Westerners accused of similar crimes. When it became clear that these people were innocent, it became equally apparent Saudis were victimizing foreigners and then setting up other foreigners to take the fall - Westerners, in particular. Anyone could see animosity developing between Saudi Arabia and the West. Yet American consulates in Saudi cities were making it remarkably easy for Saudi Arabian citizens, some of whom were quite hostile, to stay or get training in the United States.

Regardless of what they might have known about the Saudi "terror connection," the FBI was not even allowed to put Saudis on their terrorist list until after 9/11. Deputy Director and counter-terrorism expert for the FBI, John O'Neill, would claim that the US State Department – in collaboration with the oil lobbies that made up President Bush's entourage – actually blocked attempts to prove Osama bin-Laden's guilt. Was the lack of pursuit by design or omission?[72]

In January of 2001, former oilman George W. Bush was sworn in as President of the USA. His running mate, now Vice President Dick Cheney, had been up until recently Chief Executive Officer of Halliburton, the world's largest oil services company. Halliburton was very much involved in Caspian Sea oil exploration. Cheney had also been the defense secretary in George Bush Senior's "Gulf War" administration. Paul Wolfowitz, the new president's deputy defense minister, was the Under Secretary of Defense Policy for his father's administration, and a well-known advocate of aggressive military action.

George W. Bush's other top people would include: Deputy Secretary of State, Richard Armitage, a key player in the sordid Iran-Contragate Affair; National Security Adviser, Condoleeza Rice, formerly of Chevron oil; Commerce Secretary, Donald Evans, formerly the CEO of Tom Brown Inc, an American natural gas company; Secretary of the Interior, Gale Norton, a former national chairwoman of the Coalition of Republican Environmental Advocates – funded by, among others, BP Amoco; Secretary of Energy, Spencer Abraham, (up through his failed bid for senatorial reelection in 2000, he received more oil and gas money than all but three other senators from January 1997 through July 2000); and Secretary of the Army, Thomas White, the former Vice-Chairman of Enron and a major shareholder of that company's stock. One could see that this was a wartime administration with a very pointed interest in oil – and some rather questionable integrity.

The affiliations to the oil industry were by no means an accident. The key figures pulling the strings had obviously determined the selection process long ago. But even Americans who were aware of the industrial/military monopoly now running their country would never have believed the scope of the foreign power-grabs it was planning.

By now, American intelligence agencies had been training regional agents for a while in Central Asian languages, at the Defense Language

Institute (DLI) in Monterey, California and at its East Coast branch in Washington DC.

It did not take the new Republican President long to start tampering with his country's Defense policies, surrounding himself in scandal. One of the first things George W. did was cancel the ongoing missile control talks that had been taking place with North Korea, an aggressive move in the wrong direction in the opinion of most. According to analysts, Bush probably felt that this would help him sell his plan for a missile defense system to the US public.

But it certainly did not impress the Carlyle Group, his father's colleagues and employers, who had huge money invested in South Korea. The ensuing instability between north and south that would come as a result of the President's decision would not be good for the economy of South Korea. But not long after, George W. Bush reversed his decision on the missile talks. Only days later, the *New York Times* reported, "In an effort to influence one of his son's most crucial foreign policy decisions, former President George Bush sent to the President through his aides a memo forcefully arguing the need to reopen negotiations with North Korea, according to people who have seen the document."

As an ex-President, George Bush Sr. is permitted access to regular CIA briefings. He also holds considerable influence over many of the White House's top politicians, plus many international ones as well. All of this could give the Carlyle Group a distinct edge over their competitors. Judicial Watch is a non-partisan, non-profit organization serving as an ethical and legal "watchdog" over the US government, as well as American legal and judicial systems. This Washington law firm has asked for George H.W. Bush's resignation from The Carlyle Group many times, citing conflict of interest.

After years of controversy and well over a million dollars worth of lobbying alone, the Carlyle Group pawned off a line of bogus attack vehicles on the American military through one of its companies, United Defense. *The Wall Street Journal* had called this fighting machine, *the Crusader,* a dinosaur. Its many critics unanimously asserted it was virtually useless for the type of war the US would be fighting in the future. But before the George W. Bush administration finally conceded that the critics were right and scrapped the unit, Carlyle had raked in hundreds of millions of dollars in profit, courtesy of the American public.[73]

As the new Bush administration finalized its plans to secure the oil reserves of Central Asia, a separate sequence of back room meetings and events also unfurled in the months counting down to 9/11. They would eventually cast a shadow on the simple version of who and what motivated the scourge of September 11, 2001.

In January of 2001, right after George W. Bush assumed power, the White House blocked an FBI investigation monitoring the activities of certain members of Osama bin Laden's family.74 The probe included Abdullah and Omar bin-Laden, both residing in the town of Falls Church, Virginia, practically next door to the Central Intelligence Agency headquarters. Because President Bill Clinton had issued a similar order in 1996, Bush's move seemed to establish a pattern.

The limitations imposed on him by moves such as this, plus the government's lack of interest in terrorist intelligence he had been hired to collect, would soon lead FBI counter-terrorism expert, John O'Neill, to resign.[75] Before the end of the year, he would be offered the job as director of security at the World Trade Center and would strangely start working there only two weeks before 9/11. He and his knowledge perished in the ashes of the twin towers.

In July of 2001, according to the French news journal, *Le Figaro,* an American hospital in Dubai, United Arab Emirates, admitted Osama bin-Laden for kidney problems. He allegedly met with a CIA agent while there at the hospital. Although the CIA denied the allegation, they would have obviously done so regardless of the facts. It was interesting to note that the Carlyle Group held majority shareholder status of *Le Figaro* at the time, and yet the editor did not retract the news item. This leads one to believe in the accuracy of the report.[76]

Two months earlier, US Deputy Secretary of State Richard Armitage, and CIA director George Tenet, both flew to Asia. Armitage engaged in well-publicized discussions in India, while Tenet slipped into Islamabad for a lengthy meeting with General Musharraf, a key ally now running Pakistan.[77] Tenet's Pakistani counterpart, ISI head, MAHMUD AHMAD, could only have been allowed his position after being officially approved by Washington. This approval would have necessitated his working intimately with the CIA. His absence during this meeting would have been highly unusual.

That same summer, Mahmud Ahmad arranged for an aide to transfer one hundred thousands dollars to Mohammad Atta, the chief conspirator in the September 11 attacks according to the FBI.

The money transfer was later confirmed by the FBI.[78] This was an influential man who served American Foreign Policy interests.[79] And on 9/11, Mr. Ahmad was relaxing in Washington. He had arrived there on September 4th on a regular visit of consultations.[80] He met with some of America's most powerful politicians and intelligence figures during his stay. After news of Mr. Ahmad's payment to the top terrorist leaked out in India and garnered an FBI confirmation, Mahmud Ahmad simply resigned. The whole affair has been hushed up in the US with the greatest of care. But there are still more pieces of the 9/11 puzzle that do not readily fit into place.

Although there was plenty of cause for concern, the US virtually tossed aside a succession of warnings before 9/11. Some singled out the World Trade Center for the week of September 9th and spoke about twenty-five recently tutored suicide pilots. In August, President Vladimir Putin even warned in the strongest possible terms of impending attacks on US airports and government buildings. There were actually many warnings that arrived throughout the course of the year 2001 and a lot of them came from friendly governments.

Richard Clarke, the President's personal counter-terrorism adviser at the time, would come to charge that Bush refused to regard the hunting down of bin-Laden or the terrorist threat in general as an "urgent issue" in the months before 9/11. This was despite repeated warnings by Clarke and others, including his colleague, John O'Neill. Richard Clarke was frustrated by Bush's refusal to hunt down Bin Laden or treat the terrorist threat as serious in the months before 9/11. He wrote a memo to National Security Adviser Condoleeza Rice just days before 9/11. It chastised defense officials for their refusal to act, suggesting they "imagine a day after hundreds of Americans lay dead at home or abroad after a terrorist attack and ask themselves what else they could have done."

★   ★   ★

Massoud's strategic pursuits in the first eight months of 2001 would present a modest backdrop to the clandestine activity throughout this section of the globe, but at least he was visible. He arrived with a delegation in Paris on April 4, for a press conference during which he once again slammed Pakistan and pleaded with the Western World to remove the country from the Afghan picture. Massoud took the time to mention a number of members of the United Front Leadership Council. This was partly to illustrate the ethnic diversity within the northern coalition. These were men who the commander insisted held no conflicts among them. The leaders who received special mention were Haji Abdul-Qadir, Mawlawi Atta Mohammad, General Sayed Hussein Anwari, Ustad Khalili, Commander Piram Qol and Emir Ismail Khan.[81] Although Khalili and many of his Hazara followers had bitter memories of Massoud from his days as defence minister in Kabul, they had begun to appreciate him as the last bastion of resistance against the Taliban. There is an old Arab saying: the friend of my friend is my friend; the friend of my enemy is my enemy; the enemy of my friend is my enemy; and the enemy of my enemy is my friend.

Dr. Abdullah accompanied Massoud on to Strasbourg, Germany, where the commander's speech to a packed session of the European Parliament drew a standing ovation. They held another press conference in Dushanbe, Tajikistan, a week and a half later. During one of his invectives on the speaking tour, Massoud quipped that although the West should pressure Pakistan to leave Afghanistan alone, Pakistan probably wouldn't anyway.

Whether invited to come along or not, Rabbani, still the official president of the country, did not join Massoud in Europe. Perhaps there was some controversy surrounding Massoud's decision to go in the first place. The trip created a situation where the commander once again overshadowed others in the international recognition category. Some may have felt Massoud was stepping on their toes, so to speak.

By now, the world clearly recognized Massoud as the real leader of Taliban opposition. In any leadership structure, however, there are those who feel they have earned too great a role, with more leverage in decision-making than they have been allotted. I wonder if the US had already identified several such individuals and targeted these men to lead in a post-Massoud landscape.

Although the rival factions of Afghanistan continued to joust throughout 2001, no significant holdings changed hands during its first three seasons. Massoud reported renewed civilian resistance in a variety of provinces and once again stressed that the Taliban were beatable, but nothing of any significance really changed. It was an ominous calm before a storm that would blow in a new era.

CHAPTER 12

AFGHANISTAN:
SUMMER-FALL, 2002

We have about 50% of the world's wealth, but only 6,3% of its population...In this situation, we cannot fail to be the object of envy and resentment. Our real task in the coming period is to develop a pattern of relationships which will permit us to maintain this position of disparity... To do so, we will have to dispense with all sentimentality and daydreaming; and our attention will have to be concentrated everywhere on our immediate national objectives... We should cease to talk about vague and...unreal objectives such as human rights, the raising of the living standards, and democratization. The day is not far off when we are going to have to deal in straight power concepts. The less we are then hampered by idealistic slogans, the better.

– Policy Planning Study 23,
U.S. State Department, 1948

On September 9, 2001, two suicide attackers posing as reporters were granted an audience with Ahmed Shah Massoud. They had cleared his last line of defence and were asking suspicious questions about bin-Laden when they detonated an explosive hidden inside their camera. The commander, severely maimed, died inside one of his helicopters on the way to the hospital in Tajikistan.

Massoud had hardly slept at all the night before his murder. He stayed awake until 3:00 a.m. reading the Qur'an with friends. Then, almost immediately after retiring, he received a call from Bismillah Khan, an Alliance general. The phone call lasted until after dawn. He did catch about one and a half hours rest after the lengthy conversation, but that was all. With the inevitable fatigue gnawing away at Massoud later that morning, he could very easily have let his guard down. Perhaps the commander did not have the energy to summon the intuition that had saved him so many times before in his life.[82]

The view held by most at the time was that a Taliban/ al-Qaeda connection was responsible for Massoud's assassination, but other possibilities floated about as well. At least a handful of Afghans I spoke with during personal investigations there in 2002 pulled US intelligence out of a new lineup of suspects. Many people in Afghanistan believed Massoud was eliminated because his nationalistic fervor would have put him at odds with the foreign forces that came to occupy his country shortly following his death. The theory made some sense, since the Northern Alliance without Massoud did indeed cooperate and merge with the new US-led interim government.

The Taliban had probably known for months that a collision with the US was imminent, and that it would render them extremely vulnerable to a full Alliance assault. In July of 2001, according to the BBC and several respected publications, three American diplomats, Tom Simmons, Karl Inderfurth and Lee Coldren had assembled with Russian and Pakistani intelligence in Berlin. The Americans forewarned everyone that if Osama bin-Laden were not quickly turned over to their government, the US military would strike Afghanistan in October.[83] Allegedly, Mr. Simmons directed an ultimatum the Taliban's way. It was to be their choice: a "carpet of gold" or a "carpet of bombs."[84] The Pakistanis would, of course, pass the message along to their Afghan friends. This was later verified by the British press.

One of the men who received advance notice of US plans to attack Afghanistan was former Pakistani Foreign Secretary, Niaz Naik. He would come to claim that after 9/11 he doubted the US would have cancelled these plans even if the Taliban had immediately given them bin-Laden.[85]

A bewildering concentration of Allied troops converged in the areas surrounding Afghanistan in the months and days preceding September 11. Over twenty-three thousand NATO troops were joined in Egypt by an additional seventeen thousand from the US, for yearly maneuvers. Two US aircraft carrier battle groups coalesced as well in the Arabian Sea, right off the shores of Pakistan. To top off this impressive gathering, twenty-five thousand British soldiers sailed toward their destination in Oman, in a seamless deployment obviously in the planning for a while.[86] Given the massive military presence, plus the recent verbal threat from the Americans, the Taliban must have been aware they had a serious fight on their hands. It would have given them plenty of incentive to see Massoud eliminated before September 11, when the situation would escalate. This was, of course, assuming they knew about 9/11 in advance. In any event, the Taliban must have been growing somewhat desperate as 9/11 approached. It was doubtful they were naïve enough to believe the US had left any option on the table other than military intervention by this time.

Regardless of motive and conjecture, the Taliban vehemently denied any involvement in the murder, a plea of innocence that most Afghans believed. Bin-Laden would have been another obvious suspect. How could the Taliban have refused him the sanctuary he would soon so desperately need if he had just eliminated Ahmed Shah Massoud, their most potent enemy?

The strange meetings and events leading up to 9/11 would continue both on that day and for a few more afterward. At 8:19 a.m. on the morning of Sept. 11, a flight attendant phoned an American Airlines flight service manager at Boston's Logan Airport to announce the hijacking of her aircraft, American Airlines Flight 11.[87] Flight control had lost all radio contact some five or six minutes earlier.[88] Around 8:20, the plane started to veer dramatically off course.[89] **Within another minute, the transponder, an electronic device providing the controllers with the plane's exact location and altitude, stopped transmitting**. By 8:25, air traffic controllers just heard a transmission of the hijackers speaking on-board Flight 11, and could no longer deny the plane was hi-jacked.[90]

Boston flight control finally contacted the FAA at 8:32 to report the hijacking. The FAA did not immediately contact NORAD to scramble fighter jets to go after Flight 11. A couple of minutes later, the air traffic controllers attempted to reach the military through the FAA's Cape Cod facility, before going through the usual NORAD channels. At 8:37 they reached NORAD's North East Air Defense Sector, and this was apparently the first time NORAD heard anything about the hijacking.[91] FAA Administrator Jane Garvey would testify in 2003 that the FAA contacted NORAD at 8:34. NORAD, however, originally claimed they were not notified until 8:40. The later time of 8:40 a.m. was reported by many media sources before the 9/11 Commission's report.[92] (If NORAD did, in fact, receive their first notification of the hijacking from Boston air control at 8:37 a.m., this meant they were not contacted by anyone until twenty-three or twenty-four minutes after radio contact was lost. This was about seventeen minutes after the transponder signal had disappeared and the flight had strayed far from its path. It was also a good twelve or thirteen minutes after the voices of hijackers being transmitted from Flight 11 had erased any remaining doubt the plane had been hijacked. Flight 11 found its target only nine minutes later.

ABC news would later say, "There doesn't seem to have been alarm bells going off, traffic controllers getting on with law enforcement or the military. There's a gap there that will have to be investigated."[93]

The FAA and NORAD also had their share of explaining to do. The FAA said it opened a phone line with NORAD to discuss both American Airlines Flight 77, which was headed for the Pentagon, and United Airline's Flight 93, later presumed to be headed for Washington, if not the White House itself. If this was a fact, NORAD had as long as fifty minutes to scramble fighter jets to intercept Flight 93 in its path toward Washington, DC. But it crashed in Pennsylvania. The FAA and NORAD also had at least 42 minutes to decide what to do about Flight 93, before it slammed into the Pentagon. There were so many questions left unanswered about the day.[94]

Many eye-opening reports have surfaced about 9/11 since the year 2001. One of the most noteworthy is that Donald Rumsfeld, Secretary of Defense, issued a new directive to the Pentagon in June of 2001. Under the new rule, any such order, including the tracking of hijacked aircraft, would have to go through the Secretary of Defense – him.[95] The timing was rather curious.

Other accounts have claimed that three different war games. exercises were taking place on September 11, 2001. One was a mock hi-jacking, another a live hi-jacking, and the other involved false images on radar screens in the Northeast Air Defense Sector. The Northeast of the US, of course, was where the real hijackings took place that day. And the false blips created confusion for fighter jet pilots assigned to track these planes down.[96]

Dr. Robert M Bowman, the President of the Institute for Space and Security Studies, believes that if normal communication and common sense action were used by the airlines, air-traffic control, FAA, NORAD and the interceptor bases, the interceptors would have saved both the World Trade Center and the Pentagon with time to spare. As an ex-fighter pilot, he does not feel the pilots themselves were in error. He believes those responsible were too high up to be blamed – an act of treason in his opinion.[97]

About forty-eight hours later, while the White House maintained a lockdown in the skies above the US, three planes carrying the bin-Ladens and the Saudi Royal family were cleared to leave the US at a time when no one else in the country was allowed to fly.

On November 1, 2001, the White House was involved in yet another suspicious development. An unprecedented executive order was issued, enabling George W. Bush to seal presidential records as far back as 1980.[98] The announcement came shortly before the scheduled release of a cache of Reagan administration documents.

★ ★ ★

The Northern Alliance showered Kabul with Scud missiles on the night of September11, just after finding out their beloved commander had died. They may have emptied their entire reservoir of Scuds on the Taliban. If they were looking for revenge, they would not need to wait long. Wave after wave of American aircraft raged through the Afghan skies only a month later, dropping hi-tech explosives into every possible enemy stronghold. The Northern Alliance assembled under the next in command, Mohammed Fahim. They followed Fahim into battle, in cooperation with the US forces, killing or running off all remnants of the Taliban, at least for the time being. Massoud's pleas to the international community for help in eliminating his enemies had finally been granted, but he was no longer available to participate in the mission. Like Moses, he never got to cross into the Promised Land.

Western press lavished attention on every American casualty during the abrupt dismissal of the Afghan dictators. Flattering eulogies about honor and decency were bestowed upon the young men, mostly pilots and soldiers. Media reports particularly praised the first ground casualty, a CIA agent named Johnny "Mike" Spann. He died while a group of Taliban captives attempted escape from a makeshift American prison in Mazar e Sharif. Shortly after the prison riot, Oliver August, a Times of London correspondent who had witnessed it, was interviewed on BBC's "Newsnight." He said that Spann and a CIA colleague, Dave, were believed to have provoked the violence by interrogating foreign Taliban prisoners aggressively. August claimed Spann pulled a gun, before his CIA colleague shot three prisoners dead in cold blood. This was when the situation went awry.[99] About 500 prisoners were killed according to many accounts, but hundreds more according to others. Few of the inmates at the prison, if any, survived.

Most if not all of the prisoners who died in the unfortunate incident were foreigners from a variety of countries. Many of the Afghans initially among them had already been allowed to return home to their farms, before the captives who remained were transferred to the prison. Some of the so-called foreigners, however, were simply Pushtun Afghans who came from the other side of the Durand Line, in Pakistan. All of these men were hoping they would receive fair treatment as prisoners of war. They obviously did not. The American solution was to eventually bomb the facility before anyone could escape the confined space. Yet the media applauded American efforts to bring order to the land.

Plenty of Northern Alliance troops also sacrificed their lives in the brief war against the Taliban. The most heroic in my opinion, though, were the thousands of Afghan citizens who succumbed to errant American rocket blasts and assorted crossfire. Others lost their livelihoods, homes and loved ones. These issues, however, disappeared from the international press before authorities could accurately tally the numbers of deceased innocents.

The US directed a lot of money and energy into their lengthy air attack on Afghanistan. Their proclaimed purpose was to catch both Osama bin-Laden and Mullah Mohammed Omar dead or alive. But they didn't find either of these men and it didn't seem to bother them much. It certainly did not slow down their pursuit of pipelines and new military bases. One could easily be left wondering why they did not start their war on terrorism in Saudi Arabia, where fifteen of the nineteen alleged perpetrators of the 9/11 attacks came from. There were no Afghans in the group. No Iraqis either.

The US could not logically blame the Taliban as a whole for 9/11. The only crime against the US the zealots could really be accused of was sheltering their friend, Osama bin-Laden. They had not, however, demonstrated the spirit of cooperation required to make American pipeline dreams a reality. This was probably the main reason the Taliban had to be rooted out. It was doubtful the US would ever be allowed to build the military bases they needed to protect the region for themselves. By all appearances, Afghanistan had to be taken swiftly and efficiently so these bases could be put into place quickly and the American administration could make some headway with their other urgent plans for the region. Afghanistan had always been the strategic crossroads of Central Asia, which made it the strategic crossroads of the world to this very day. It would be a perfect launch pad from which to access the surrounding countries that interested them in their plans to secure global dominance. Their uncontrollable pawn, the Taliban, made an excellent scapegoat.

It did not take the US long to begin taking inventory on the oil wealth the war against terrorism could help secure. During a visit to Kazakhstan on December 8 of 2001, Secretary of State Colin Powell divulged that over the next five to ten years, US oil companies would likely invest $200 billion in this one Central Asian country alone.[100] Shortly thereafter, *The Observer* reported that an anonymous source in the Kazakh government had commented, "It is clear that the continuing war in Afghanistan is no more than a veil for the US to establish political dominance in the region. The war on terrorism is only a pretext for extending influence over our energy resources."[101]

The aggressive American quest for oil was accompanied by a concerted effort to condemn those who stood in the way. Defense Secretary Donald Rumsfeld and his deputy, Paul Wolfowitz, assembled an elite intelligence unit to "second-guess" CIA information.[102] In 1997, these men were two of the initiators of the "Project for a New American Century." They now hoped the new agency, The Office of Special Plans (OSP), would be able to draw the conclusions necessary to justify military maneuvers being planned, specifically in Iraq. The group functioned under the careful watch of hard-line conservatives at the top of the Pentagon and White House, including Vice-President Dick Cheney. Cheney was, of course, also behind the "Project for a New American Century."

An article in "The Guardian" referred to the OSP as an "ideologically driven network" and compared it to "a shadow government." Much of the network operated aside from the official payroll and free from congressional scrutiny. It was, however, extremely influential. It would manage to win a heated debate with the State Department and the CIA to produce a justification for an invasion of Iraq.[103]

In an interview with the the Scottish Sunday Herald, former CIA officer Larry Johnson would describe the OSP as "dangerous for US national security and a threat to world peace". He accused them of manipulating intelligence so they could carry out their agenda to overthrow Saddam Hussein. Mr Johnson went on to call them "idealogues" with a pre-existing view of truth and reality. According to the former agent, they used fragments of intelligence to reinforce their agenda, while ignoring any information to the contrary. He said "they should be eliminated".

Amidst the usual secrecy, Rumsfeld also formed an operation entitled the "Strategic Support Branch," in 2001. *The Washington Post* would eventually expose the organization to the public. The Defense Secretary was alleged to have designed the unit to function without detection, under his direct command. According to the *Post* article, it used "small teams of case officers, linguists, interrogators and technical specialists alongside newly empowered special operations forces." The group operated in Afghanistan, Iraq and other countries. The foreign language training undertaken by American intelligence agents was reaping benefits.

Of course, Rumsfeld's office denied the existence of any intelligence unit that replied directly to him for clandestine operations. But the report said the Strategic Support Branch had been created to furnish Rumsfeld with independent tools for the "full spectrum of human operations." [104]

The formation of these two custom-designed spy networks, the OSP and SSB, clearly marked the defense department's efforts to bring American intelligence under the Pentagon's control, separate from the CIA, to integrate with its war machine.

In January of 2002, the *Christian Science Monitor* claimed the US was working on thirteen different bases in nine countries in and around Central Asia. The *Los Angeles Times* added that the centers now employed 60,000 workers. The new ones would add to the total of about 700 military bases the Americans already operated throughout the world. Amongst the five Central Asian Republics of the former Soviet Union, only Turkmenistan continued to refuse to offer the US military comfortable quarters. A small portion of this buildup could be rationally attributed to a battle against terrorism. Most of it was established to protect their new investments along the Eurasian corridor and to intimidate Russia, not to mention China. American Foreign Policy initiatives have never reflected a desire to exterminate terrorism as much as they seem designed to nurture it – for use against countries they seek to weaken, control or exploit. And if an American administration ever becomes sincerely concerned about it, it will need to curb its own violence first.

The US appointed a former employee of UNOCAL to the interim presidency of Afghanistan in December of 2001. It was a selection guaranteeing them capital gain more than anything else. UNOCAL, of course, was the American pipeline contender before all the controversy in Afghanistan had temporarily sidelined their plans. The Americans must have figured this Afghan, Hamid Karzai, fit all of the necessary criteria. He had fought as Mujahideen against the Soviets, and had been Deputy Foreign Minister in Rabbani's government as well. He was a Pushtun, and of chieftain blood, but he was also educated in the ways of the West. Many newspapers reported Karzai had been a Deputy Foreign Minister for the Taliban. [105] These details were barely a matter of interest compared to claims made by the Saudi journal, Al-Watan. This publication stated Karzai had been a covert CIA operative since the 1980s. According to their sources, he had collaborated with the Central Intelligence Agency to secure US aid for the Taliban as of 1994.[106] This was well before the Taliban seized power in Afghanistan.

At Karzai's presidential inauguration ceremony, most news wires claimed that even in death Massoud stole the show. His huge portrait dominating the dais, his empty chair sitting in a special place of honor, and the cries of grief whenever his name arose, all paid homage to the revered man's life. Massoud was becoming Afghanistan's Che Guevara.

Burhanuddin Rabbani, Massoud's longtime cohort, offered his assessment of the country's present day obstacles during the proceedings: "Everyone is well aware that the main cause of the endless tragedies of our nation..... has been the aggressive interference in the internal affairs of our country..... Taliban mercenaries and terrorist cells in our country have had no other reason than outside interference..." was an excerpt from the former president's short statement at the swearing in of the new one.

The proclamation did not impress many of the foreign diplomats present. Some may have thought it ironic that many Arabs who now comprised the very terrorist cells Rabbani was referring to had initially been admitted into the country by himself and given citizenship. Dr. Rajwali Shah Khattak would make the following comment about the Afghan Arabs: "By default they were left to the Taliban...... the Taliban inherited the Arabs."

Karzai was obviously aware the Afghan presidency had ended the lives of many of his predecessors. The US Special Forces soldiers assigned to protect him eased much of his concern. But an assassin almost did away with Karzai eight months into his first term, when he traveled to Kandahar for his brother's wedding. The gunman fired a couple of shots into the president's car and one of the bodyguards died in the exchange.

My Taloqan acquaintance Haji Qadir did not fare so well. He had just been appointed one of the vice presidents when assailants took his life in a bloodbath. Abdul Haq, Haji's brother and business partner living in United Arab Emirates, had already been removed in the early stages of the American incursion. The people's prime candidate for the Afghan presidency, Mr. Haq had been called home to head up an opposition backed by the last monarch – King Zahir Shah. The CIA supported it. After some weeks of preparing in Peshawar (ISI territory), Haq snuck into Afghanistan to rally the tribes who had promised their allegiance, but the Taliban intercepted the small caravan. The CIA took their time responding and even then only sent in drones to help. The Taliban accused Haq of being aligned with the Americans and executed him. Because Karzai's family was from Taliban territory in the south, perhaps the Taliban thought Karzai would supply more leverage for them and killed his competition.

Rumors swirled that the CIA had suddenly aborted their allegiance to Abdul Haq, seemingly deciding the most expedient solution to a potential presidential selection crisis was to simply feed him to the wolves · the Taliban. Whether or not the hearsay derived from fact, the popular Afghan most certainly would have held the favour of just about any national assembly in an election battle with Karzai. Using whatever savvy required to insert their preferred implant, the US managed to maneuver Karzai into the presidency with little fanfare other than Rabbani's articulate complaints about foreign manipulation in Afghan politics.

On January 1, 2002, Zalmay Khalizad was appointed by the US president as Special Envoy to Afghanistan.[107] Khalilzad had been holding a position on the US National Security Council as Special Assistant to the President and Senior Director for Gulf, Southwest Asia and Other Regional Issues. Khalilzad was previously an official in the Reagan and Bush Sr. administrations. During the Clinton years, he worked for Unocal.[108] He was also a founding member of the Project for a New American Century. To call this man an important figure in US plans for this part of the world would be a gross understatement. For a long while, he had been America's kingpin in Central Asia. He practically ran the entire show. Khalilzad had written his own highly touted blueprint for American world domination nearly a decade earlier, although it was revised under the supervision of Paul Wolfowitz before its release. Khalilzad's proposal, called Defense Planning Guidance, was heartily praised by Dick Cheney, defense secretary at the time under George Bush Senior. This Republican recommendation for a global US military stranglehold not only influenced the foreign policy of the elder Bush's administration, for which it was written, but it also would go on to affect the decisions of George W. Bush and his team of hard-line politicians eight years later. This would not be surprising since so many of the people who the younger Bush brought in to help him devise strategy had held key positions in the father's government.

Zalmay Khalilzad, an Afghan American, also played a crucial role in negotiating with the Taliban to build the pipeline through Afghanistan. Although according to the US this war in Central Asia had nothing to do with oil or natural gas, the Bush administration's top political appointments in Afghanistan appeared to be telling an entirely different story. Mr. Khalilzad would soon go on to play a substantial role in setting up the provisional government in Iraq.

In an interview with a Berkeley California radio station in March of 2002, Democrat Representative Cynthia McKinney voiced certain opinions and questions pervading the minds of more and more world citizens as time goes by. She said, "Persons close to this administration are poised to make huge profits off America's new war," mentioning the Carlyle Group as an example. She also stated, "An administration of questionable legitimacy has been given unprecedented power...We know there were numerous warnings about the events to come on September 11... What did this administration know and when did it know it? Who else knew and why did they not warn the innocent people of New York who were needlessly murdered?.. What do they have to hide?"

Not only had Carlyle already made a fortune from 9/11 and the fledgling war on terror, but weapons, truck and plane manufacturers were pumping out orders as well. The oil conglomerates with their multiple subsidiaries were signing deals worth billions of dollars and decades of time. Rising oil prices reflected the value of the Euro plus the "terrorism premium." Information and technology companies now had burgeoning defense contract divisions, capitalizing on the fear of terrorism that had gained control over North America's emotions. These were the same patrons and profiteers who covered the bulk of George W's exorbitant campaign costs. Communities such as Colorado Springs, with five major military posts and the IT company, SI International, would boom, with billions of dollars of defense spending from the Pentagon.

IT companies have become the backbone of the US war machine. In recent times, advancements in communications and weapons technology have enhanced the destruction efficiency of the US military exponentially. These umbrella companies provide a wide range of specialized services. They secure intelligence data through computer (data base) design and data base control, provide weapon maintenance, tank and plane maintenance, and provide private mercenary personnel for training, fighting and protection. Some IT companies have even branched off into construction. With the various construction projects undertaken by the military, a lot of money can be made. George W. Bush's 2001 declaration of a war with no bounds must have sent a profound surge of jubilation through the ranks of these corporations and their major shareholders.

Another blatant beneficiary of American military aggression was Halliburton, the mammoth oil services and construction company headed up by Vice President Dick Cheney until he resigned to run for public office with George W. Bush. In December of 2001, Halliburton, via its subsidiary, Kellogg, Brown & Root, had signed an exclusive no-bid deal to provide the American military with all of its theater and base logistical support requirements for a ten-year period. If Halliburton could provide the service, no one else anywhere in the world would be able to tender a bid. It was a sweet deal worth billions to Cheney's associates. One could not be blamed for wondering how much this tycoon-turned-politician might stand to gain from decisions made in the White House today. After leaving Halliburton, Cheney received a $26 million compensation package. He also held $46 million of the company's stock. [109]

★   ★   ★

In search of information about Massoud's death, 9/11 and the dramatically changing Afghan situation in general, I flew to New Delhi, India in February of 2002. I had already offered my condolences via letter through Dr. Abdullah, but I considered the commander's passing a profound loss to the world and naturally wanted to know

more. In New Delhi, I dined at the home ofMassoud Khalili, the
Afghan Ambassador to this allied nation. It was difficult to avoid being
distracted by the excellent quality of the cuisine on both occasions.
Mr. Khalili had been an extremely close companion of the newly
deceased commander for almost twenty-five years. The bomb that
ended Massoud's life had also scarred and burned Ambassador Khalili,
now unable to walk without a cane. There was none of the bitterness
one might expect from someone who had recently suffered such a
tragedy. I was immediately struck by the man's pleasant and generous
demeanour.

The eloquent Ambassador held his beloved friend in the greatest
esteem. Khalili explained that a mutual affinity for Muslim poetry
characterized his relationship with Ahmed Shah. Every time in each
other's company they would recess for an hour or so to recite and
analyze Islamic poetry. As they had on so many other occasions, this
is how they spent Massoud's last night. The two Arab imposters had
camped out for fifteen days to earn their interview with the absent
commander, and Massoud, upon his return, consented to see them. At
the last minute, Khalili could see they were not real journalists and told
Massoud so. But it wouldn't have necessarily been easy to change the
course of events at this point, and the commander probably realized it.
His security had obviously scrutinized the Arabs to their satisfaction,
so perhaps Massoud felt relatively at ease. He simply said he'd like to
get the interview over with. Only moments later, he lay dying. No one
could have known Ahmed Shah Massoud's death would somehow,
strangely, herald an age of increasing suicide attacks.

Mr. Khalili responded to my questions about possible co-
conspirators around the globe, citing bin-Laden as the most likely
suspect. Like many others, he believed the murder of Massoud could
have bought the terrorist continued asylum in Afghanistan, despite the
pressure the Taliban came under to give him up. The sophistication of
a bomb-bearing camera also led Khalili to suspect bin-Laden, right
from the start. The Afghan diplomat believed the Pakistan ISI, forever
foe to Massoud, must have in some way contributed to the plan, as
well

I asked Mr. Khalili if he thought the people who planned the
commander's assassination were aware of 9/11 in advance. He replied,
"The strategy of Osama bin-Laden...the strategy of ISI of Pakistan......
was indeed to get Afghanistan totally occupied ...they needed... one

person to be killed.......he (bin–Laden) needed protection from Mullah Omar, nothing else...both Osama bin Laden and ISI of Pakistan consulted and organized this. Right? Period. Maybe leaders of Taliban were informed, Mullah Omar was informed, I don't know. But ISI and Osama bin-Laden knew very well what they were doing against Commander Massoud."

Earlier on, Mr. Khalili had commented, "You kill somebody, you make him a hero, but a dead hero cannot win the war. He was...... the most talented organizer of that area...such a leader...he was the symbol of resistance."

I did not necessarily agree with all of Mr. Khalili's assessments, and at times the interview took on minor elements of debate. For instance, I said that Massoud's assassination could have been counter-productive for the Taliban in one way. If Mullah Omar and bin-Laden had been aware of what was about to happen on 9/11, they would have also understood the probability of the Americans retaliating. Why then would they have wanted to create a martyr on top of their approaching troubles?

But the ambassador believed the men who planned 9/11 had no idea how much damage and loss of life would occur from the attacks on the World Trade Center. He therefore felt no one could have known the Americans would retaliate so strongly. Again, I found this simplistic, but he has a right to his point of view, as do I. The benefits of killing Massoud consequently outweighed the disadvantages of making him a martyr, in Mr. Khalili's opinion. He also firmly believed that 9/11 would not have been carried out at all had bin-Laden known ahead of time the magnitude of the resulting devastation. For the rest of the interview, I found his views on these matters most agreeable.

Khalili went on to explain that the commander "...could see the Taliban were in a very, very bad position as far as the society and the common people were concerned... [Shortly before his death, Massoud] was working very hard, day and night, giving his people training, motivation, force, high morale, going around to find some helpers...In the region, Pakistan was isolated, Taliban was isolated. He was not isolated. He had friends in Central Asia, he had them in India, in Russia, in Iran, and so they all wanted him to win the war. Not because of Afghanistan, but because of the regional problems, the Taliban; they are extremists." All of this implied Massoud was not in the gravely weakened military position many people believed him to be when he was killed. Without the commander in the way, the Taliban would have been in a much better position to make their push for the remaining provinces of Afghanistan.

Khalili also spoke about the sharpness of Massoud's mind, his ability to assimilate everything being discussed, even if two or three people debated points on top of one another. He praised the commander's personality, stating, "He was generous like a sea and kind like a sun, always. But humble like an elf, just like an elf." And he referred to Massoud's optimism as eternal. Apparently it shone through even in the bleakest of moments.

The Ambassador, himself a Masters graduate in political science, heartily complimented the commander's intellect. He saw Massoud not only as a military strategist, but also as a born leader of people. Khalili claimed Massoud had wished to eventually retire to a quiet space and read poetry, somewhere far from the mountains that held memories of combat, and from whose confines the commander had gazed down upon such misery.

In May of 2002, I tracked down Amrullah Saleh in a thoroughly battered, but slowly recovering, Kabul. We met at the old Pakistan Embassy, across the street from the famous Marco Polo Restaurant. With his intimate Northern Alliance connections, the shrewd young professional had managed to earn an important position in the several-month-old national security and intelligence program. It was an occupation warranting enough secrecy for me not to press for details. Surprisingly, he treated me rather coolly at first, almost with annoyance. I believe the Pushtun-style clothing I had chosen to wear did not blend in very well with his painful memories of the Taliban. I told him the sparkle in his eyes had faded somewhat since our last encounter. He responded by explaining how weary he was from the recent fighting. We then proceeded into reminiscences about comic moments we shared in Taloqan and the Panjshir, and he once again smiled like the Amrullah of old. I learned from him that Engineer Ishaq had gone to Washington, while Mr. Registani had accepted work in Moscow. As for Amrullah, his selection as Afghanistan's Chief of Intelligence only a year and a half later would make the *New York Times*. My charming young Afghan friend would become the country's top spy and top spy catcher. Afghans are indeed fortunate to have Amrullah serving their country.

That June, Kabul hosted a Loya Jurga. This was a tribal council with representatives from all corners of the country, for the appointment of the new interim government's political heads. Campaign posters were pasted all around town, but those promoting Rabbani particularly caught my attention. Massoud's image hovered in the background. From what I understood, a democratic electoral process was supposed to decide the victors, but the US intervened somewhere along the way. They appointed their chosen favorites to all administrative positions important to them, leaving only the most trivial to democratic selection. Some ministers were Afghans who had been in America and not seen Afghan soil for decades. Rabbani, the former president, failed to gain a posting.

Even before the election fiasco aggravated matters, most Afghans viewed Hamid Karzai, the new presidential appointee, with suspicion. The familiar ring of foreign political tampering does not sit lightly with these people. It likely didn't surprise many informed citizens of the country when the assassination attempt on Karzai's life took place a little over half a year later.

Only a month or so after I left Afghanistan, a Rand Corporation analyst named Laurent Murawiec gave a briefing to the American Defense Policy Board. It recommended Saudi Arabia be given an ultimatum to either cease funding terrorism or face confiscation of their oil fields and very considerable assets invested in the United States.[110] The view that "there is an Arabia, but it need not be Saudi," was part of the proposal. The briefing concluded with a "grand strategy" for the Middle East, pinning Iraq as the tactical pivot, Saudi Arabia the strategic pivot, and, curiously, Egypt the prize.[111]

Egypt would without doubt be a prize for the men who ran the USA. It was the heart, soul, and intellectual center of the Arab world. Al-Azhar, the university attended by Azzam, Hekmatyar, Rabbani and so many other renowned Muslims, could illustrate this to a degree. Back in the eighteenth century, when Europeans were still stuck in the Dark Ages, Al-Azhar was the Middle-Eastern center of sciences, literature and art. The medical teachings of the legendary Persian physician and philosopher, Avicenna, were one example. His medical knowledge was more advanced than Europe's, even some seven hundred years after his death. To this day, this genius' work remains the foundation for many medical textbooks around the world.

In 1798, Al-Azhar became the center of resistance against

Napoleon's bid to conquer the East. During the reign of the Ottoman Empire, it was the powerful sheiks running the Egyptian university who made the recommendation that determined the new King of the land. The university churned out many of the intellectual and cultural heads of the entire Arab world. It was known as something of a "king-maker." And this was only one Egyptian institution. Accordingly, the many other Arab countries in the region would be rendered more fragmented and much weaker without the cultural lifeblood pumped into them by Egypt. The US had every incentive it needed to place its own seal on the nation. My experience examining this country, sometimes from inside of it, would lead me to conclude that Cairo was indeed an intended center of a new US-controlled empire in the Middle East.

With press discoveries such as the Rand Corporation's briefing to the American Defense Policy Board, the "war on terrorism" had already begun to take on some remarkably economic and imperialistic overtones. As if further evidence of such intentions were necessary, the US finally broke ground on the Baku-Tbilisi-Ceyhan pipeline. The pipeline would travel a one thousand seven hundred kilometre stretch from the western shores of the Caspian Sea in Azerbaijan all the way down to the shores of the Mediterranean in Turkey. It would cleverly detour Armenia, going instead through Georgia, now a NATO partner of the US. The deal was pushed through despite loud objections from both Amnesty International and a bevy of international environmental groups. The more direct route through Iran would of course be unthinkable. The idea was to take power away from the Persian Gulf, and from Russia too for that matter. An east–west swath across the south Caucasus seemed to be the appropriate design.[112]

I spent more time in and around Afghanistan in fall of 2002, crossing into both Pakistan and Iran for short periods. Massoud's brother, Ahmed Wali, very kindly issued me a multiple entry visa from his Ambassador 's desk in England, which allowed for more latitude than usual in my travel plans.

The Afghan government had plastered posters of Ahmed Shah Massoud all over many of the places I visited, but particularly in Kabul. The display struck me as a rather ostentatious effort by the new regime to promote itself. The English captions read THE GREAT MASSOUD, THE WAY FORWARD, as though the national hero was calling the shots posthumously, from some mysterious sanctum deep inside the administrative buildings. Plaques and framed prints of the beloved Afghan legend were everywhere, even in taxis. The main road leading to and from Kabul city to the Airport had suddenly been renamed THE GREAT MASSOUD ROAD or MASSOUD WAY. Some humans speak louder from the grave than most of us do while living.

On this trip, I landed in Kandahar first, home of the Taliban not long ago but American headquarters now. The plane descended to the runway on an evasive zigzag path, accompanied by an announcement that this was standard procedure. Rocket attacks against the Americans were a regular occurrence at the time and the erratic landing reflected the precarious situation, especially in Kandahar. The density of US military presence in the airport caught me a little off guard. I soon saw quite a few armed soldiers in other centers such as Jalalabad and Gardez, but nothing compared to this concentration.

I was fortunate to interview a wide range of people this time around, including some street vendors, a doctor, a professor, a warlord, the Assistant Commander of Northern Alliance troops responsible for Gardez, and the Inspector General of Police in Jalalabad. There seemed to be a general theme in the conversation of the people I spoke with. In these eastern and southeastern Pushtun provinces, it was not only Taliban who regularly discharged rockets at the GIs. It seemed like an elite sport increasing in popularity.

Further evidence of cultural disintegration exposed itself along the road running southeast from Kandahar towards Spin Boldak and beyond. Here, one would expect to see fragments of nomadic tribes passing through. Instead, a significant number of Kouchie youth had resorted to begging alongside the rougher sections that slowed traffic to a crawl. This was new. For centuries, maybe even millennia, the nomadic tribes of Afghanistan had moved about this land in total self-sufficiency. They were a very resourceful lot, traditionally requiring very little for their survival. But a year after the war with the US, many of the children appeared so haggard it made me wonder if they would last the winter. I remember wishing a few conscientious reporters could have been with me to witness how American occupation had brought these people to this sad state of affairs. Occupation is not really such an abstract form of violence. Neither is hunger.

Billions of dollars of foreign aid had been promised to Afghanistan after the Taliban defeat. The country needed it badly and quickly. But outside of $200 million to rebuild the highway connecting Kandahar to Herat, most of the financial relief seemed to be taking a rather roundabout route to get there. Even the $200 million for the highway could not be seen as a sincere, selfless contribution. The Americans needed to refurbish this particular transportation route anyway, for pipeline construction. The US had apparently contributed very little actual financial relief. They spent their own money on bullets instead. Ali Ahmad Jalali, another Afghan "American," was put in charge of regulating all donations that came in from the other countries. He was Karzai's new Afghan Minister of Internal Affairs

In Quetta, an Afghan reporter I spoke with accused the Northern Alliance of complicity in Haji Qadir's murder. The well-publicized assassination had taken place just a few months before. Hearsay would abound that it was the work of the Shura Nazeem, Massoud's most intimate circle of fighting men. Some thought these men, all of them Tajik, were rudderless without the commander's leadership. Because the Shura Nazeem of the Northern Alliance was now largely incorporated into Kabul's central command, the rumor pretty much meant that Haji Qadir had died at the hands of his own government.

Truth or fiction, there was a certain ring to it. Aside from the fact that assassins managed to riddle Qadir with bullets while his own guards surrounded him, Haji had protested Tajik domination within the new interim regime from day one. He had even walked out in a huff from the Bonn Conference, a UN-sponsored assembly determining Afghanistan's new government structure just before Karzai's inauguration. Mr. Qadir, unlike Massoud and most of his associates in the Northern Alliance, was not Tajik, but Pushtun. And just because Massoud's vision of a democratic government in Afghanistan had included respected Pushtun leaders such as Qadir, did not mean each one of the officers he left behind necessarily shared the same sentiment.

Haji Qadir's murder troubled a great many citizens of Jalalabad, who viewed the man as a noble and heroic figure. He had governed their city and province for years back in the 1990s, and was still regarded with affection. I went to Jalalabad, in pursuit of a few insights on Haji Qadir's murder. I asked the Inspector General of Police for Nangarhar if he knew who might have assassinated Mr. Qadir. He replied, in his broken English, "Kabul government should know who was killed to him." The inspector went on to say, through an interpreter, "I can tell you that Afghan have more enemies and Haji Qadir have enemies, so I cannot say to you exactly that that guy kill him. But I can tell you that the enemy of Afghanistan, the enemy of peace, the enemy of Islam is kill him."

The young policeman's responses were sincere and touching. They also suggested to me that Haji's death had increased tensions between Jalalabad, with its mainly Pushtun population, and Kabul, which houses the mainly Tajik central government.

A similar type of rumor circulated about the assassination of Dr. Abdul Rahman, Afghanistan's Civil Aviation Minister, back in February of the same year. Karzai himself had taken very little time pointing out the guilty in this instance. He alleged that five senior military and defense officials in his own government were involved. Three of them, the head of intelligence, the technical deputy of the Defence Ministry, and a Supreme Court judge, were all top members of the Northern Alliance. The head of intelligence who stood accused by Karzai held the position before Amrullah Saleh's appointment.[113]

An Afghan told me both Abdul Rahman and Haji Qadir wanted to see the former king, Zahir Shah, play a key role in the new Afghan government. If this information was accurate, both these politicians could have been considered threats to the Tajik hegemony in the new administration.

Even though Ahmed Shah's former associates dominated the upper echelons of the new administration, the government would surely miss his voice of moderation. And to what degree these men would represent their former commander's vision for Afghanistan looked like a highly debatable issue.

It appears to me that serious trouble continues to brew in Afghanistan. The Pushtuns perceive their lack of representation within the largely American- regulated political process as disrespectful and threatening. They have lost power since the defeat of the Taliban. Things have changed. Although a variety of Pushtuns enjoyed Pakistani support throughout the nineties, the ISI no longer has much room to maneuver in Afghanistan. And Pakistan still produces plenty of fundamentalist Muslims who despise the US. This probably bothers the Americans more than it used to, with such far-reaching economic plans underway throughout the region.

The Afghan-Uzbek, General Dostum, is back from Turkey again. He returned to Northern Afghanistan in November of 2001. Now he must deal with his longtime local Tajik rival, Atta Mohammed. At least he no longer needs to worry about his former subordinate-turned-enemy, Malik Pehlawan. Malik appears to have received a US visa and has purportedly sought asylum there. So Dostum once again controls Mazar e Sharif, or so I've been told. As long as Karzai and the Americans allow him to, he probably won't present too much of a threat to the government.

Gulbuddin Hekmatyar is another story altogether. Perhaps not surprisingly, the always ready-to-rumble military commander has resurfaced as a leader of the masses opposing US control over the government and country – much to the CIA's indignation. Hekmatyar is a powerful Pushtun leader who has headed the same political party, the Hizb-e-Islami, for more than fifteen years. The fairest way to deal with him might be to allow his group to participate in the election under their own banner. This would be democratic process. However, it is very unlikely to happen. Instead Hekmatyar was greeted with a missile shot from a "predator" drone when he returned to Afghanistan from Iran not long ago. The missile, which nearly hit its mark, could only have been sent by the US military.

Perhaps one day the Americans will want true democracy in Afghanistan. But judging by the inhibitions of most Afghans to speak candidly to me about the US presence in their country, freedom of speech is apparently not yet part of the plan. Neither is a determined and well-armed resistance movement. In the meantime, the US tortures many of the perceived enemies they do manage to capture, at facilities such as Bagram Air Base with its private torture chambers.

With or without a powerful rebel like Gulbuddin Hekmatyar on the loose, Hamid Karzai's security personnel will probably find themselves working overtime if they wish to keep him out of harm's way. The President has earned a fair measure of displeasure from his own people, as the Pushtun figurehead of yet another meddling alien power. Still, public elections will be held, if sanctioned by the US and the UN according to their initial promise, long before this handpicked regime grows too old.

The American military lingers in Afghanistan to promote political and economic stability inside the country and to combat terrorism within and without. Of those who live there, very few Afghans buy this US rhetoric. Furthermore, millions of well-informed citizens around the globe insist the bottomless war on terrorism is only a smokescreen for the Americans' ambition to economically dominate the world. The fear of terrorist retribution has granted Western leaders an ideal opportunity to tighten their grip on the masses at home as well. They have begun chipping away at the civil liberties of US citizens and have influenced some of its allies to do the same.

The Bush Administration's so-called "War on Terrorism" is dripping with oil. The attacks of 9/11 have provided Cheney and his corporate elite with the Pearl Harbor referred to in their Project for the New American Century; or the "truly massive and widely perceived direct external threat" referred to by Zbigniew Brzezinski in his infamous book. September 11, 2001 is the catalyst everyone said would be required to swing public opinion towards implementation of a Home Security crackdown and a foreign policy permitting pre-emptive war. It has given them a legitimate reason to invade Afghanistan, whisk away the Taliban obstacle to their pipeline dreams, and plant themselves strategically on Central Asian soil, stepping up their quest for control of the hemisphere.

Whether or not one considers present American military commitments in the Muslim world to be honorable, no one can deny that their past involvement in assorted Middle Eastern, Central Asian and African nations has induced an escalating animosity toward the US. More and more radical detractors are answering the aggression of American foreign policy throughout the area. The sentiment at least is resurfacing closer to home in South America as well.

White House officials want us to believe that the many Muslims who actively oppose US militancy abroad do so because they hate democracy and freedom. I would instead propose that people who resort to acts of violence against seemingly unbeatable foes usually do so because they feel their freedom is threatened. Many of them, in fact, value their liberty to the extent that they would rather die for it than subjugate themselves to oppression. Organizations such as al-Qaeda feed on the disillusionment that exists because of the lack of true democracy in their respective lands.

For many people in Middle East and Central Asia, a dictator who has gained or held power due to the colonization of their country is the only "democracy" they have ever known. Morocco, Algeria, Egypt, pre-occupation Iraq, Saudi Arabia, and pre- revolution Iran are all cases in point. If George Bush's adversaries in the Muslim world are suspicious at all of democracy, it is because of this false version imposed on them. In reality, no denial of freedoms or abuse of human rights will prevent the White House from doing business with someone who can make money for them.

By the end of 2002, the George W. Bush administration, with its seemingly infinite military and intelligence resources, studied a substantial catalogue of nations in the Middle East, Central Asia, Asia and Africa. Who to accuse? Who to attack? Where will the financial rewards warrant military action? Ominously, it pays only token attention to the on-going crisis in Israel, the conflict from which much of the hemisphere's ill sentiment toward the US and its allies actually stems. The US perennially offers a massive dose of foreign aid to the wealthy nation, which is often translated into weaponry used on Palestinians.

By the US government's own admission, we will learn only as much about its operations in the war against terror as it deems compatible with their best chances for success. This is a buffer that can nicely conceal hidden agendas. Likewise, I tend to suspect that as the war heats up, the definition of the term "terrorist" will expand to include many who simply protest too loudly against American aggression in countries where the US doesn't belong in the first place. Maybe it already has.

But, of course, Uncle Sam admits to no ulterior motives anywhere. Not even in Iraq which the US is determined to invade because of hidden weapons of mass destruction. Few believe they exist. Nevertheless, it is not difficult to imagine that the prospect of replacing Saddam Hussein with a friendly leader excites Western kings of commerce, who pursue riches with a passion that far exceeds any sense of morality. They would have their very own oil-rich country to exploit - tax-free.

As George W. Bush and his powerful friends ring in 2003, toasting their grand plans for the new year, America the Good spruces up its superhero image, battling the forces of darkness on foreign soil. US politicians address the masses in their evangelical tones, spreading fear among us while promoting their case for major military confrontation in the Middle East. They also do everything in their power to bait other UN countries into the volatile scenario to bolster their own credibility. And as they do, their relentless jabber about the need for war starts to sound more and more to me like the sales pitch of a used car salesman.

CHAPTER 13

AFGHANISTAN:
EARLY JULY to EARLY AUGUST 2003

I think, legally speaking, there's a very solid case for impeaching every American President since the Second World War. They've all been either outright war criminals or involved in serious war crimes.
– Noam Chomsky,

arguably the most important intellectual alive
in *The New York Times*

Well in advance of my last trip to Afghanistan, the Australian press had uncovered yet another absorbing US government report revealing the real reasons behind their war on terror. This one, submitted to Vice-President Dick Cheney in April of 2001, was commissioned by former US Secretary of State James Baker III and the Council on Foreign Relations. It was called "Strategic Energy Policy Challenges for the 21st Century." The document stated, "The United States remains a prisoner of its energy dilemma," in reference to its lack of ability to meet demands from US citizens. It concluded once again that one of the "consequences" of this perceived shortage was a "need for military intervention" to gain the necessary oil supply. It also said quite clearly that the US needed to specifically overthrow Iraq in order to facilitate control of its oil. James Baker III was the former Secretary of State under George Bush Sr. and had led five different Republican Presidential campaigns. He also fought hard in the trenches of Florida to assure that the 2001 Presidential vote recount went George W.s way. Furthermore, he held a prestigious position within the Carlyle Group. To top off the influential credentials, James Baker III was principal attorney of the law firm Baker and Botts, representing the Baku-Tbilisi-Ceyhan pipeline (Azerbaijan, Georgia, Turkey). The Australians released this information at the same time the Americans and Brits were lying to the world about their motives for military intervention in Iraq, but it did nothing to alter the outcome of the lobbying[114].

I took an overland route into Afghanistan for my final trip there, in early July of 2003. My teenaged daughter accompanied me on the journey. On this occasion, I went primarily to line up interviews with controversial and difficult-to-access Afghans for CBC Radio News, so I spoke with some influential people.

At behest of CBC, I went to see Dr. Sharif Fayez, Afghanistan's Minister of Higher Education, at his office in Kabul University. He told me in great detail about his friend, Ismail Khan of Herat, now facing new challenges under Hamid Karzai's presidential control. Khan is called "Emir" in his own territory, which illustrates the deep respect he holds among many of his people.

I also visited with a senior professor at the university named Dr. Askar, already a friend from his days teaching in Oxford, England. Apart from being a sensitive and brilliant human being, Dr. Askar has written a very insightful book on the Hazara ethnics of Afghanistan and Central Asia. After some conversation, I asked the doctor to point me in the direction of Afshar, the Kabul suburb where a great many Hazara civilians, plus some other ethnic groups, were slaughtered back in 1993. I then set out to explore the area. The near twenty years of war in the country had taken its toll on the district. Entire villages were filled with multi-tiered dwellings missing roofs. In some cases, one could make out only the outline of the building and the boundary walls of the compound. Some displayed three walls but none had roofs. I saw adults and children leaving buildings that did not look habitable. Despite the absence of basic living requirements, these Afghans did not act like destitute people. Several times I noticed an innocence and sincerity in their eyes that was almost childlike in its beauty.

Another person I spent some time with in Kabul was a man named Faizullah Zaki, General Dostum's second in command. I met him while trying to arrange a CBC interview with the General himself. I was grateful for the moments he spared me, as the man had important business to tend to. I could not have imagined a more pleasant setting for conversation than the garden he took me to.

Zaki spoke to me about the unfairness of the press Dostum had received lately. I had read the General stood accused of war crimes involving up to a thousand Taliban captives who had surrendered in 2001. He had imprisoned these soldiers within a day or two of the Mazar e Sharif prison massacre in October. Dostum was also defending himself against allegations of impropriety regarding certain witnesses who could have testified against him on the war crimes issue.[115] I did not discuss the details of the allegations with Mr. Zaki.

On a positive note, Zaki spoke to me about a disarmament program Dostum had proposed in his new role of Deputy Defence Minister of Afghanistan. The two men were probably hoping the program would finally net the general some press with a positive spin.

The Taliban would not forget about their comrades who perished in the incidents allegedly involving General Dostum. In the coming years, someone attempted to assassinate him, using a suicide bomber.

Perhaps the most notable difference in Afghanistan from the previous fall was the extent to which the remaining Taliban forces had multiplied. Even without the considerable support they once received from the US, the Saudis and Pakistan, the Taliban just won't admit defeat. I interviewed a member of the Taliban militia who was heading back from Peshawar, Pakistan to fight in Afghanistan. He assured me they would continue to fight all foreign intervention and that starvation was preferable to occupation. Such resilience from a group that recently toyed with the pipeline plans concerns the Americans more than they let on.

If the US were to offer the Taliban legitimacy, the fundamentalists would need to dispense with their leader, Mullah Omar. George Bush could not allow this man to remain their head after promising to bring both him and bin-Laden "to justice" a few years back. But the Taliban proved stubborn about protecting bin-Laden, so it stands to reason they will be stubborn about protecting their own leadership. Such recognition would also require the Taliban to adopt a more moderate political philosophy. The White House would have to include provisions for human rights and the treatment of women in any discourse. It would have to continue to keep the West believing that all the death and destruction since their invasion of the country was an unfortunate side effect of the noble quests for freedom and peace.

Despite the pious pledge for democracy in Afghanistan, I believe the Bush government couldn't really care less who ran the country, as long as its pipeline construction and military bases are guaranteed to remain free from sabotage. The Taliban's vision for a pure Islamic society, however, does not embrace American imperialism. An extensive fundamentalist resurrection in Afghanistan would surely endanger US investment. It would also embarrass the American president as he campaigns for re-election.

The lackadaisical pace at which the rebuilding of Afghanistan has moved ahead suggests US leaders view the land as little more than an expensive public relations exercise they would like to walk away from at the soonest possible moment. Their presence is no longer necessary to camouflage their Caspian Sea ambitions. The leaders of Turkmenistan, Afghanistan and Pakistan signed the pipeline agreement late last year, and this was a top priority out of the way. American corporations have had sufficient time to build military bases in the country. The US State Department also paid Kellogg, Brown and Root, the Halliburton subsidiary, over 100 million dollars for construction of the US embassy in Kabul, under a ten-year deal with Halliburton.[116]But the Pentagon realizes it must at least help establish a stronger army for the Afghan central government if it wishes to get the oil flowing and keep it free from attack down the line. The paltry few thousand or so soldiers that comprise Karzai's national army certainly can't accomplish this alone, when some of the warlords' militias are much bigger. Little is being done to create a land of content, law-abiding citizens. Many thousands of people in the country still live in the tattered remains of their once happy homes. Understandably, there is resentment.

How well the new Afghanistan works depends on who you are, where you live, your gender, and what ethnic group you belong to. Women do enjoy a few rights they were not permitted in recent years. Girls can go to school if their parents want them to and women can attend university, at least in some parts of the country. But any woman who strays from home without a mature male escort runs serious risk of harassment, physical attack, or sexual assault. Such violence has become extremely common, despite the presence of foreign troops in the land. In certain parts of the country, if the escort is an improper one, the woman might be accused of sexual impropriety and interrogated, or worse. An adulteress wife may no longer face an execution, but she will probably suffer a very severe prison sentence. And she might be the victim of an honour killing in certain areas of the land. During my stay in the country, I attended a press conference held in response to a Human Rights Watch report exploring such women's issues. The gathering was convened by a military general who had been accused by the group of extorting bribes.

Many women in Afghanistan still wear the traditional burqa with a full-face veil, although the law does not force it upon them. Some leave their eyes uncovered and the bolder ones wear scarves over their heads. Females are permitted to work now, if they can find a job, and they can also drive – another impossibility under the Taliban. But it remains to be seen to what extent the male-dominated society will eventually welcome them into professions where they could truly influence the long-standing policies restricting them.[117] Warlords still rule the vast majority of the nation, most of them with the central government's blessings. Some have been given positions in President Karzai's government, reflecting the old Cosa Nostra adage of keeping your friends close and your enemies closer. The warlords and tribal chiefs still independently control varying amounts of territory and wield assorted degrees of power, while possessing a fair measure of autonomy in their own regions. Although conceptually a good thing, this ancient tribal system is like governments everywhere, vulnerable to corruption. Too many align with whomever and whatever assures them maximum personal gain. The loyalties of some of these men can be bought by anyone for the right price. The US military has even hired a number of the warlords to help hunt down the Taliban, which sometimes results in the warlords' personal enemies being detained for months. Others have been paid to play peacekeeper within an American version of peace.

The warlords and their militia are sometimes the most frequent perpetrators of crime in their own provinces. This creates obvious problems, but Afghans are certainly not novices at dealing with it. On the other hand, a serious breakdown of order could come about due to the lack of inclusion being offered to the Pushtun majority by Karzai and his mainly Tajik cabinet. They are angry and it's not difficult to see why.

Bacha Khan is a man of influence in Paktia province. His son was killed by a US missile while guarding an unauthorized checkpoint – intentionally in his opinion. Khan is also a warlord who claimed to be unfairly treated by the new Afghan President when I spoke with him through an interpreter in both 2002 and 2003. He stated that he, along with Hamid Karzai and Abdul Haq – all three Pushtun – were the first three Afghans the Americans invited back into Afghanistan to help establish order in the fall of 2001. Khan said the US gave him the task of tracking down Taliban troops as they dispersed, and then calling in American air strikes against them.

Bacha Khan and Karzai started feuding shortly before Karzai was sworn in as President. Either by design or through error, Khan called in an American air strike against some of Karzai's friends as they made their way to the inauguration ceremonies in Kabul. Karzai stripped Khan of his governor's title. The President has continued to marginalize the man ever since.

Bacha Khan is a minor player in the grand scheme of Afghan politics. There are many with much more at stake who would do the president harm if given the chance. Jalaluddin Haqqani is a concern. A commander and scholar from the same "Zadran" tribe as Bacha Khan, Haqqani fought in Afghanistan against the Russians before sitting out the civil war in Kabul. Later, he took on posting with the Taliban as responsible for the southern command, and has not yet forfeited his position. The people Karzai reports to are probably more concerned about Mr. Haqqani than Karzai himself is. And Haqqani is only one of a number of prominent Taliban figures who passionately oppose the central government and its American partners. Karzai knows this, so when inside the country he rarely strays from the comfort and security of his headquarters in the capital city.

The Afghan President's welfare is now largely in the hands of a private military contractor named DynCorp, a company that began fifty years ago as an aviation contractor and was absorbed in 2003 by the IT company Computer Sciences Corporation. The task of protecting Karzai was handed over to these freelancers shortly after the attempt on his life in September of 2002. DynCorp, with about twenty-three thousand employees and about two billion dollars income per annum, is one of the most successful of many such corporations now doing business all over the globe. Others of note include Kellogg, Brown and Root, ArmorGroup, Vinnell, MPRI and Sandline International. About thirty-five of them are based in the US alone. DynCorp, like many others, likes to be considered a security contracting company, but some see it as a mercenary machine, with staff consisting mostly of finely tuned private soldiers. Already controversial without further scandal, DynCorp personnel working for the United Nations police service in Bosnia were allegedly involved in buying and selling prostitutes, some as young as twelve. [118]

One of the many problems in Afghanistan today is the resurging opium and heroin trade. After the Taliban all but eliminated poppy farms in the vast majority of the nation, Afghanistan, under American occupation, has once again become the world's largest producer. Karzai says this alarms him, and rightly so, as violence, guns and instability tend to increase proportionately to the industry's growth. The US professes concern over the poppy growth spike. If it truly bothers those powerful enough to set policy, I suspect this would simply be because they fear revenues may have made their way into the hands of the wrong parties, such as the Taliban, al-Qaeda or Gulbuddin Hekmatyar.

The most perilous issue in Afghanistan today continues to involve the Pushtuns. After more than two hundred years of control, the ethnic majority of the nation now finds the Pushtu language marginalized in the country's higher education system, in favor of the Tajik Persian (or Dari) tongue. The Pushtuns may take offense at this linguistic realignment. It has happened to them before, under British colonial. rule in the nineteenth century, and they do not wish to see it happen again. There have recently been several Pushtun student uprisings at the University of Kabul.

Partly because of this issue, a significant number of Pushtun Afghan natives are receptive to seeing the neo-Taliban, a predominantly Pushtun group, gain a measure of control in the country once again.

The present rendition of the Taliban dilemma has become an interesting one. A great many Afghans came to value the law and order they effectively established and maintained everywhere they took charge. The fundamentalists transformed a land filled with crime into one where people could safely leave their doors unlocked. And they did it quickly.

The punishments doled out to those who insisted on breaking the law were considered excessive according to Western standards. The oppression of women during their tenure also won them little favor outside of Afghanistan and Pakistan. It still brings them well-deserved opposition. But the common banditry and assaults against women that regularly transpire in some developing countries did not occur under Taliban rule. They took place before the Taliban came into being and are happening again now, but they disappeared when the fundamentalists were in control. Whether true or not, the Taliban always claimed that after disposing of Massoud and winning the civil war, the wives, daughters and mothers of Afghanistan would be granted much more freedom.

The restrictions the Taliban government placed on sports, games, dancing, music and education were severe, even by Afghan standards. Afghans must have dearly missed the music, which they love. But many considered these inconveniences alone a small price to pay for the stability the strict disciplinarians provided.

Given the benefit of hindsight, I don't believe the Taliban was so difficult to understand. They saw that their society had fallen prey to all manner of Western, anti-Islamic behavior, and set out to realign it. One could argue that at least their ultimate goal was pure. Furthermore, their policing may have stopped more violence than that which they inflicted. The Taliban put forth a set of rules and then stuck to them religiously. They carried out their mandates, agreeable or not, with honesty and in plain view. Rarely did people just disappear to be tortured to death in a secret prison, as they had under other regimes. If something happened, the Taliban responded immediately and everyone knew what to expect. In their own eyes, the Taliban operated with integrity and honor, according to their own ideology.

The fact that this group allowed the world to know what they were up to may have turned us against them, but one should keep in mind their legal doctrine evolved from a region of the world where many civilians suffer cruel punishments from their governments. Consequently, when we look at the Taliban from a broader perspective, it should not surprise us that a great many Afghans do not view the Taliban resurgence with the same horror we think they should. Once again, this is especially true of the Pushtuns, many of them extremely upset with the disregard of the largely Tajik administration currently in Kabul.

Rahimullah Yusufzai, the world-renowned Pushtun reporter from Peshawar, said to me in 2002, "The Taliban are biding their time. They did it once so they know they can do it again. They will remain a relevant political party."

President Karzai is well aware of dissension amongst the Pushtun majority and obviously tries to keep the situation under reasonable control. Although the Americans have offered millions of dollars for the capture of one of the more militant Pushtun leaders, Gulbuddin Hekmatyar, Karzai seems to have allowed a great many members of the man's political party to infiltrate the secondary tiers of his own government. Since the US would obviously be aware of this, one has to doubt their sincerity. What the Americans say is often different from what they want. Its difficult to know America's primary agenda. But the potential for a future uprising concerns the US enough that the ever-changing pipeline route is lately circumventing provinces where

Pushtun are a majority. These areas run the greatest risk of a Taliban revival.

Rather than alter their master plan for Afghanistan by granting some solid concessions to the Pushtuns, Karzai and his US colleagues have decided to strand hundreds of thousands of them in Pakistan. The mid-western borderlands known as North West Frontier Province belonged to Afghanistan until the late nineteenth century, when British colonial bureaucrats decided to transfer them onto a map of British India. A great many Pushtuns living in the area have continued to call themselves "Afghan" until this very day.

Karzai has made a great effort to seal off portions of the Afghan border with Pakistan. His fellow Pushtuns on the Pakistan side now have a much more difficult time gaining access to their ancestral country – a move which truly hurts these people, who value their dual citizenship dearly.

Regardless of what happens to the Pushtun vote on the Pakistan side of the border, more than seventy-five percent of Pushtuns still live in Afghanistan. This is enough to change their fate if the elections are conducted fairly. But from what I have seen so far, it does not look like the Pushtuns will be adequately represented in the parliamentary election, scheduled for 2005. And how can the Pushtuns exercise their voice in the country's politics if some of their most respected leaders are not allowed to participate?

Another conundrum facing many Afghans is that Hamid Karzai retains the support of most countries offering foreign aid to Afghanistan. A vote against him would therefore be a vote against food on the table. One way or another, Karzai's angles are covered.

I doubt very much that Massoud, even though he was Tajik, would have agreed to marginalize the Pushtuns to the extent we see today. And he didn't want foreign military personnel to defeat the Taliban, either. He probably wouldn't have refused weaponry without too many onerous conditions attached. But basically the commander only wanted the US to aid him diplomatically, to terminate Pakistan's involvement. I highly doubt Massoud would have signed on for aggressive foreign soldiers kicking in Afghan doors. Right up until the end of his life, the commander contended that if Pakistan forces in the Taliban militia were called home, his enemies could be defeated within a year. He also said many times that it should be Afghans, and only Afghans, who solve their country's problems. Massoud would likely not have collaborated with a foreign power to the extent the Northern Alliance has since his assassination.

In the end, Afghanistan and the world are both better off for having known Ahmed Shah Massoud. May God Bless the commander and finally bring him the peace his soul so fervently sought. After more than twenty years of non-stop fighting, not only is he free from the burden of his responsibilities to his countrymen, but he will also be spared the dark cloud of war threatening Central Asia and the Middle East.

Most people in these areas consider militarization by Americans in Muslim lands to be a threatening scenario rather than a welcome safety net. More are also coming to believe that suicide attacks against Americans and other occupying Westerners are justified. Considering the superior weaponry of the Americans and the grossly unbalanced ratio of Muslim deaths to American casualties, any resistance is little more than a suicide mission anyway. It is easy for us to overlook the fact that hundreds of thousands of people in Afghanistan and Iraq have had many friends or loved ones die in a relatively short period of time, at the hands of foreigners who have come into their countries without invitation. Those who have chosen to fight back believe they are simply resisting foreign control and oppression.

Other Muslim nations are becoming concerned that they, too, may be invaded and occupied in the name of "freedom and democracy." Should this occur, it may lead to the Muslim world experiencing an even greater sense of polarization from the West. And if this polarization becomes pronounced enough, it could be answered by a united Islamic community in Central Asia and the Middle East. The Islamic peoples' obligation to defend their lands against aggressors is a profound responsibility dictated by their religion.

No one can deny that in both Afghanistan and Iraq tyrants have been deposed, but to what avail if lawlessness rules the land? Under American-led occupation, both countries have been systematically stripped of their nationhood and dignity. The main difference might be that the Iraqis, having lived in relative peace for ten years, have more energy to fight. Some might also be incensed over the fact that sanctions aimed at Saddam Hussein recently killed over a million of the country's people.

As time goes by more and more dissidents, not fewer, appear on the horizon in a multitude of Muslim nations. The belief that this will magically stop when enough of the "freedom haters" are exterminated could be a dangerously optimistic one. The violence in Iraq and Afghanistan is not just a temporary condition a "democratic" and foreign-controlled government can easily transform. A leadership whose priorities lie with external economic interests may garner more fury than favour.

In the view of most 9/11 researchers, the attacks on the World Trade Center and the Pentagon did not represent an American intelligence failure, but an intelligence success. What the American government says happened on that day does not stand up to any reasonable presentation of the facts. A poll taken in New York State a few years after 9/11 suggests that about 50% of New York City's residents believed upper level American officials knew about the terrorist attacks in advance and allowed them to be carried out anyway. About 41% of the state's residents felt the same way.[119] The evidence regarding 9/11 does seem to suggest a much broader plot than the official version. It likely involves members of the American intelligence community, Pakistan's ISI, some very influential corporate interests and perhaps a small group of politicians with household names.

A substantial mound of evidence exists to support a widespread contention that the "War on Terrorism" is fraudulent. It is also a war that could not have been launched without a 9/11 or Pearl Harbor-style attack to bait the American public, as per policy conclusions given by George W. Bush's top advisors even before their administration took power. Once one has taken a serious look at the evidence left in their wake, it appears very much like 9/11, the invasions of Afghanistan and Iraq, and the war against terror as a whole, are all parts of a singular plan with multiple tiers.

The global power play we see before us has nothing to do with spreading freedom and democracy. Nor is it designed to create a world where more people can enjoy a decent standard of living. It is certainly not about a quest for universal peace, unless true peace can be achieved at gunpoint. Some of our best minds claim that the men behind this push for supremacy seek to usher in a new world order in which totalitarianism will eventually rule and human rights may well cease to exist.

The unveiling of time has demonstrated these views to be less and less farfetched. We would be well advised not to dismiss this assertion as a foolhardy conspiracy theory. As the machinations of corporate globalization proceed to ravage the earth's remaining treasures, global poverty and starvation continue to spiral out of control. Afghanistan and Iraq are but two of many nations that have been humbled by the industrial/military complex. The only means of survival for much of the world's population is to toil for foreign corporations, under the most unhealthy and exploitive working conditions, earning pitiful wages. Contrary to the American dream, the Western world is not immune from these grim economic trends either. Homelessness runs rampant. The gap between rich and poor increases at an alarming pace. The world's middle class is disappearing, a sobering tribute to our blind faith in unrestricted capitalism.

A FINAL WORD FROM THE AUTHOR

First they came for the communists,
and I did not speak out because I was not a communist;
Then they came for the socialists,
and I did not speak out because I was not a socialist;
Then they came for the trade unionists,
and I did not speak out because I was not a trade unionist;
Then they came for the Jews,
and I did not speak out because I was not a Jew;
And when they came for me, there was no one left to speak out.
– Pastor Martin Niemoeller
anti–Nazi activist, 1940s Germany

I met Massoud in 1998. It was an experience that didn't let me down. He was daring and adventurous, challenging and direct. He was playful, witty and astute. Massoud, the visionary, was shining.

The political climate and public opinion had swayed towards the Taliban. Ahmed Shah Massoud's national appeal and 20–year reputation was fading from the minds of a great many Afghans. A leading academic explained Massoud's career to me as having three distinct stages: 1. The visionary; 2. The uncouth Mujahideen; and 3. A visionary again after departing Kabul. His country eventually honoured him with the title of "National Hero."

Afghanistan, for a number of generations, had seen warlords and militias engage in acts that by today's language would be deemed terrorism. Yet Timothy McVeigh's act of carnage in Oklahoma City did not merit the word "terrorist" in the national press. It seems the term is now reserved for Muslims who challenge an imperial agenda.

We managed to devolve with this "war on terror" — a war with neither borders nor accountability. The lessons of Vietnam have been lost. "Flower power" has become "violence power". It probably wouldn't have surprised Sigmund Freud. "Civilized society," he said, "is perpetually menaced with disintegration through this primary hostility of men towards one another."

How did we degenerate to this state of affairs?

In 1984 thousands of famine victims in Ethiopia and Sudan were not enough to elicit a world response to desertification and drought. The West sent aid but Africa's climate problems remained local concerns. Meanwhile a self-centered two percent of the global population spewed close to forty percent of the world's greenhouse gases. The ensuing meltdown of polar ice caps and continued demise of plant and animal life can be traced to the two percent's refusal to sign the Kyoto Accord.

In May of 2001, the Taliban began to smash two immense and ancient Buddha statues with anti-aircraft and tank fire. When the Buddhas remained unmoved, they used dynamite to eliminate a 1,500–year link with the past. The senseless destruction of these treasures understandably drew a negative reaction around the globe. Yet what was less understandable was that the outcry was louder and longer than for the destruction of children's lives. In 1999 homeless children in Afghanistan died of hypothermia and starvation while the ravages of neglect were blatant. Sometimes hundreds died in a single night. The U.N. estimated that four million people in the country were on the brink of starvation, but two statues took all the press.

Despite their sometimes severe tactics, in the mid 1990s the Taliban were useful to the oil companies. They stabilized the regions the pipeline would traverse. It would begin in the north in Turkmenistan, cut across Afghanistan, and continue to the southern Pakistan port of Gwadar.

In late 1996, Zalmay Khalilzad of the American Enterprise Institute claimed in *The Washington Post* that the Taliban did "not practise the anti-US style fundamentalism practised by Iran." He added, "We should...be willing to offer recognition and humanitarian assistance and to promote international economic reconstruction. It is time for the United States to engage."

But as the millennium neared, oil companies began to grow wary of the Taliban's ability to maintain control. Central Asia possesses almost forty percent of the world's gas reserves and six percent of its oil, an enormous and virtually unexploited energy potential. Staggering amounts of foreign funding and manpower had been invested in the pipeline project.

By the end of the 1990's, Zalmay Khalilzad with his University of Chicago fellow, Paul Wolfowitz, were occupied with plans to depose Saddam Hussein in Iraq. Now Mr. Khalilzad issued a proclamation contrary to his earlier plea, saying Afghanistan was "a haven for some of the world's most lethal terrorists" who "pose a threat to US soldiers and civilians at home and abroad, to the Middle East peace process, and to the stability of our allies in the region." Khalilzad suggested his government take measures to weaken the Taliban and support the Northern Alliance.

The tables quickly turned. *The New York Times, National Geographic* and *The Washington Post* printed articles decrying the Taliban and praising Massoud and his forces.

Human rights violations apparently had carried no weight when the Taliban's presence was perceived as instrumental for projected oil profits. Their seemingly barbaric attitudes towards women, education, the arts, liberties and freedoms had been well known to any who cared to see. When it became clear Taliban's absence would serve the same cause, their ex benefactors initiated an extraordinary interest in the "burqa". Western press campaigned against this "dreaded burqa" representing the Taliban as inventors of the head-to-toe female covering.

In reality, women in rural Afghanistan often wore clothing similar to men's when working shoulder to shoulder with them in the fields. The traditional family burqa would be taken out when the village women travelled to more urban centres. The burqa was a socio-economic issue, even more than a cultural one.

Islamic fundamentalism became the source of alarm, replacing communism and the war on drugs. Although Massoud was involved with the movement, I personally could not readily say whether he was a fundamentalist, a trend that crosses ethnic and religious boundaries. Christian fundamentalism however is readily apparent in the oval office.

The same hypocrisy is visible in the war on drugs. The Taliban at first tolerated poppy production because it wasn't the local citizens who consumed most of the opium and heroin. But eventually the Taliban signed an agreement with the UN to abolish the crop. They became the first and last government in Kabul ever to come close to accomplishing this promise.

The edict was deeply resented by a desperate populace. To a great many people, income derived from an opium harvest was their only means of survival. To add to the Taliban's problems, a severe drought hit southwest Afghanistan. People began to think it was God's Will to punish the leaders of their country. All in all, a great many people blamed the Taliban for their increasing poverty. It did not help these fundamentalists closer to the end of their reign.

As a basis for entering Afghanistan, Tony Blair claimed eighty percent of heroin on the streets of London came from Afghanistan. Illusions have replaced 'fact'. Our news has become virtual. We as a people would be well advised to heed the words of Malcolm X, "You're not supposed to be so blind with patriotism that you can't face reality. Wrong is wrong no matter who does it or who says it."

By the year 2000 Massoud and his men were pushed into a corner of Afghanistan. Forgotten by the world, Ahmed Shah traveled to Paris to deliver an unscheduled speech to a gathering of world leaders. He was a man of dust and charm in a room of shiny suits, seeking assistance to bring an end to the Taliban. On this day the words of Massoud brought world attention to Afghanistan, the Northern Alliance, and the Taliban.

Global assistance was not increased even though Massoud's presence supplied the only thread of cohesion to his country at the time. While the other warlords directed their parties from safe havens in Peshawar and Tehran, Massoud stayed in Afghanistan. It is one of the few things Afghans of every persuasion agree upon as Massoud's legacy.

When I finally met Massoud and experienced his honest dedication and indomitable spirit firsthand, I recalled my excitement ten years earlier while visiting my mother in 1992. A story about the commander had come on the television news. I beckoned her to watch, feeling like a child captivated by a famous sports hero. But indeed, in my mind Massoud was a hero. Together we watched him rise from meditation to announce he would not participate in the shelling of his country's capital even though other Mujahideen forces were moving on Kabul from several directions. He struck a strong and dashing figure with his tilted pakool cap. Seeing the northern resistance military commander speak so compassionately and eloquently edged my mother towards understanding that Afghanistan was indeed a tapestry of cultures, where warlords could be heroes, and military men poets.

Massoud was already a prominent Afghan visionary when few had heard of the Northern Alliance. He may have been assassinated at the peak of his influence. Alive, the Western oil cartels may have seen Massoud as an obstacle in the Central Asia oil game. He had forged significant strides in Afghanistan's struggle against tyranny, generating disquiet for any whose plans included dominating Afghanistan.

Massoud's assassination may remain an unsolved mystery. But still we can learn from what transpires in his wake. Ahmed Shah Massoud's work to preserve a unified Afghanistan in dangerous times was his life. Not money, not oil, but Afghanistan.

The Taliban's reign in Afghanistan was a brief moment in a long and complex history. Western powers helped them to rise and govern for five years, then pushed them to collapse. Taliban ideals continue to resonate in the southeast, but Afghanistan has broken its long-standing tradition of majority Pushtun governance, and Kabul is no longer independent of foreign authority.

"Through arms [and] technology, you can rule these people, but they will never be loyal to you," Dr. Raj Wali Khattak advised. "You must win their hearts and the winning is much easier. The best friend can be a Pushtun and the worst enemy can also be a Pushtun. If you earn their confidence they will sacrifice everything for you."

There are many around the world who echo these essential sentiments. Perhaps it is time for us to try something radical. To try for a world where those with the biggest guns no longer dictate agreements between nations. Where the hunt for weapons of mass destruction begins in the US, Britain and Russia. Where the political environment of our planet is everybody's concern. It's an opportunity for people from all walks of life, from all faiths and nationalities, to rise in unison and confront the outdated colonial mentality still governing our world.

How we treat the most vulnerable among us is the standard upon which we, as the global village, should be judged. We need to make an attempt to meet others without bias, to not be drawn into fearing all that is different from us.

Those who think we still have time to sit on the fence risk waking up one day to discover voices silenced and civil liberties merely a memory.

Endnotes

1 Wikipedia. <<http://en.wikipedia.org/islam_Karimov>>.

2 English Pravda, 30 May 2001.

3 Houston Chronicle, 30 June 1996.

4 Thomas Hunter. "Bomb School: International Terrorists Training Camps". Jane's Intelligence Review (March 1997).

5 Intelligence Newsletter 312 (May 29, 1997).

6 "Ahmed Shah Massoud". Biography. <<http://afgha.com>>

7 "Ahmed Shah Massoud". Biography. <<http://afgha.com>>

8 Zbigniew Brzezinski, interview, "The CIA Intervention in Afghanistan", Le Nouvel Observateur 15-21 January 1998.

9 A. H. Guernsey. "The English in India," Harper's New Monthly Magazine 25:149 (October, 1862).

10 "Percentages: CIA World Factbook 2001"

11 Radio Free Europe/RL 07 August 1999.

12 Ahmed Rashid, Taliban, (2000). Bin Laden (Alleged), audiocassette calls for Jihad, CBS News, 8 April 2003. JemaahIslamiyah, "Damaged but still dangerous", ICG Asia Report 63 26 August 2003. PWHCE, Abdullah Azzam biography.

13 Sam Vaknin, "Afghan MYTHS", Interview with Anssi Kristian Kullberg, 16 December 2003.

14 Michel Chossoudovsky, War and Globalization, (2002): 32. War and Globalization chapter 2, Jane's Intelligence Review. Michael Griffin, Reaping the Whirlwind, (Pluto Press, 2001): 132.

15 Ahmed Rashid, "The Taliban: Exporting Extremism" Foreign Affairs, (November/December 1999)

16 RAWA Revolutionary Association of the Women of Afghanistan, "Statement on the Terrorist attacks in the US", CRG Center for Research on Globalisation, 16 September 2001 <http://globalresearch.ca/articles RAW109A.html>.

17 Reaping the Whirlwind 145-46. War and Globalization 20, 22, 23.

18 Mohammed Yousef and Mark Adlin, The Bear Trap, (1992).

19 Biography Ahmed Shah Massoud - Afgha.com

20 David C. Isby, War in a Distant Country: Afghanistan, Invasio and Resistance, (Britain, Arms and Armour Press, 1989): Chapter 4.

21 Reaping the Whirlwind, 1.

22 Sam Vaknin, interview.

23 George C. Wilson, Washington Post Staff Writer, 4 July 1988: A01.

24 Jamie McIntyre, Cold War Postscript: Legacy of Afghanistan Haunts Both Cold War Superpowers, CNN 7 March 1999 - 9:30 p.m. ET.

25 Barnett R. Rubin, The Search For Peace in Afghanistan, (Yale University Press, 1995).

26 afghan.com - Afgha culture days - ahmed shah mas'ud

27 Reaping the Whirlwind.

28 Human Rights Watch. The Nation. Ahmed Rashid

29 Reaping the Whirlwind, 30.

30 Ahmad Rashid, "Pakistan and the Taliban", The Nation Lahore Pakistan, 11 April 1998.

31 International Media Corporation Defence and Strategy Policy, "US Commits Forces, Weapons to Bosnia", London, 31 October 1994 in War and Globalization.

32 Global Policy Forum Security Council, "CIA Aided Kosovo Guerilla Army All Along", London Sunday Times 12 March 2000.

33 Pravda, 21 March 2001.

34 <http://kyber.org/pahtonpeople/Ayub Afridi>.

35 Ishtiaq Ahmad, "How America Courted Taliban", Pakistan Observer 20 October 2001

36 John Pilger, "This War is a Fraud", Daily Mirror, 29 October 2001.

37 Economist Intelligence Unit, March 1996. Reaping the Whirlwind, 46-47

38 Jane's Intelligence Weekly, 27 Nov. 1996.

39 Reaping the Whirlwind.

40 United States Senate Committee on Foreign Relations, Testimony on the Situation in Afghanistan, CFR.org.

41 A. H. Guernsey, "The English in India", Harper's New Monthly Magazine 25:149, (October 1862).

42 State Department, Official Biography of Phyllis Oakley.

43 Patrick E. Tyler, "U.S. Strategy Plan Calls for Insuring No Rivals Develop, A One-Superpower World, Pentagon's Document Outlines Ways to Thwart Challenges to Primacy of America", New York Times 8 March 1992.

44 Linda McQuaig, Peak Oil

45 Dan Briody, The Iron Triangle, (John Wiley and Sons, 2003).

46 Joel Andreas, Addicted to War, (Frank Dorrell and AK Press, 2002).

47 Noam Chomsky, What Uncle Sam Really Wants, (Odonian Press).

48 Joel Andreas.

49 Chalmers Johnson, prologue, The Sorrows of Empire: Militarism, Secrecy, and the End of the Republic, (Henry Holt and Company Incorporated, 2004).

50 The Pentagon Papers.

51 Joel Andreas.

52 Noam Chomsky.

53 John Piliger, "Recalling Pol Pot's Terror, But Forgetting His Backers", Cambodia info. http://www.antiwar.com

54 last 9 paragraphs, Joel Andreas.Noam Chomsky.

55 Harold C. Funk, a Canadian lawyer working for 30 years with the Supreme Court of Canada.

56 Commander Ahmed Shah Massoud, interview, Azadi Afghan Radio 7 August 2000. Afghanistan Online

57 Brave New World & New Work News, August 1998.

58 New York Times, 5 December 1998.

59 New York Times, 8 December 2001.

60 Michael Griffin, Reaping the Whirlwind, (Pluto Press, 2001): 191.

61 Ahmed Rashid, Taliban. F. Bamiyan, The Never-Ending War, (1998-99).

62 Anthony Lloyd, "Interview with Massoud", The Times of London 28 October 2000.

63 "Married to the Jihad: The lonely world of al-Qaeda's wives", The Independent 28 March 2004. <http://jihadwatch.com>

64 AP, 19 December 2000.

65 War and Globalization.

66 Sunday Herald, 7 September 2002.

67 LA Times, 12 January 2003.

68 Sunday Herald, 9/07/02.

69 Washington Post, 23 February 2004.

70 Brissard and Guillaume, The Forbidden Truth, (Thunder's Mouth Press/Nation Books, 20 September 2002).

71 Robert Baer, interview, Fifth Estate, CBC, 29 October 2003.

72 Brissard and Guillaume.

73 Dan Briody.

74 BBC, 6 November 2001.

75 Brissard and Guillaume.

76 Le Figaro, 31 October 2001.

77 BBC, 18 September 2001. The Guardian 22 September 2001.

78 The Times of India 11 October 2001. Agence Presse France 10 October 2001.

79 War and Globalization, 60.

80 New York Times 13 September 2001.

81 "Masood: Broad-Based Natinal Resistance to Lead Imminent Nationwide Uprising Against Pakistan and the Taliban," Omaid Weekly 470 23 April 2001.

82 Jon Anderson, "The Assassins," New York Times 10 June 2002.

83 The Guardian, 26 September 2001.

84 "The Forbidden Truth". The Guardian 22 September 2001. BBC 18 September 2001.

85 George Arney, "US Planned Attack Against Taliban", BBC 18 September 2001.

86 "US Equipment Starts Arriving in Egypt", Jordan Times AP Egypt, 5 September 2001. Francis A. Boyle, Professor International Law, "Pre-Planned US/UK War Against Afghanistan", Rense.com 12 September 2001. "US Must Not Ignore Rights Abuses", Human Rights Watch 10 October 2001."As More forces Head to Region, US Seeks Greater Access to Bases Ringing Afghanistan", Wall Street Journal 24 September 2001.

87 <u>New York Observer</u> 11 February 2004.

88 <u>New York Times</u> 16 October 2001.

89 <u>New York Times 15 September 2001.</u>

90 Independent Commission Report, 17 June 2004.<u>New York Times 15 September 2001: (C)</u>

91 Independent Commission Report.

92 NORAD 8:40 18 September 2001. AP 19 August 2002. BBC 1 September 2002. Newsday 10 September 2002.

93 <u>News</u> ABC 14 September 2001.

94 Gail Sheehy, "Stewardess ID'd Hijackers: Early Transcripts Show in Relation to the 9/11 Independent Hearings", New York Observer 16 February 2004.

95 <u>New York Observer</u> 17 June 2004.

96 Michael C Ruppert, documentary, "The Great Conspiracy: The 9/11 News Special You Never Saw", www greatconspiracy.ca. Barry Zwicker, Barry Zwicker's 9/11 Resource Guide. Aviation Week & Space Technology 3 June 2002. Newhouse News. Toronto Star 9 December 2001.

97 Dr. Robert Bowman, "A Fighter Pilot Looks Back at 9/11 and Forward to a Resurrected America", Convocation Hall, University of Toronto, 30 May 2004, in Barry Zwicker's 9/11 Resource Guide.

98 Ruth Rosen, "Enron's Secrets are Safe", San Francisco Chronicle, 28January 2002. www.sfgate.com/cgi bin/article.cgi?f=/c/a/2002/01/28/ED98382.DTL. Washington Post 1 November 2001.George Lardner Jr., "Bush Clamping Down On Presidential Papers".

99 Rashmee Z Ahmed, "US 'Hero' May Have Triggered Mazar Revolt", Times of India, Times News Network 29 November 2001.

100 <u>New York Times</u>, 16 December 2001.

101 <u>Observer</u>, 20 January 2002.

102 Julian Berger, "The spies who pushed for war", The Guardian 17 July 2003.

103 Julian Berger.

104 "Pentagon Refutes Report Over New Espionage Unit", <u>Indo-Asian News Service</u> 23 January 2005.

105 <u>Le Monde</u> 13 December 2001. <u>CNN</u> 22 December 2001. FTW.

106 Michel Chossoudovsky. BBC Monitoring Service 15 December 2001.

107 <u>BBC</u>, 1 January 2002.

108 <u>Independent</u> 10 January 2002. <u>State Department Profile</u>, 2001.

109 Gary Strauss, "Cheney as VP Faces a Serious Pay Cut", USA Today 26 July 2001,.

The World According to Bush. William Karel, documentary, CBC 17 October 2004.

110 <u>Washington Post</u> 6 August 2002.

111 Kaleem Omar, "Poetic Licence: Exit America's Prince of Darkness", Daily Times Pakistan 1 April 2003.

112 Pipeline Groundbreaking Ceremony Takes Place In Baku, 18 September 2002, http://Eurasianet.org.

113 Karzai Says Minister Assassinated; Points Finger at Afghan Officials, 15 February 2002, http://CNN.com
     WORLD

114 Sunday Herald 5 October 2002.

115 Rory McCarthy, "US Afghan Ally 'Tortured Witnesses to His War Crimes', The Guardian 18 November
     2002.

116 defense-aerospace.com, Despite being under an investigative cloud, Halliburton gets 4.3 billion in 2003.
     Source: The Center for Public Integrity, 18 August 2004.

117 Human Rights Watch Report, August 2003.

118 David Isenberg, Security for Sale in Afghanistan, 4 January 2003, Asia Times Online..

119 Zogby poll, Utica NY, 911TRUTH.ORG.

Index

D

Dari (Afghan Persian)	12, 173
Defense Planning Guidance	100, 154
Deobandi	79
Diem, Hgo (Vietnam)	111
Dostum, Rashid	74, 135, 163
Dushanbe	12, 16, 29, 31-36, 39, 40, 65, 92, 113, 115, 120-122 124, 128, 131, 143

E

Eid	93, 108, 115, 116, 125
Egypt	42-44, 46, 57, 132, 145, 159, 160. 165
El Salvador	112
Ethiopia	179

F

FCC (Federal Communications Commission)	110
Ferghana Valley	10, 34

G

Georgia	112, 133, 160, 167
Gorbachev, Mikhail	50, 51, 97,
Grenada	111
GUUAM Alliance (Georgia, Uzbekistan, Ukraine, Azerbaijan, Moldova)	133
Guatemala	110, 112

H

Haiti	110
Haq, Abdul	41, 66, 67, 153, 171
Haqqani, Jalaluddin	41, 172
Hazara	9, 27, 28, 57, 58, 84-87, 109, 130, 143, 168
Heroin	11, 14, 24, 45, 46, 66, 71, 115, 172, 181, 182
Hizb-e-Islami	48, 53, 164
Hizb-e-Wahdat	57, 84, 85
Honduras	110, 112
Horn of Africa	99

I

IMU (Islamic Movement of Uzbekistan)	10, 11, 34
India	5, 14, 26, 66, 72, 73, 96, 98, 101, 102, 124, 141, 142, 155, 157, 175
Indonesia	111
Iran	4, 6, 28, 49, 51, 65, 72, 73, 85, 97, 98, 100, 102, 121, 129, 131, 133-136, 139, 157, 160, 164, 165, 180

MEMBER OF SCABRINI GROUP

Québec, Canada
2006

www.ingramcontent.com/pod-product-compliance
Lightning Source LLC
Chambersburg PA
CBHW061151120626
46546CB00005B/2012